English Book Collectors

William Younger Fletcher

Edited by Alfred Pollard

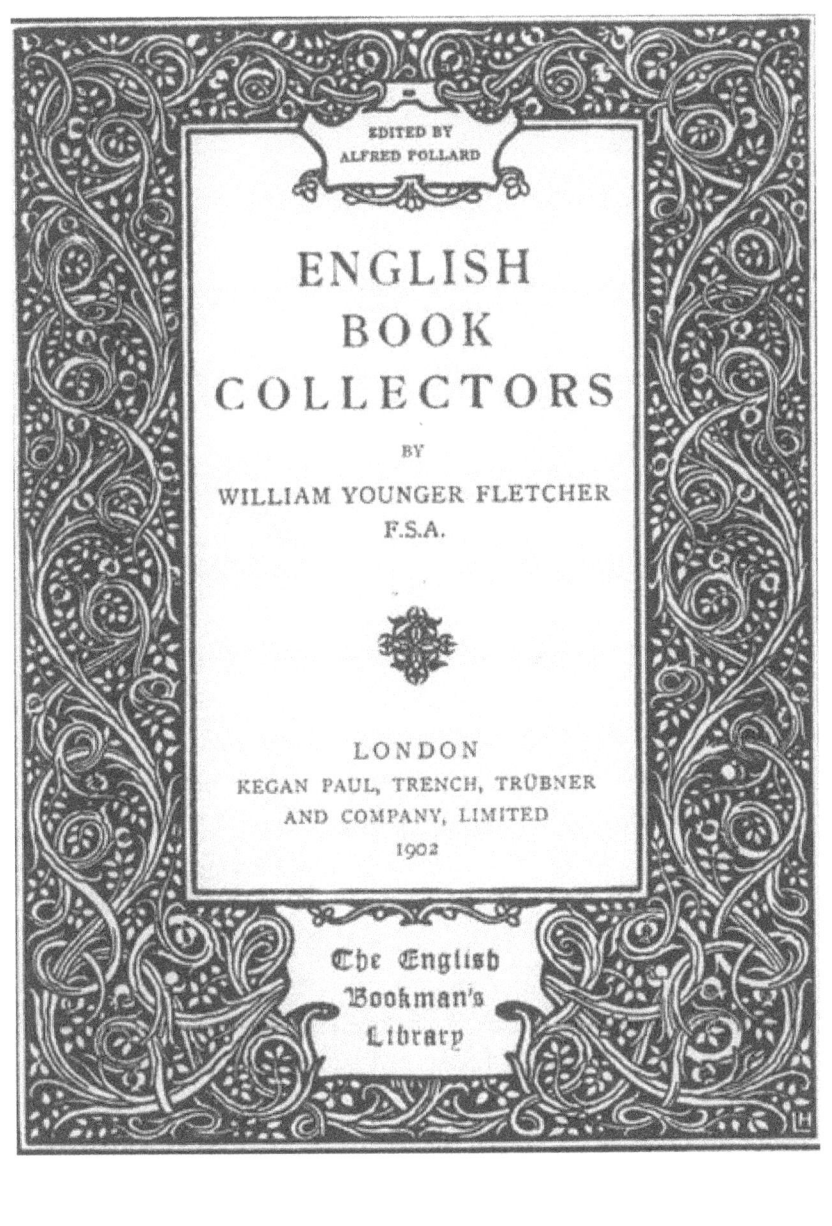

EDITED BY
ALFRED POLLARD

ENGLISH BOOK COLLECTORS

BY

WILLIAM YOUNGER FLETCHER
F.S.A.

LONDON
KEGAN PAUL, TRENCH, TRÜBNER
AND COMPANY, LIMITED
1902

The English
Bookman's
Library

GEORGE JOHN, SECOND EARL SPENCER.

PREFACE

y principal object in compiling this work on English Book Collectors has been to bring together in a compact and convenient form the information respecting them which is to be found scattered in the works of many writers, both old and new. While giving short histories of the lives of the collectors, and some description of their libraries, I have also endeavoured to show what manner of men the owners of these collections were. In doing this I have sought, where practicable, to let the accounts be told as much as possible in the words of their biographers, as their narratives are often not only full of interest, but are also couched in delightfully quaint language. As it would not be possible in a volume of this size to furnish satisfactory notices of all the Englishmen who have formed large libraries, I have selected some of those who appear to possess special claims to notice, either on the ground of their interesting personality, or the exceptional importance of their collections. I have not given any account of the collectors who lived prior to the reign of Henry VII., for until that time libraries consisted almost entirely of manuscripts; and I have also excluded men who, like Sir Thomas Bodley, collected books for the express purpose of forming, or adding to, public libraries.

My friend, Mr. Walter Stanley Graves, has in an appendix to this volume compiled a list of the principal sales of libraries in this country from an early period to the present time, which will be found to supply useful information about many of those collectors who are not otherwise mentioned in the book.

Mr. Locker-Lampson in the introduction to the catalogue of his library very pertinently remarks: 'It is a good thing to read books, and it need not be a bad thing to write them; but it is a pious thing to preserve those that have been some time written.' To collectors scholars owe a deep debt of gratitude, for innumerable are the precious manuscripts and rare printed books which they have rescued from destruction, and not a few of them have enriched by their gifts and bequests the public libraries of their country. Every lover of books must feel how greatly indebted he is to Archbishops Cranmer and Parker, the Earl of Arundel, Lord Lumley, Sir Robert Cotton, and other early collectors, for saving so many of the priceless manuscripts from the libraries of the suppressed monasteries and religious houses which, at the Reformation, intolerance, ignorance, and greed consigned to the hands of the tailor, the goldbeater, and the grocer. A large number of the treasures once to be found in these collections have been irrecoverably lost, but many a volume, now the pride of some great library, bears witness to the pious and successful exertions of these eminent men.

A love of book-collecting has always prevailed in this country, and since the end of the seventeenth century it has become very widely diffused. In the early days of the eighteenth century the Duke of Devonshire, the Earls of Oxford and Sunderland, and several other collectors, employed themselves during the winter months in rambling through various quarters of the town in search of additions to their libraries, and with some of these collectors the acquisition of books became a positive passion. In 1813 Dr. Dibdin thought that the thermometer of bibliomania had reached its highest point, and it would certainly appear to have been very high indeed, judging from the prices obtained at the Roxburghe and other sales of the time. For some years there was a period of depression, which perhaps was at the lowest between 1830 and 1850, but the desire to acquire rare books appears never to have been greater than at the present day, and for the choicest examples collectors are willing to give sums which dwarf into insignificance the prices which excited the astonishment of our fathers. These high prices may possibly be somewhat due to the spirited bidding of the great bookseller we have recently lost, and to the competition of our American cousins; but they are also distinct evidences that the beautiful and interesting volumes which issued from the presses of the old printers have not lost their charm for the bibliophiles of our own time. They have the advantage, too, of causing these treasures to be more valued, and consequently better treated, for it has been well said that nothing tends to the preservation of anything so much as making it bear a high price.

A chronological arrangement of the collectors has been adopted for several reasons as the preferable one, but an alphabetical list of their names will be found at the beginning of the volume. It ought also to be observed that accounts of the different libraries rarely mention the number of books contained in them, but when they have been sold by auction I have found by a careful examination of the sale catalogues that on an average each lot may be reckoned as consisting of about a volume and a half.

> 'For out of the olde feldes, as men saythe,
> Cometh al this newe come fro yere to yere,
> And out of olde bokes, in good faythe,
> Cometh al this newe science that men lere.'

> CHAUCER. — *Parlement of Foules.*

> W.Y.F.

ALPHABETICAL LIST OF COLLECTORS

Arundel, Henry Fitzalan, Earl of,

Ashburnham, Bertram, Earl of,

Askew, Dr. Anthony,

Bagford, John,

Banks, Sir Joseph, Bart.,

Beauclerk, Hon. Topham,

Beckford, William,

Bernard, Dr. Francis,

Bindley, James,

Brand, Rev. John,

Bridges, John,

Buckingham, Richard Grenville, Duke of,

Burghley, William Cecil, Lord,

Burney, Charles,

Burton, Robert,

Corser, Rev. Thomas,

Cotton, Sir Robert Bruce, Bart.,

Cracherode, Rev. C.M.,

Cranmer, Thomas, Archbishop of Canterbury,

Crawford, Alexander William, Earl of,

Daniel, George,

Dee, Dr. John,

Dent, John,

Devonshire, William, Duke of,

D'Ewes, Sir Symonds, Bart.,

Digby, Sir Kenelm,

Douce, Francis,

Edwards, James,

Fairfax, Brian,

Farmer, Rev. Richard, D.D.,

Fisher, John, Bishop of Rochester,

Folkes, Martin,

Gibson-Craig, James Thomson,

Gough, Richard,

Grenville, Right Hon. Thomas,

Guilford, Frederick North, Earl of,

Hamilton, Alexander, Duke of,

Hargrave, Francis,

Hearne, Thomas,

Heath, Benjamin,

Heath, Rev. Benjamin, D.D.,

Heber, Richard,

Hibbert, George,

Hoare, Sir Richard Colt, Bart.,

Huth, Henry,

Inglis, John Bellingham,

Laing, David,

Lansdowne, William Petty Fitzmaurice, Marquis of,

Laud, William, Archbishop of Canterbury,

Leicester, Robert Dudley, Earl of,

Le Neve, Peter,

Locker-Lampson, Frederick,

Lumley, John, Lord,

Luttrell, Narcissus,

Marlborough, George Spencer Churchill, Duke of,

Mead, Dr. Richard,

Miller, William Henry,

Moore, John, Bishop of Ely,

Morris, William,

Murray, John,

Norfolk, Thomas Howard, Earl of,

Oldys, William,

Orford, Horace Walpole, Earl of,

Oxford, Robert and Edward Harley, Earls of,

Parker, Matthew, Archbishop of Canterbury,

Pearson, Major Thomas,

Pembroke, Thomas Herbert, Earl of,

Pepys, Samuel,

Perkins, Frederick,

Perkins, Henry,

Phillipps, Sir Thomas, Bart.,

Ratcliffe, John,

Rawlinson, Dr. Richard,

Rawlinson, Thomas,

Reed, Isaac,

Roxburghe, John Ker, Duke of,

LIST OF ILLUSTRATIONS

Sir Hans Sloane, Bart.,

Book-plate of Robert Harley,

Book-stamp of Robert Harley,

Dr. Mead,

Earl of Sunderland,

Thomas Hearne,

Book-plate of Joseph Smith,

Dr. Richard Rawlinson,

Strawberry Hill,

Rev. C.M. Cracherode,

Book-stamp of Rev. C.M. Cracherode,

Book-plate of John Towneley,

Book-plate of James Bindley,

Rev. Dr. Heath,

Duke of Roxburghe,

Book-stamp of Michael Wodhull,

Right Hon. Thomas Grenville,

William Beckford,

Duke of Devonshire,

Small Book-stamp of the Earl of Balcarres,

Large Book-stamp of the Earl of Balcarres,

Frederick Locker-Lampson,

Book-plate of Frederick Locker-Lampson,

ROYAL COLLECTORS

lthough various books are incidentally mentioned in the Wardrobe Accounts of the first, second, and third Edwards, there is no good reason to believe that any English king, save perhaps Henry VI., or any royal prince, with the exception of Humphrey, Duke of Gloucester, and possibly of John, Duke of Bedford, possessed a collection large enough to be styled a library until the reign of Edward IV. In the Wardrobe Accounts of that Sovereign, preserved among the Harleian MSS. in the library of the British Museum, mention is made of the conveyance, in the year 1480, of the King's books from London to Eltham Palace. It is stated that some were put into 'the kings carr,' and others into 'divers cofyns of fyrre,' Several entries also refer to the 'coverying and garnysshing of the books of oure saide Souverain Lorde the Kynge' by Piers Bauduyn, stationer. Among the books mentioned are the works of Josephus, Livy, and Froissart, 'a booke of *the holy Trinite*,' 'a booke called *le Gouvernement of Kinges and Princes*,' 'a booke called *la Forteresse de Foy*,' and 'a booke called the *bible historial*.' The price paid for 'binding, gilding, and dressing' the copy of the *Bible Historiale* and the works of Livy was twenty shillings each, and for several others sixteen shillings each. Other entries show that the bindings were of 'Cremysy velvet figured,' with 'Laces and Tassels of Silk,' with 'Blue Silk and Gold Botons,' and with 'Claspes with Roses and the Kings Armes upon them.' 'LXX Bolions coper and gilt,' and 'CCC nayles gilt' were also used.

The first English king who formed a library of any size was Henry VII., and many entries are found in his Privy Purse Expenses relating to the purchase and binding of his books. The great ornament of his collection was the superb series of volumes on vellum bought of Antoine Vérard, the Paris publisher, which now forms one of the choicer treasures of the British Museum. Henry's principal library was kept in his palace at Richmond, where, with the exception of some volumes which seem to have been taken to Beddington by Henry VIII., it appears to have remained for more than a century after his death, for Justus Zinzerling, a native of Thuringia, and Doctor of Laws at Basle, states in his book of travels, entitled *Itinerarium Galliæ, etc.*, Lyons, 1616, that 'the most curious thing to be seen at Richmond Palace is Henry VII.'s library.' It was probably removed to Whitehall, for the only book in the library mentioned by Zinzerling, a *Genealogia Rerum Angliæ ab Adamo*, appears in a catalogue of Charles II.'s MSS. at Whitehall, compiled in 1666.

Henry VIII. inherited the love of his father for books, and added considerably to his collection. Besides the library at Richmond, Henry had a fine one at Westminster, a catalogue of which, compiled in 1542 or 1543, is still preserved in the Record Office. He had also libraries at Greenwich, Windsor, Newhall in Essex, and Beddington in Surrey. Some of his books were also kept at St. James's, for in the inventory of his furniture at that palace, entries occur of a *Description of the hollie lande*; 'a boke covered with vellat, embroidered with the Kings arms, declaring the same, in a case of black leather, with his graces arms'; and other volumes. Of these libraries the largest and most important appears to have been that at Westminster. It was fairly rich in the Greek and Latin classics, and in the writings of French and Italian authors. The English historians were well represented, but the principal feature of the collection was the works of the Fathers, which were very numerous. The library also contained no less than sixty primers, many of them being bound in 'vellat,' or in 'lether gorgiously gilted.' In the succeeding reign this library was purged 'of all massebookes, legendes, and other superstitiouse bookes' by an Order in Council, which also directed that 'the garnyture of the bookes being either golde or silver' should be delivered to Sir Anthony Aucher, the Master of the Jewel House.

The library at Greenwich contained three hundred and forty-one printed and manuscript volumes, besides a number of manuscripts, kept in various parts of the palace. An inventory, taken after the King's death, mentions among other books 'a greate booke called an Herballe,' 'twoo great Bibles in Latten,' and 'a booke, wrytten on parchment, of the processe betweene King Henry th' eight and the Ladye Katheryne Dowager.' The Windsor and Newhall libraries were smaller; the first comprising one hundred and nine, and the second sixty volumes. At Beddington were some remarkably choice books, including many beautiful editions printed for Antoine Vérard, probably some of those purchased by Henry VII. Among these was 'a greate booke of

2

parchment, written and lymned with gold of gravers worke, *de confessione Amantis.'*

Edward VI. and Mary during their short reigns added comparatively few books to the royal collection, nor are there many to be now found in it which were acquired by Elizabeth. It is difficult to say what became of this Queen's books, of which she appears to have possessed a considerable number; for Paul Hentzner tells us in his *Itinerary* that her library at Whitehall, when he visited it in 1598, was well stored with books in various languages, 'all bound in velvet of different colours, although chiefly red, with clasps of gold and silver; some having pearls and precious stones set in their bindings.' Probably the richness of the bindings had much to do with the disappearance of the books.

James I. is undoubtedly entitled to a place in the list of royal book-collectors, and the numerous fine volumes, many of them splendidly bound, with which he augmented the royal library, testify to his love of books. When but twelve years of age he possessed a collection of something like six hundred volumes, about four hundred of which are specified in a manuscript list, principally in the handwriting of Peter Young, who shared with George Buchanan the charge of James's education. This list is preserved in the British Museum, and was edited in 1893 by Mr. G.F. Warner, Assistant-Keeper of Manuscripts, for the Scottish History Society. After the death of the learned Isaac Casaubon, the King, at the instigation of Patrick Young, his librarian, purchased his entire library of his widow for the sum of two hundred and fifty pounds.

If James I. is entitled to be regarded as a collector, his eldest son Henry has even a better claim to the title. This young prince, who combined a great fondness for manly sports with a sincere love for literature, purchased from the executors of his tutor, Lord Lumley, the greater portion of the large and valuable collection which that nobleman had partly formed himself, and partly inherited from his father-in-law, Henry Fitzalan, Earl of Arundel, the possessor of a fine library at Nonsuch, comprising a number of manuscripts and many printed volumes which had belonged to Archbishop Cranmer. Henry's first care

3

after the acquisition of the books was to have them catalogued, and in his Privy Purse Expenses for the year 1609 we find the following entry: 'To Mr. Holcock, for writing a Catalogue of the Library which his Highness hade of my Lord Lumley, £8, 13s. 0d.' He also unfortunately had the volumes rebound and stamped with his arms and badges, a step which must have destroyed many interesting bindings. Henry only lived three years to enjoy his purchase, but during that time he made many additions to it. Edward Wright, the mathematician, who died in 1615, was his librarian, and received a salary of thirty pounds a year. As Henry died intestate his library became the property of his father, and passed into the royal collection which was given to the British Museum by George II.

Prince Rupert also appears to have inherited to some extent the love of books possessed by his grandfather James I. and his uncle Prince Henry, for he formed a well-selected library of about twelve hundred volumes, of which a catalogue is preserved among the Sloane manuscripts in the British Museum.[1]

King Charles I., although he bought some books, and had a number of valuable volumes given to him by his mother, can hardly be classed with the royal book-collectors. He had a greater inclination to paintings and music than to books, and it is said that he so excelled in the fine arts, that he might, if it were necessary, 'have got a livelihood by them.' One very precious addition to the royal library was, however, made during his reign: the famous *Codex Alexandrinus*, which Cyril Lucar, Patriarch of Constantinople, in 1624 placed in the hands of Sir Thomas Roe, the English ambassador to the Porte, as a gift to King James, but which did not reach England till four years later, when that sovereign was no longer alive. The royal library, which had narrowly escaped dispersion in the Civil War, was largely increased during the reign of Charles II., and at his death the works in it amounted to more than ten thousand. A love of books can scarcely be attributed to Charles, and although he certainly caused some important additions to be made to the collection—notably a number of valuable manuscripts which had belonged successively to John and Charles Theyer—the greater part of the increase may be ascribed to the operation of the Copyright Act, which was passed in the fourteenth year of this reign, and enabled the royal library to claim a copy of every work printed in the English dominions. From the death of Charles until the library was given to the nation by George II. in 1757 little interest was taken in it by the kings and queens who reigned in the interval.

HENRY, PRINCE OF WALES.

Although George III. was a man of somewhat imperfect education, he keenly regretted the loss of the royal collection, and no sooner was he seated on the throne than he began to amass the magnificent library which has now joined its predecessor in the British Museum. In this labour of love he was assisted by the sympathy and help of his Queen, who, Dr. Croly tells us, was in the habit of paying visits, with a lady-in-waiting, to Holywell Street and Ludgate Hill, where second-hand books were offered for sale. The King commenced the formation of his collection in 1762 by buying for about ten thousand pounds the choice library of Mr. Joseph Smith, who for many years was the British consul at Venice, and 'for seven or eight years the shops and warehouses of English booksellers were also sedulously examined, and large purchases were made from them. In this labour Dr. Johnson often assisted, actively as well as by advice.'[2] It is said the King expended during his long reign, on an average, about two thousand pounds a year in the purchase of books. In 1768 he despatched his illegitimate half-brother, Mr. Barnard, afterwards Sir Frederic Augusta Barnard, whom he had appointed his librarian, on a bibliographical tour on the Continent, during which so many valuable acquisitions were obtained for the library, that it at once took its place amongst the most important collections in the country, and after the death of the King, when the books it contained were counted by order of a select committee of the House of Commons, they were found to number 'about 65,250 exclusive of a very numerous assortment of pamphlets, principally contained in 868 cases, and requiring about 140 more cases to contain the whole.' These tracts, which number about nineteen thousand, have since been separately bound. The manuscripts belonging to the library amount to about four hundred and forty volumes, and there is also a magnificent collection of maps and topographical prints and drawings. The library is very rich in bibliographical rarities as well as in general literature. The Gutenberg Bible, the Bamberg Bible, the first and second Mentz Psalters (the first, a superb volume, is kept at Windsor Castle), and no less than thirty-nine Caxtons are among the most conspicuous of the many treasures of this splendid collection. The Caxtons were principally purchased at the sales of the libraries of James West in 1773, John Ratcliffe, the Bermondsey ship-chandler, who had acquired the remarkable number of forty-eight, in 1776, and of Richard Farmer in 1798. Edwards, in his *Lives of the Founders of the British Museum*, informs us that 'Ratcliffe's forty-eight Caxtons produced at his sale two hundred and thirty-six pounds, and that the king bought twenty of them at an aggregate cost of about eighty-five pounds. Amongst them were *Boethius de Consolatione Philosophiæ*, the first editions of *Reynard the Foxe* and the *Golden Legende*, the *Curial*, and the *Speculum Vitæ Christi*. The *Boethius* is a fine copy, and was obtained for four pounds six shillings.'

George III.'s library was first kept in the old Palace of Kew, which was pulled down in 1802, and afterwards in a handsome and extensive suite of rooms at Buckingham House; the site which at one time had been proposed for the British Museum. Scholars and students were at all times liberally permitted by the King to consult the books, and he also showed his kindly consideration for them by instructing his librarian 'not to bid either against a literary man who wants books for study, or against a known collector of small means.' A handsome catalogue of the library was compiled by Sir F.A. Barnard, who had charge of the collection from its commencement to the time when it was acquired by the nation. He died on the 27th of January 1830, aged eighty-seven.

The library in which George III. took so keen an interest was regarded by his successor as a costly burden, and there is little doubt he intended to dispose of it to the Emperor of Russia, who was very anxious to obtain it. The design of the King having become known to Lord Farnborough and Richard Heber, the collector, they communicated intelligence of it to Lord Liverpool and Lord Sidmouth, who were fortunately able to prevent the proposed sale of the books by offering the King an equivalent for them, the amount of which has not transpired, out of a fund known as the Droits of the Admiralty. On the completion of the bargain, George IV. addressed to Lord Liverpool a letter, dated January 15th, 1823, in which occur the following words: 'The King, my late revered and excellent father, having formed during a long series of years a most valuable and extensive library, consisting of about 120,000 volumes, I have resolved to present this collection to the British Nation.' This letter, printed in letters of gold, is preserved in the British Museum. In addition to the first edition of the Mentz Psalter; the Aldine Virgil of 1505, the Second Shakespeare folio which once belonged to Charles I., four Caxtons forming part of the collection, viz., *The Doctrinal of Sapience*, on parchment, *The Fables of Æsop*, *The Fayts of Arms*, and the *Recueil des Histoires de Troye*, with a few other volumes, were retained at Windsor.

Of the sons of George III., the Duke of Sussex alone appears to have inherited his father's love of collecting books, and he formed a magnificent library in his apartments at Kensington Palace. The collection consisted of more than fifty thousand volumes, twelve thousand of which were theological. It included a very considerable number of early Hebrew and other rare manuscripts, and about one thousand editions of the Bible. An elaborate catalogue of a portion of it, entitled *Bibliotheca Sussexiana*, was compiled by Dr. T.J. Pettigrew, the Duke's librarian, in two volumes, the first of which was printed in 1827, and the second in 1839.

After the Duke's death his books were sold by auction by Evans of Pall Mall. They were disposed of in six sales, the first of which took place in July 1844, and the last in August 1845; and they occupied altogether sixty-one days. The number of lots was fourteen thousand one hundred and seven, and the total amount realised nineteen thousand one hundred and forty-eight pounds.

The Duke of York possessed a good library, which was sold by Sotheby in May 1827, but it consisted almost entirely of modern books, and the Duke could hardly be considered a collector.

On his succession to the throne William IV., as he remarked, found himself the only sovereign in Europe not possessed of a library, and speedily took steps to acquire one. He did more than this, for in July 1833 he caused a special codicil to his will to be drawn up which sets forth that 'Whereas His Majesty hath made considerable additions to the Royal Libraries in His Majesty's several Palaces, and may hereafter make further additions thereto, Now His Majesty doth give and bequeath all such additions, whether the same have been or may be made by and at the cost of His Majesty's Privy Purse or otherwise unto and for the benefit of His Majesty's successors, in order that the said Royal Libraries may be transmitted entire.'

When on November 30th, 1834, the King signed this document, he made it yet more emphatic by the autograph note: 'Approved and confirmed by me the King, and I further declare that all the books, drawings, and plans collected in all the palaces shall for ever continue Heirlooms to the Crown and on no pretence whatever be alienated from the Crown.'

Thus explicitly protected from the fate which befell its two predecessors, this third Royal Library throve and prospered under Queen Victoria till it fills a handsome room at Windsor Castle. The few books reserved by George IV. give it importance as an antiquarian collection; but its development has been rather on historical and topographical than on antiquarian lines, though it possesses sufficient fine bindings to have supplied materials for a handsome volume of facsimiles by Mr. Griggs, edited with introduction and descriptions by Mr. R. R. Holmes, M.V.O., the King's Librarian at Windsor.

FOOTNOTES:

[1] Sloane MSS. 555.

[2] Edwards, *Lives of the Founders of the British Museum*, p. 469.

JOHN FISHER, BISHOP OF ROCHESTER, 1459?-1535

John Fisher, Bishop of Rochester, was born at Beverley in Yorkshire, and was the eldest son of Robert Fisher, a mercer of that town. The date of his birth is uncertain, some of his biographers placing it as early as 1459, and others as late as 1469. He was educated in the school attached to the collegiate church of his native place, and afterwards at Michael House, Cambridge (now incorporated into Trinity College), of which he became a Fellow in 1491, and Master in 1497. In 1501 he was elected Vice-Chancellor, and in 1504 Chancellor of the University. The respect in which Margaret, Countess of Richmond, the mother of Henry VII., held him, induced her to appoint him her chaplain and confessor, and it was principally through his exertions that the Countess's designs for founding St. John's College, Cambridge, were carried out, Fisher himself subsequently founding several fellowships, scholarships, and lectureships in connection with the college. He was appointed the first 'Lady Margaret's Professor of Divinity' in the University of Cambridge in 1503, and in 1504 was consecrated Bishop of Rochester. The firmness with which he opposed the royal supremacy, and the divorce of Henry VIII., brought on him the displeasure of the King, and in 1534, having given too ready a credence to the 'revelations' of Elizabeth Barton, 'the nun of Kent,' he was attainted of misprision of treason, and soon afterwards, on his refusal to acknowledge the King's supremacy and the validity of his marriage with Anne Boleyn, was committed with Sir Thomas More to the Tower. During his imprisonment Pope Paul III. created him a cardinal, an act which greatly increased the irritation of the King against him, and on the 22nd of June 1535 Fisher was beheaded on Tower Hill.

Bishop Fisher, who was the author of a considerable number of controversial tracts, was a man of great learning, and is said to have possessed the finest library in the country. In an account of his life and death first published in 1665, which was professedly written by Thomas Baily, a royalist divine, but is said to have been really the work of Dr. Richard Hall of Christ's College, Cambridge, who died in 1604, a relation is given of the seizure of his goods and books after his attainder. 'In the meantime lest any conveyance might be made of his goods remaining at Rochester, or elsewhere in Kent, the King sent one Sir Richard Moryson, of his Privy Chamber, and one Gostwick, together with divers other Commissioners, down into that Countrey, to make seisure of all his moveable goods that they could finde there, who being come unto Rochester, according to their Commission, entred his house; and the first thing they did was, they turned out all his Servants; then they fell to rifling his goods, whereof the chief part of them were taken for the Kings use, the rest they took for themselves; then they came into his Library, which they found so replenished, and with such kind of Books, as it was thought the like was not to be found againe in the possession of any one private man in Christendom; with which they trussed up and filled 32 great vats, or pipes, besides those that were imbezel'd away, spoyl'd and scatter'd; and whereas many yeares before he had made a deed of gift of all these books, and other his household stuffe to the Colledge of St John in Cambridge, ... two frauds were committed in this trespasse; the Colledge were bereaved of their gift, and the Bishop of his purpose.' An account of his library and its confiscation is also to be found in a manuscript treatise concerning his life and death, preserved among the Harleian MSS. in the British Museum. 'He had ye notablest Library of Books in all England, two long galleries full, the Books were sorted in stalls & a Register of ye names of every Book at ye end of every stall. All these his Books, & all his Hangings, plate, & vessels for Hawl, Chamber, Buttry, & Kitchin, he gave long before his death to St Joh: College, by a Deed of gift, & put them in possession thereof; & then by indenture did borrow all ye sd: books & stuff, to have ye use of y^m during his life, but at his apprehension, the Lord Crumwell caused all to be confiscated, which he gave to Moryson, Plankney of Chester, and other that were about him, & so ye College was defrauded of all this gift.'

Erasmus represents Fisher as a man of the greatest integrity, of deep learning, incredible sweetness of temper, and grandeur of soul; and Sir Thomas More declared that there was 'in this realm no one man, in wisdom, learning, and long approved vertue together, mete to be matched and compared with him.'

An excellent portrait of Fisher is preserved among the Holbein drawings at Windsor Castle, and others are to be found in several of the Colleges of the University of Cambridge.

THOMAS CRANMER, ARCHBISHOP OF CANTERBURY, 1489-1556

Thomas Cranmer, Archbishop of Canterbury, the events of whose life are so well known that it is not necessary to give an account of them here, possessed a very fine library, both of manuscripts and printed books. Many of the volumes it contained are still in existence, and fortunately they can be identified without difficulty, as almost all of them bear the Archbishop's name written, it is believed, by one of his secretaries. As might be expected, the books are principally of a theological nature, although copies of the Greek and Latin Classics, and of works treating of historical, scientific, legal, medical, and miscellaneous subjects are fairly numerous. Strype tells us 'that the library was the storehouse of ecclesiastical writers of all ages: and which was open for the use of learned men. Here old Latimer spent many an hour; and found some books so remarkable, that once he thought fit to mention one in a sermon before the King.' Strype adds that Cranmer both annotated the books in his library, and also made extracts from them, and the notes which are found in many of those which have been preserved to our time confirm his statement.

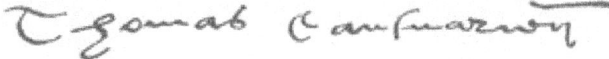

The fate of the library after the fall of its owner can only be conjectured.

Soon after the accession of Mary to the throne Cranmer was put on his trial for high treason, and sentence of death was passed upon him; and although at that time his life was spared, he was included in the Act of Attainder passed in Parliament against the Earl of Northumberland, deprived of his archbishopric, and committed to the Tower. He had to produce an inventory of his goods; and a list of all the property found in the Archbishop's palaces is still preserved in the Record Office, but, with the exception that it is stated that a 'bible with other bookes of service' were 'conveyed and stolen awaie' from the chapel, no mention is made of the books. They probably shared the fate of the goods of Robert Holgate, Archbishop of York, who was deprived of his see in 1554, and imprisoned in the Tower, and while confined there had his houses at Battersea and Cawood rifled of all their valuables.

It is evident that many of Cranmer's books were acquired by Lord Lumley, then a young nobleman in high favour at Court; and others by Lord Lumley's father-in-law, Henry Fitzalan, Earl of Arundel, the Lord Steward, who at that time was forming a library at Nonsuch, which he had recently purchased of the Queen; as a number of the volumes which were in their libraries have the Archbishop's name inscribed in them.

By far the larger portion of Cranmer's books which have survived to the present time are preserved in the British Museum, whither they came in 1757 as part of the old Royal Library, Henry Prince of Wales having purchased the Lumley and Arundel collections in 1609. But some are also possessed by the Cambridge University Library, the Bodleian Library, and the Archiepiscopal Library at Lambeth, while others are to be found on the shelves of various cathedral and collegiate libraries, and a few are in private hands. Those belonging to the two University Libraries were probably gifts of Lord Lumley, who presented eighty-four volumes to the Cambridge University Library in 1598, and forty to the Bodleian in the following year.

Cranmer was the author of several theological books, and he also wrote the prologue to the second edition of the 'Great Bible,' printed in 1540. His works were collected and arranged by H. Jenkyns, and published in four volumes at Oxford in 1833. There is a portrait of the Archbishop, at the age of fifty-seven, by G. Fliccius in the National Portrait Gallery, and others are at Cambridge and Lambeth. Cranmer was born at Aslacton Manor, in Nottinghamshire, on the 21st of July 1489, and burned at the stake at Oxford on the 21st of March 1556.

MATTHEW PARKER, ARCHBISHOP OF CANTERBURY, 1504-1575

ARCHBISHOP PARKER.

Matthew Parker, the second Protestant Archbishop of Canterbury, was born at Norwich on the 6th of August 1504. He was the son of William Parker, a calenderer of stuffs, who, Strype says, 'lived in very good reputation and plenty, and was a gentleman, bearing for his coat of arms on a field gules, three keys erected. To which shield, in honour of the Archbishop, a chevron was added afterwards, charged with three resplendent estoilles.' Parker was first privately educated, and afterwards proceeded to Corpus Christi College, Cambridge, of which college he was elected a Fellow in 1527. In the same year he took holy orders, and in 1535 was appointed Chaplain to Queen Anne Boleyn, who shortly afterwards conferred on him the Deanery of the College of St. John the Baptist at Stoke, near Clare in Suffolk. In 1538 he was created a Doctor of Divinity, and made one of the King's chaplains; and in 1544 he was elected Master of Corpus Christi College. He was chosen to the office of Vice-Chancellor of the University of Cambridge in 1545, and again in 1549. In 1552 he was appointed to the Deanery of Lincoln, of which he was deprived in 1554. During the reign of Mary, Parker lived quietly pursuing his studies, as he himself tells us, 'Postea privatus vixi, ita coram Deo lætus in conscientiâ meâ; adeoque nee pudefactus, nec dejectus, ut dulcissimum otium literarium, ad quod Dei bona providentia me revocavit, multo majores et solidiores voluptates mihi pepererit, quàm negotiosum illud et periculosum vivendi genus unquam placuit.' On the accession of Elizabeth he was summoned from his retirement and made Archbishop of Canterbury. His consecration took place on the 17th of December 1559. He died on the 17th of May 1575, and was buried in his private chapel at Lambeth, in a tomb which he had himself prepared. His remains, however, were disinterred in 1648 by Colonel Scot, the regicide, and buried under a dunghill, but after the Restoration they were replaced in the chapel.

Parker married in 1547 Margaret, daughter of Robert Harlestone of Matsal, in the county of Norfolk, by whom he had four sons, of whom two died in infancy, and a daughter. John, the eldest son, was knighted in 1603, and died in 1618.

Archbishop Parker was not only a great churchman, a distinguished scholar, and a warm promoter of learning, but he was also an ardent collector of books, and formed a very fine and valuable library, composed to a great extent of rare and choice manuscripts which had once belonged to the suppressed monasteries and religious houses. He also appears to have purchased Bale's fine collection of manuscripts.

Some of his books he presented to the Cambridge University Library during his lifetime, and in his will he made bequests of other volumes from his collection to that library. He also gave books to the libraries of the colleges of Caius and Trinity Hall, but the great bulk of his manuscripts and printed books he left to his own college of Corpus Christi.[3] An original list of these volumes is preserved in the college, with a note by John Parker, the Archbishop's son, stating that the missing volumes 'weare not found by me in my father's Librarie, but either lent or embezeled, whereby I could not deliver them to the college.' Some singular conditions were attached to this bequest by the Archbishop. 'Every year on the 6th of August, the collection is to be visited by the masters or *locum tenentes* of Trinity Hall and Caius, with two scholars on Archbishop Parker's foundation, and if, on examination of the library, twenty-five books are missing, or cannot be found within six months, the whole collection devolves to Caius. In that case the masters or *locum tenentes* of Trinity Hall and Benet, with two scholars on the same foundation, are the visitors: and if Caius College be guilty of the like neglect, the books to be delivered up to Trinity Hall: then the masters or *locum tenentes* of Caius and Benet, with two such scholars, become the inspectors; and in case of default on part of Trinity Hall, the whole collection reverts back to its former order. On the examination day, the visitors dine in the College Hall, and receive three shillings and four pence, and the scholars one shilling each.'[4] It is also probable that he was a benefactor to the library at Lambeth, for some of the manuscripts preserved there contain notes in his handwriting. The books which he did not specially bequeath he left to his son John, afterwards Sir John Parker.

In addition to the books which Parker gave to Corpus Christi College he founded several scholarships in connection with it, and bestowed upon it large sums of money and presents of plate. He also gave various pieces of plate to Gonville and Caius College and Trinity Hall.

Parker's love for books, and the pains he took to rescue the precious volumes which, after the dissolution of the abbeys and religious houses, were being destroyed or sold for common purposes, is so well told by Strype that his account is worth giving at length: 'His learning, though it were universal, yet it ran chiefly upon antiquity. Insomuch that he was one of the greatest antiquarians of the age. And the world is for ever beholden to him for two things; viz., for retrieving many ancient authors, Saxon and British, as well as Norman, and for restoring and enlightening a great deal of the ancient history of this noble island. He lived in, or soon after, those times, wherein opportunities were given for searches after these antiquities. For when the abbeys and religious houses were dissolved, and the books that were contained in the libraries thereunto belonging underwent the same fate, being miserably embezzled, and sold away to tradesmen for little or nothing, for their ordinary shop uses; then did our Parker, and some few more lovers of ancient learning, procure, both by their money and their friends, what books soever they could: and having got them into their possession, esteemed many of them as their greatest treasures, which other ignorant spoilers esteemed but as trash, and to be burnt, or sold at easy rates, or converted to any ordinary uses.

'He was therefore a mighty collector of books, to preserve, as much as could be, the ancient monuments of the learned men of our nation from perishing. And for that purpose he did employ divers men proper for such an end, to search all England over, and Wales, (and perhaps Scotland and Ireland too), for books of all sorts, some modern as well as ancient; and to buy them up for his use; giving them commission and authority under his own hand for doing the same. One of these, named Batman,[5] in the space of no more than four years, procured for our Archbishop to the number of 6700 books. It seems to be almost incredible, then, what infinite volumes all the rest of his agents in many more years must have retrieved for him.

'It was in those times that many of our choicest MSS. were conveyed out of the land beyond sea. Of this our Archbishop complained often; taking it heavily, as he wrote in one of his letters to Secretary

Cecyl, "that the nation was deprived of such choice monuments, so much as he saw they were in those days, partly by being spent in shops, and used as waste paper, or conveyed over beyond sea, by some who considered more their own private gain than the honour of their country." This was the reason he took so much pleasure in the said Secretary's library; "that such MSS. might be preserved within the realm, and not sent over by covetous stationers, or spoiled in the apothecaries' shops." ... For the retrieving of these ancient treatises and MSS. as much as might be, the Archbishop had such abroad, as he appointed to lay out for them wheresoever they were to be met with, as was shewn before.

'But he procured not a few himself from such in his own time as were studious in antiquity: as, namely, several Saxon books from Robert Talbot,[6] a great collector of such ancient writings in King Henry the Eighth's time, and an acquaintance of Leland, Bale, etc. Some of which writings the said Talbot had from Dr. Owen,[7] the said King Henry's physician; and some our archbishop likewise had from him; as appears in one of the Cotton volumes:[8] which is made up of a collection of various charters, etc., written out by Joh. Joscelyn.[9] Where at some of these MSS. collected, the said Joscelyn adds these notes, *The copy of this Dr. Talbot had of Dr. Owen. The Archbishop of Canterbury had this charter from Dr. Owen, etc.* There be other collections of this nature now remaining in Benet College, sometime belonging to this Talbot, which we may presume the Archbishop, partly by his own interest, and partly by the interest of Bale, Caius, and others, obtained; particularly his annotations upon that part of Antoninus's *Itinerarium* which belongs to Britain. And another *De Chartis quibusdam regum Britannorum.* These are mentioned by Anthony à Wood.

'And he kept such in his family as could imitate any of the old characters admirably well. One of these was Lyly, an excellent writer, and that could counterfeit any antique writing. Him the Archbishop customarily used to make old books complete, that wanted some pages; that the character might seem to be the same throughout. So that he acquired at length an admirable collection of ancient MSS. and very many too: as we may conjecture from his diligence for so many years as he lived, in buying and procuring such monuments. The remainders of his highly valuable collections are now preserved in several libraries of the Universities of Oxford and Cambridge, but chiefly in that of Benet College, Cambridge.'

Archbishop Parker was one of the founders of the Society of Antiquaries in 1572. He took a special interest in the early English Chronicles, and endeavoured to revive the study of the Saxon language. Among other works he caused to be printed *Flores Historiarum*, attributed to Matthew of Westminster, Matthew Paris's *Historia Major*, and the Latin text of Asser's *Alfredi Regis Res Gestæ* in Saxon characters, cut by John Day, the printer. He also, says Strype, 'laboured to forward the composing and publishing of a Saxon Dictionary.' His great work, *De Antiquitate Britannicæ Ecclesiæ et Privilegiis Ecclesiæ Cantuariensis, cum Archiepiscopis eiusdem 70*, which, if not written by him, was produced under his immediate supervision, was printed by John Day in Lambeth Palace in 1572. A very limited number of copies of this work, the first book privately printed in England, were struck off; not more than twenty-five are known to exist, and no two are found quite alike. The preparation of the Bishops' Bible, which was completed in 1568, was performed under his auspices. A presentation copy to Queen Elizabeth from the Archbishop of the *Flores Historiarum*, very handsomely bound, with the royal arms on the covers; and a copy of the work *De Antiquitate Britannicæ Ecclesiæ, etc.*, in a fine embroidered binding, which is also believed to have been presented to the Queen by the Archbishop, are preserved in the British Museum. These books were probably bound in Lambeth Palace, for in a letter to Lord Burghley, dated the 9th of May 1573, the Archbishop writes, with reference to the last-named work, 'I have within my house on wagis, drawers and cutters, paynters, lymners, wryters, and boke-bynders'; and he adds that he has sent Lord Burghley a copy of it 'bound by my man.'

A list of Parker's writings, and his editions of authors will be found in Coopers' *Athenæ Cantabrigienses*. There are portraits of him in Lambeth Palace, the Guildhall at Norwich, Corpus Christi College, and in the Master's Lodge, Trinity College, Cambridge. There is also a rare portrait of him, engraved in 1573, by Remigius Hogenberg, who appears to have been in the service of the Archbishop.

FOOTNOTES:

[3] An interesting account of the sources of the manuscripts, by Montague Rhodes James, Litt. D., Director of the Fitzwilliam Museum, was published in 1899 by the Cambridge Antiquarian Society.

[4] Hartshorne, *Book Rarities in the University of Cambridge*, p. 9.

[5] Dr. Stephen Batman, one of the Archbishop's domestic chaplains, editor of *De Proprietatibus Rerum*, by Bartholomeus Anglicanus.

[6] Robert Talbot, Rector of Haversham, Berkshire, and Treasurer of Norwich Cathedral, was the son of John Talbot of Thorpe Malsover, Northamptonshire. He was born about 1505, and was educated at Winchester and New College, Oxford. Camden calls him 'a learned antiquary,' and Lambarde describes him as 'a diligent trauayler in the Englishe hystorye.' He died in 1558, and was buried in Norwich Cathedral. His choicest manuscripts were left by him to New College.

[7] Dr. Owen, physician to King Henry VIII., King Edward VI., and Queen Mary. He died in 1558, and was buried in St. Stephen's, Walbrook.

[8] Vitellius D. 7.

[9] An antiquary who resided in the Archbishop's house, and who wrote the lives in *De Antiquitate Britannicæ Ecclesiæ*.

HENRY FITZALAN, EARL OF ARUNDEL, 1513?-1580

Henry Fitzalan, twelfth Earl of Arundel, was born about the year 1513. He was the only son of William Fitzalan, eleventh Earl of Arundel, K.G., by his second wife, Anne, daughter of Henry Percy, fourth Earl of Northumberland.

THE EARL OF ARUNDEL'S DEVICE.

When fourteen years of age his father was anxious to place him in the household of Cardinal Wolsey, but he preferred to offer his service to his godfather, King Henry VIII., 'who did nobly receave him, and well esteemed of him for the same.'[10] In 1534 he was summoned to Parliament in his father's barony as Lord Maltravers,[11] and in 1536, although only twenty-three years of age, he was appointed Governor of Calais, a post he held until the death of his father in January 1544. On the 24th of April in the same year he was made a K.G., and in the following July he received the appointment of 'Marshal of the Field' in the army which invaded France. He greatly distinguished himself at the siege of Boulogne, and on his return home he was made Lord Chamberlain, which office he held until the fourth year of King Edward VI.'s reign, when, on a false and ridiculous charge of abusing the privileges of his post to enrich himself and his friends, he was deprived of it, and fined twelve thousand pounds, eight thousand pounds of which was afterwards remitted.[12]

On the death of Edward, Arundel took a prominent part in the proceedings which placed Mary on the throne, and as a reward for his exertions he was made Lord Steward of the Household, and was also given a seat on the Council Board. Queen Elizabeth, on her accession to the crown, continued him in all the appointments which he had held in the preceding reign, and on several occasions visited him at Nonsuch, his residence at Cheam in Surrey. These marks of kindness led him, it is said, to aspire to a union with his royal mistress; but being disappointed in gaining her hand, and 'being miscontented with sundry things,' in 1564 he resigned his post of Lord Steward 'with sundry Speeches of Offence,'[13] which so displeased Elizabeth that she ordered him to confine himself to his house. He afterwards partially regained the favour of the Queen, but having endeavoured to promote the marriage of his widowed son-in-law, the Duke of Norfolk, with Mary Queen of Scots, he was once more placed under arrest, and although after a time he obtained his release, it was followed by further imprisonment, and he did not finally regain his liberty until some months after the execution of Norfolk on the 2nd of June 1572.

Arundel passed the remainder of his life in retirement, affectionately tended until her death in 1577 by 'his nursse and deare beloved childe' Lady Lumley. He died on the 24th of February 1580 at Arundel House in the Strand, and was buried in the Collegiate Chapel at Arundel, where a monument, with an inscription by his son-in-law, Lord Lumley, was erected to his memory.

Arundel was twice married. By his first wife, Katherine, second daughter of Thomas Grey, Marquis of Dorset, he had one son, Henry, Lord Maltravers, who died in 1556, and two daughters: Jane, who married Lord Lumley, and Mary, who became the wife of Thomas Howard, Duke of Norfolk, beheaded in 1572. His second wife, Mary, who died in 1557, was a daughter of Sir John Arundell of Lanherne, Cornwall, and widow of Robert Ratcliffe, first Earl of Sussex. By her he had no issue.

With the assistance of Humphrey Llwyd, the physician and antiquary, who married Barbara, sister of Lord Lumley, Lord Arundel formed at his residence of Nonsuch a fine collection of books, many of which had once been the property of Archbishop

Cranmer. An account of this mansion is given in the manuscript Life of Lord Arundel, to which we have already alluded, and it also contains a reference to his library. 'This Earle moreover continewed allwayes of a greate and noble mynde. Amonge the number of whose doings, that past in his tyme, this one is not the least, to showe his magnificence, that perceivinge a sumptuous house called Nonsuche to have bene begon, but not finished, by his first maister Kinge Henry the eighte, and thearfore in Quene Maryes tyme, thoughte mete rather to have bene pulled downe and solde by peacemeale then to be perfited at her charges, he, for the love and honour he bare to his olde maister, desired to buye the same house, by greace, of the Quene, for wch he gave faire lands unto her Highnes; and having the same, did not leave till he had fullye finished it in buildings, reparations, paviments and gardens, in as ample and perfit sorte as by the first intente and meaninge of the saide Kinge his old maister, the same should have bene performed, and so it is nowe evident to be beholden of all strangers, and others, for the honour of this Realme as a pearle thereof. The same he haith lefte to his posterity, garnished and replenished with riche furnitures; amonge the wch his Lybrarye is righte worthye of remembrance.'

Lord Arundel left Nonsuch, with its library and furniture, together with the greater part of his estates, to his son-in-law, Lord Lumley.

There are portraits of the Earl of Arundel by Holbein and Sir Anthony More. That by Holbein, which is in the collection of the Marquis of Bath, is engraved in Lodge's *Portraits of Illustrious Personages*.

FOOTNOTES:

[10] MS. Life of the Earl of Arundel, evidently written by one of his most intimate servants, probably a chaplain.—*Royal MSS.*, 17 A ix., British Museum.

[11] *Complete Peerage of England, etc.* Edited by G.E.C.

[12] 'Th' erle of Arrundel committed to his house for certaine crimes of suspicion against him, as pluking downe of boltes and lokkes at Westminster, giving of my stuff away, etc., and put to a fine of 12,000 pound to be paide a 1000 pound yerely, of which he was after released.' — *Journal of King Edward VI.*, Cotton MSS., C. x., British Museum.

[13] Strype, *Annals* (London, 1709), i. 413.

SIR THOMAS SMITH, 1513-1577

SIR THOMAS SMITH'S
BOOK-STAMP.

Sir Thomas Smith, who was Secretary of State to King Edward VI., and afterwards to Queen Elizabeth, was born at Saffron Walden, Essex, on the 23rd of December 1513. He was the son of John Smith of Saffron Walden and Agnes Charnock, a member of an old Lancashire family. When eleven years old he was sent to Queens' College, Cambridge, as he himself informs us in his *Autobiographical Notes*, now preserved in the British Museum,[14] which he wrote for the purpose of having his nativity cast: '1525. Sub fine II āni circa festū Michis Cantabrigiam sū missus ad bonas I[r]as.' Here he so greatly distinguished himself that King Henry VIII. chose him and John Cheke, afterwards tutor to Prince Edward, to be his scholars, and allotted them salaries for the encouragement of their studies. Cheke makes mention of this honour in an epistle to the King prefixed to his edition of Two Homilies of St. John Chrysostom, published at London in 1543: 'Cooptasti me et Thomam Smithum socium atque æqualem meum, in scholasticos tuos.' Smith specially applied himself to the study of the Greek classics, and also to the reformation of the faulty pronunciation of the Greek language which then prevailed; and in a short time, so Strype, in his *Life of Sir T. Smith*, tells us, his more correct way 'prevailed all the University over.' He also endeavoured to introduce a new English alphabet of twenty-nine letters, and to amend the spelling of the time, 'some of the syllables,' he considered, 'being stuffed with needless letters.' As early as 1531 he had become a Fellow of his college, and in 1534 he was chosen University Orator. In 1540 Smith paid a visit to the Continent, and proceeded to Padua, where he took the degree of D.C.L. On his return to England in 1542 he was made LL.D. at Cambridge, and at the beginning of 1544 was appointed Regius Professor of Civil Law at the University. In the succeeding year he served as Vice-Chancellor, and also became Chancellor to Goodrich, Bishop of Ely, by whom in 1546 he was collated to the rectory of Leverington, Cambridgeshire, and also ordained priest, a fact unknown to Strype. About the same time he received a prebend from the Dean of Lincoln, and soon after he became Provost of Eton and Dean of Carlisle. Towards the end of February 1547, Smith was summoned to court, and 'mutata clericali veste, modoque, ac vivendi forma,'[15] he was made Clerk of the Privy Council, and Master of the Court of Requests of the Duke of Somerset, then Lord Protector. On the 14th of April 1548 he was sworn one of the King's Secretaries, and knighted in the beginning of the following year. Shortly after his appointment Smith was sent as ambassador to the Emperor Charles V., and in 1551 he took part in the embassy to France to arrange a match for the King with the French sovereign's eldest daughter. On the accession of Mary he lost all his offices and preferments, but he managed to pass through this dangerous reign in safety; and Strype says of him, 'that when many were most cruelly burnt for the profession of the religion which he held, he escaped, and was saved even in the midst of the fire, which he probably might have an eye to in changing the crest of his coat-of-arms, which now was a salamander living in the midst of a flame; whereas before it was an eagle holding a writing-pen flaming in his dexter claw.' When Elizabeth came to the throne, Smith returned to court, and was engaged in several embassies to France. In 1572 the Queen conferred on him the Chancellorship of the Order of the Garter; and shortly afterwards, on Lord Burghley's preferment to the office of Lord Treasurer, vacant by the death of the Marquis of Winchester, made him Secretary of State, a post which, four-and-twenty years before, he held under Edward VI. Smith died at his residence called Mounthaut, or Hill-hall, in Essex on the 12th of August 1577, and was buried in the parish church of Theydon Mount, where a monument was erected to his memory. He was twice married, but had no children by either of his wives.

Sir Thomas Smith possessed a fine library of about a thousand volumes. He bequeathed all his Latin and Greek books, as well as his great globe, of his own making, to Queens' College, Cambridge, or, if that college did not care to have them, to Peterhouse. Some of his Italian and French books he gave to the Queen's Library, and many volumes were also left to friends. Strype gives a list of the contents of the library at Hill-hall in 1566.

Smith was the author of several works, the principal one being *De Republica Anglorum; the Maner of Gouvernement or Policie of the Realm of England*, London, 1583, 4to. Between 1583 and 1640 this work passed through ten editions, and several Latin and other translations of it have been published.

A portrait of him by Holbein is at Theydon Mount, and another is preserved at Queens' College, Cambridge.

FOOTNOTES:

[14] Sloane MSS. 325, f. 2.

[15] *Autobiographical Notes* by Sir T. Smith.

WILLIAM CECIL, LORD BURGHLEY, 1520-1598

William Cecil, Lord Burghley, a relation of whose life would be the history of England during the reign of Elizabeth, was born in 1520 and died in 1598. This great statesman, who at the age of sixteen delivered a lecture on the logic of the Schools, and at nineteen one on the Greek language, found time amid the cares and anxieties attendant on his high position to form a library, which Strype tells us was a very choice one. The same authority also mentions that he gave many books to the University of Cambridge, 'both Latin and Greek, concerning the canon and civil law and physic.' In 1687 a considerable portion of his printed books and manuscripts was sold by auction. The title-page of the sale catalogue reads 'Bibliotheca Illustriss: sive Catalogus Variorum Librorum in quâvis Linguâ et Facultate Insignium ornatissimæ Bibliothecæ Viri Cujusdam Prænobilis ac Honoratissimi olim defuncti, Libris rarissimis tam Typis excusis quàm Manuscriptis refertissimæ: Quorum Auctio habebitur Londini, ad Insigne Ursi in Vico dicto Ave-Mary-Lane prope Templum D. Pauli, Novemb. 21, 1687. Per T. Bentley and B. Walford, Bibliopolas. Lond.'; and in the Preface we read:—'If the catalogue, here presented, were only of Common Books, and such as were easie to be had, it would not have been very necessary to have Prefac'd any thing to the Reader: But since it appears in the World with two Circumstances, which no Auction in England (perhaps) ever had before; nor is it probable that the like should frequently happen again, it would seem an Oversight, if we should neglect to advertise the Reader of them. The first is, That it comprises the main part of the Library of that Famous Secretary William Cecil, Lord Burleigh: which consider'd, must put it out of doubt, that these Books are excellent in their several kinds and well-chosen. The second is, That it contains a greater number of Rare Manuscripts than ever yet were offer'd together in this way, many of which are rendred the more valuable by being remark'd upon by the hand of the said great Man. This Auction will begin on Monday the 21st day of November next 1687, at the sign of the Bear in Ave-Mary-Lane, near the West-end of St. Paul's Church, continuing day by day the first five days of every Week, till all the Books are sold, from the Hours of Nine in the Morning till Twelve, and from Two till Six in the Evening.' There were three thousand eight hundred and forty-four lots of printed books, and four hundred and thirteen manuscripts in two hundred and forty-three lots in the sale. A copy of the catalogue, marked with the prices, is preserved in the British Museum. The printed books in the sale do not appear to have been exceptionally choice or rare, but there were some valuable manuscripts. A few of the most notable, together with the prices they fetched, are given in the following list: —

Biblia Sacra Antiquissima, folio magno, vellum—six pounds, twelve shillings; *Polychronicon vetus MS. per Radulphum Hygden, nunquam Latine impressum*, vellum—eleven pounds; *Wicklif's Book of Postils or Sermons in Old English*—seven pounds, two shillings and six pence; *Other Discourses by him*—ten pounds, two shillings and six pence; *Wilhelmus Malmesburiensis de gestis Regum Angliæ*, vellum—seven pounds, three shillings; *L'Histoire du Roy Arthur, avec des Figures d'orées*, folio grand on vellum—three pounds, two shillings; *Le Chronique de Jean Froissart des guerres de France et D'Angleterre*, folio grand, *avec des belles Figures*, vellum—three pounds, nine shillings; *Norden · Speculum Britanniæ*—four pounds, seven shillings. It is not known to whom these books belonged at the period of the sale, but it appears probable they were the property of James Cecil, fourth Earl of Salisbury (a descendant of Lord Burghley's younger son), who succeeded to the title in 1683, and died in 1694. He was mixed up in the troubles of the time, and was, says Macaulay, 'foolish to a proverb,' and the 'prey of gamesters.' John Cecil, Earl of Exeter, from 1678 to 1700, who was descended from Lord Burghley's elder son, was himself a book collector, and therefore not likely to part with the library of his illustrious ancestor.

LORD BURGHLEY'S BOOK-STAMP.

The bindings of Lord Burghley's books are generally stamped with his arms, which are sometimes encircled by the order of the Garter, but a little volume preserved in the library of the British Museum simply bears his name and that of his second wife, his affectionate companion for forty-three years. Lord Burghley left an immense mass of papers, which are now preserved at Hatfield House, the Record Office, the British Museum, etc. Those in the British Museum, which consist of one hundred and twenty-one folio volumes of state papers and the miscellaneous correspondence of Lord Burghley, together with his private note-book and journals, passed from Sir Michael Hickes, one of the statesman's secretaries, to a descendant, Sir William Hickes, by whom they were sold to Chiswell, the bookseller, and by him to Strype, the historian. On Strype's death they came into the hands of James West, and from his executors they were acquired by William Petty, first Marquis of Lansdowne, whose manuscripts were purchased by the Trustees of the British Museum in 1807.[16]

THOMAS WOTTON, 1521-1587

Thomas Wotton was born in 1521 at Bocton or Boughton Place, in the parish of Boughton Malherbe, in the county of Kent, and succeeded his father, Sir Edward Wotton, in that estate in 1550. He was appointed sheriff of the county of Kent in the last year of Queen Mary, and in July 1573 he entertained Elizabeth and her court at his residence, Bocton Place, when she offered him knighthood, which he declined. Wotton was twice married. By his first wife, Elizabeth, daughter of Sir John Rudstone, he had three sons: Edward, knighted by Elizabeth, and afterwards raised to the peerage as Baron Wotton by James I.; and James and John, who were also made knights by Elizabeth. His second wife was Eleanora, daughter of Sir William Finch of Eastwell in Kent, and widow of Robert Morton, Esq., of the same county, by whom he had a son, Henry, the poet and statesman, who was knighted by James I. He died in London on the 11th of January 1587, and was buried in the parish church of Boughton Malherbe, where a monument was erected to his memory.

ARMS OF
THOMAS WOTTON.

Wotton was celebrated for his hospitality, and was much beloved and respected by all who knew him. He was also a patron of learning, and possessed a fine and extensive collection of books, remarkable for their handsome bindings. They are generally ornamented in a style similar to that used on the volumes bound for Grolier, whose motto he adopted. Although the majority of the bindings executed for him bear the legend THOMAE WOTTONI ET AMICORVM as the only mark of their ownership, they are sometimes impressed with his arms.

Izaak Walton, in his *Life of Sir Henry Wotton*, states that Thomas Wotton 'was a gentleman excellently educated, and studious in all the liberal arts, in the knowledge whereof he attained unto great perfection; who though he had—besides those abilities, a very noble and plentiful estate, and the ancient interest of his predecessors— many invitations from Queen Elizabeth to change his country recreations and retirement for a court life:—offering him a knighthood, and that to be but as an earnest of some more honourable and more profitable employment under her; yet he humbly refused both, being a man of great modesty, of a most plain and single heart, of an ancient freedom, and integrity of mind.'

FOOTNOTES:

[16] Edwards, *Lives of the Founders of the British Museum* (London, 1870), p. 426.

DR. DEE, 1527-1608

Dr. John Dee, 'that perfect astronomer, curious astrologer and serious geometrician,' as he is styled by Lilly, was born in London on the 13th of July 1527. He was the son of Rowland Dee, who, according to Wood, was a wealthy vintner, but who is described by Strype as Gentleman Sewer to Henry VIII. In his *Compendious Rehearsal* Dee informs us that he possessed a very fine collection of books, 'printed and anciently written, bound and unbound, in all near 4000, the fourth part of which were written books. The value of all which books, by the estimation of men skilful in the arts, whereof the books did and do intreat, and that in divers languages, was well worth 2000 lib.'; and he adds that he 'spent 40 years in divers places beyond the seas, and in England in getting these books together.' He specially mentions 'that four written books, one in Greek, two in French, and one in High Dutch cost 533 lib.' His library also contained a 'great case or frame of boxes, wherein some hundreds of very rare evidences of divers Irelandish territories, provinces and lands were laid up; and divers evidences ancient of some Welsh princes and noblemen, their great gifts of lands to the foundations or enrichings of Sundry Houses of Religious men. Some also were there the like of the Normans donations and gifts about and some years after the Conquest.' Dee, in a letter from Antwerp to Sir William Cecil, afterwards Lord Burghley, dated February 16, 1563, also states that he had purchased a curious book (probably a manuscript), *Steganographia*, by Joannes Trithemius, which was so rare that '1000 crowns had been offered in vain' for a copy. Dee placed his library in his house at Mortlake, Surrey, and so great was its repute, that on the 10th of March 1575, Queen Elizabeth, attended by many of her courtiers, paid him a visit for the purpose of examining it; but learning that his wife had been buried that day, she would not enter the house, but requested him to show her his famous magic glass, and describe its properties, which he accordingly did 'to her Majesty's great contentment and delight.' In 1583, during his absence on the Continent, the populace, who execrated him as 'a caller of divels,' broke into his house and destroyed a great part of his furniture, collections, and library. On his return to his home in 1589, he succeeded in regaining about three-fourths of his books; but these were gradually dispersed in consequence of the pecuniary difficulties he was in during the latter years of his life. Lilly states that 'he died very poor, enforced many times to sell some book or other to buy his dinner with.' An autograph catalogue of both his printed and manuscript books, dated September 6, 1583, is preserved among the Harleian manuscripts in the British Museum.[17] His private diary, and a catalogue of his manuscripts, were edited in 1842 for the Camden Society by Mr. J.O. Halliwell, F.R.S., from the original manuscripts in the Ashmolean Museum and Trinity College, Cambridge. Another portion of his diary, preserved in the Bodleian Library, was edited by Mr. J.E. Baily, F.S.A., and printed (twenty copies only) at London in 1880. In 1556 Dee presented to Queen Mary 'A Supplication for the recovery and preservation of ancient Writers and Monuments.' In this interesting document he laments the spoil and destruction of so many and so notable libraries through the subverting of religious houses, and suggests that a commission should be appointed with power to demand that all possessors of manuscripts throughout the realm should send their books to be copied for the Queen's library, so that it might 'in a very few years most plentifully be furnished, and that without one penny charge to the Queen, or doing injury to any creature.' He himself undertook to procure copies of the famous manuscripts at the Vatican, St. Mark's, Venice, Bologna, Florence, Vienna, etc.

Dee wrote a large number of works, but comparatively few of them have been printed. No fewer than seventy-nine are enumerated in Coopers' *Athenæ Cantabrigienses*. A catalogue of his writings, printed and unprinted, is given in his *Compendious Rehearsal*. Many of his manuscripts came into the possession of Elias Ashmole, the eminent antiquary.

Aubrey says of Dee that 'he was a great peace-maker; if any of the neighbours fell out, he would never let them alone till he had made them friends. He was tall and slender. He wore a gown like an artist's gown, with hanging sleeves, and a slit. He had a very fair, clear, sanguine complexion, a long beard as white as milk. A very handsome man.'

DR. DEE. From the Ashmolean portrait as engraved by Schencker.

He died in December 1608, and was buried in the chancel of Mortlake Church.

FOOTNOTES:

[17] *Harl. MSS.* 1879.

ROBERT DUDLEY, EARL OF LEICESTER, 1532?-1588

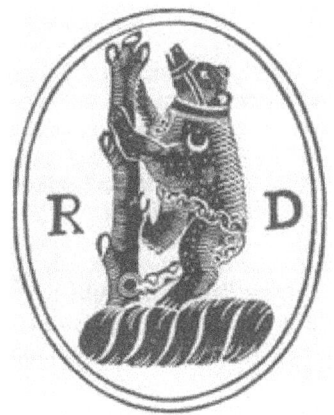

BOOK-STAMP OF LORD LEICESTER.

Robert Dudley, Baron Denbigh, and Earl of Leicester, the favourite of Elizabeth, was born on the 24th of June in 1532 or 1533. He was the fifth son of John Dudley, Duke of Northumberland, who was executed in August 1553 for maintaining the claims of Lady Jane Grey, his daughter-in-law, to the crown. He was himself condemned to death for the part he took in the attempt of his father to place Lady Jane upon the throne; but on the intercession of the Lords of the Council was pardoned by Queen Mary, who received him into favour, and appointed him master of the English ordnance at the siege of St. Quentin, where his brother Henry was killed. On the accession of Elizabeth, Dudley soon became a great favourite of the Queen, who advanced him to the highest honours, and, there is little doubt, at one time contemplated a marriage with him. Leicester was a generous supporter of learning, and his letters show that he was himself possessed of considerable literary ability. Geoffrey Whitney, in his dedication of his *Choice of Emblems* to the Earl, mentions 'his zeale and honourable care of those that love good letters,' and states that 'divers, who are nowe famous men, had bin through povertie longe since discouraged from their studies if they had not founde your honour so prone to bee their patron.' Little is known respecting Leicester's library, which must have been a large and fine one, for many handsomely bound volumes which once belonged to it are found both in public and private collections. This dispersion of his books may probably be accounted for by the sale of his goods after his death, as mentioned by Camden in his *Annals of the Reign of Elizabeth*: 'But whereas he was in the Queen's debt, his goods were sold at a public Outcry: for the Queen, though in other things she were favourable enough, yet seldom or never did she remit the debts owing to her Treasury.' In the *Notices of London Libraries*, by John Bagford and William Oldys, it is stated: 'At Lambeth Palace over the Cloyster is a well-furnished library. The oldest of the books were Dudley's, Earl of Leicester.' Not more, however, than nine or ten which belonged to the Earl are to be found there now. Almost all his books have his well-known crest, the bear and ragged staff, stamped upon the covers, but a few of them bear his arms instead.

Leicester was suddenly seized with illness on his way to Kenilworth, and died at his house at Cornbury, in Oxfordshire, on the 4th of September 1588. The suddenness of his death gave rise to a suspicion that it was caused by poison; and Ben Jonson tells a story that he had given his wife 'a bottle of liquor which he willed her to use in any faintness, which she, not knowing it was poison, gave him, and so he died.' He was buried at Warwick.

JOHN, LORD LUMLEY, 1534?-1609.

John, Lord Lumley, was born in or about the year 1534. He was the only son of George Lumley of Twing, in the county of Yorkshire, who was executed in 1537 at Tyburn, for high treason. On the death of his grandfather, Lord Lumley, in 1544, John succeeded to the family estates, and in 1547 he was permitted to take the title of Baron Lumley. He matriculated in May 1549, as a fellow-commoner of Queens' College, Cambridge, and was also educated in the court of King Edward VI., whose funeral he attended. On the 29th of September 1553 he was created a Knight of the Bath, and, two days later, was present, together with his wife, at the coronation of Queen Mary;[18] Lady Lumley riding in the third chariot with five other baronesses.

LORD LUMLEY. From the Cheam portrait as engraved for Sandford.

On the accession of Queen Elizabeth, he, with other lords, was appointed to attend her Majesty on her journey from Hatfield to London. In 1559 his father-in-law, the Earl of Arundel, at that time Chancellor of the University of Cambridge, nominated him High Steward of the University. Lord Lumley was sent to the Tower in 1569 on suspicion of being implicated in intrigues to bring about the marriage of his brother-in-law the Duke of Norfolk with Mary, Queen of Scots, and to re-establish the Roman Catholic religion. In the next year he was released, but in October 1571 he was again imprisoned, and he did not obtain his liberty until April 1573, ten months after the execution of the Duke of Norfolk. At a later period he appears to have quite regained the favour of the Queen, for we read that she accepted as a New Year's gift from him in 1584 'a cup of cristall graven and garnished with golde,' and that at the New Year 1587 he presented to her 'a booke, wherein are divers Psalmes in Lattin written, the boards greate, inclosed all over on the outeside with golde enamuld cut-worke, with divers colours and one litle claspe.'[19] In 1580 Lord Lumley lost his father-in-law, who by a deed, dated March 14th, 1566, had conveyed a great part of his estates to Lord Lumley and Jane his eldest daughter, Lord Lumley's wife; and after her decease, Lord Arundel confirmed the same to Lord Lumley by his will, which he made a few months before his death. Among the estates bequeathed were the palace and park of Nonsuch, which in 1590 Lord Lumley conveyed to the Queen in exchange for lands of the yearly value of five hundred and thirty-four pounds. Lord Lumley died on the 11th of April 1609 at his residence on Tower Hill, in the parish of St. Olave, Hart Street, and was buried in Cheam church, in the county of Surrey, where a monument was erected to his memory in the Lumley aisle, which he had built. By his first wife, Jane, who died in 1577, Lord Lumley had three children, who all died in infancy. He had no issue by his second wife, Elizabeth, daughter of John, Lord Darcy of Chiche, who survived him nine years.

Lord Lumley, Bishop Hacket says, 'did pursue Recondite Learning as much as any of his Honourable Rank in those Times, and was the owner of a most precious Library, the search and collection of Mr. Humfry Llyd.'[20] This fine library, which to a great extent was formed by the books bequeathed to him by his father-in-law in 1580, contained many volumes which had evidently been once the property of Archbishop Cranmer, as they bear his name, which is sometimes accompanied by the signature of Lumley, and in other instances by the signatures of both Arundel and Lumley. Lord Lumley also collected a number of portraits.

Lord Lumley made liberal donations of books to the University Library of Cambridge and the Bodleian Library during his lifetime, and also 'bestowed many excellent Pieces printed and manuscript upon Mr. Williams[21] for alliance sake.' After his death in 1609 the remainder of his library, 'which was probably more valuable than any other collection then existing in England, with the exception of that of Sir Robert Cotton,'[22] was purchased by Henry, Prince of Wales. At the Prince's decease in 1612 the books went to augment the old royal library of England, which was given to the nation in 1757 by King George II. A curious and interesting inventory of the 'moveables' found at Lumley Castle after the death of its owner is given in Surtees's *History of Durham*, vol. ii. pp. 158-163. The goods comprised pictures, sculptures, 'peeces of hangines of arras with golde of the Storie of Troye, Quene Hester, Cipio and Haniball,' etc., hangings of 'gilte leather,' 'Beddes' of gold, silver, and silk, splendid chairs, and velvet and Turkey carpets, and were valued at fourteen hundred and four pounds, seventeen shillings and eightpence, but no mention is made of any books. Most of these treasures were sold by auction at the beginning of the nineteenth century. Among the Royal MSS. preserved in the British Museum is a translation of Erasmus's *Institutio Principis Christiani*, signed 'Your lordshippes obedient sone, J. Lumley, 1550.' As Lord Lumley's own father was put to death in 1537, this was evidently addressed to his father-in-law, who has written his name Arundel on the first page. Lord Lumley was a member of the old Society of Antiquaries, and in conjunction with Dr. Caldwell[23] he founded a surgery lecture in the Royal College of Physicians, endowing it with forty pounds per annum.

The Lumley family was one of considerable importance and antiquity, and an amusing account is given by Pennant[24] and

41

Hutchinson[25] of a visit paid by King James I. to Lumley Castle on the 13th of April 1603. In the absence of Lord Lumley the King was received by Dr. James, Dean of Durham, 'who expatiated on the pedigree of their noble host, without missing a single ancestor, direct or collateral, from Liulph to Lord Lumley, till the King, wearied with the eternal blazon, interrupted him, "Oh mon, gang na further; let me digest the knowledge I ha gained, for on my saul I did na ken Adam's name was Lumley."'

Lord Lumley's first wife was a very learned lady, and several volumes containing the exercises both of herself and her sister, the Duchess of Norfolk, are preserved among the Royal MSS. in the British Museum, having been handed down with the Lumley books. A quarto volume,[26] upon the first leaf of which is written 'The doinge of my Lady Lumley, dowghter to my L. Therle of Arundell,' contains Latin translations of several of the Orations of Isocrates, and 'The Tragedie of Euripides called Iphigeneia, translated out of Greake into Englisshe.' Among the royal manuscripts is also to be found a beautiful little volume of fourteen vellum leaves,[27] containing copies of moral apophthegms, in Latin, which Sir Nicholas Bacon had inscribed on the walls of his house at Gorhambury. On the first page, above the arms of Lady Lumley, which are splendidly emblazoned, is written in gold capitals, 'Syr · Nicholas · Bacon · Knyghte · to · his · very · good · ladye · the · ladye · Lumley · sendeth · this,' and on the second page this title, 'Sentences printed in the Lorde Kepar's Gallery at Gorhambury: selected by him out of divers authors, and sent to the good ladye Lumley at her desire.' The sentences, which are thirty-seven in number, are inscribed in gold capital letters upon grounds of various colours.

There are three portraits of Lord Lumley at Lumley Castle, and one at Arundel Castle. A fine engraving of another portrait, which was formerly in the Lumley aisle at Cheam, is in Stebbing's edition of Sandford's *Genealogical History*. There are also engravings of Lord Lumley by Fittler and Thane. Lumley Castle also contains a portrait of Lady Lumley, inscribed 'Jane Fitzalan, daughter to Henry Earle of Arundele, first wife to John Lord Lumley.'[28]

FOOTNOTES:

[18] Cooper, *Athenæ Cantabrigienses*, vol. ii. p. 517.

[19] Cooper.

[20] Humphrey Llwyd, physician and antiquary, Lord Lumley's brother-in-law.

[21] Afterwards Archbishop of York, a relative of Lord Lumley.

[22] Edwards, *Lives of the Founders of the British Museum*, p. 162.

[23] Richard Caldwell, M.D., elected President of the Royal College of Physicians in 1570.

[24] Pennant, *Tour in Scotland, etc.*

[25] Hutchinson, *History of County of Durham.*

[26] *Royal MSS.*, 15 A ix.

[27] *Royal MSS.*, 17 A xxiii.

[28] Cooper.

GEORGE CAREW, EARL OF TOTNES, 1555-1629

George Carew, Baron Carew of Clopton and Earl of Totnes, was born in 1555. He was the son of George Carew, Dean of Windsor, by his wife Anne, daughter of Sir Nicholas Harvey. In 1564 he was sent to the University of Oxford, which he left in 1573, and in the following year went to Ireland and entered the service of his cousin Sir Peter Carew, who was then engaged in prosecuting his claims to his Irish property. Carew held various posts in that country, and remained there, save for visits to England and the Low Countries, until 1592, when he entered upon his duties as Lieutenant-General of the Ordnance, to which office he had been appointed in 1591. He took part in the expeditions of Essex to Cadiz in 1596, and to the Azores in 1597, and in 1599 returned to Ireland as Lord President of Munster, a post he held until 1603. In 1605 he was made Vice-Chamberlain to Queen Anne, and in the same year was created Baron Carew. Three years later he was made Master of the Ordnance, and in 1611 he again went to Ireland as 'Sole Commissioner for the reformation of the army and improvement of his majesties revenew.' On the 5th of February 1626, Carew, who had been knighted in 1585, was created Earl of Totnes, and later in the year received the appointment of 'Treasurer and receaver-general to queene Henriette Marie.'

BOOK-STAMP OF EARL OF TOTNES.

He died at London on the 27th of March 1629, and was buried in the Church of Stratford-on-Avon, where a monument was erected to his memory by his widow, a daughter of William Clopton, of Clopton House, near Stratford-on-Avon. He left no children by her.

Carew, who was much attached to antiquarian pursuits, maintained a large correspondence with Camden, Sir Walter Raleigh, Sir Robert Cotton, and Sir Thomas Bodley, and many of his letters have been printed by the Camden Society. He bequeathed his books and manuscripts, of which he had acquired a considerable number, to Sir Thomas Stafford, who was said to be his illegitimate son. They afterwards became the property of Archbishop Laud, who placed forty-two of the volumes of manuscripts, which principally relate to Irish history in the time of Queen Elizabeth, in the Archiepiscopal Library at Lambeth, and four in the Bodleian Library. Others are preserved in the Department of M., British Museum, the State Paper Office, and at Hatfield.

SIR ROBERT BRUCE COTTON, BART., 1571-1631

Sir Robert Bruce Cotton, who is styled by Sir Symonds D'Ewes 'England's Prime Antiquary,' was born in 1571. He was the eldest son of Thomas Cotton, of Connington, Huntingdonshire, by his first wife, Elizabeth, daughter of Francis Shirley of Staunton-Harold, Leicestershire. He received his early education at Westminster School, and in 1581 matriculated at Jesus College, Cambridge, where four years later he took the degree of B.A. At a very early age he became a member of the Elizabethan Society of Antiquaries, which met for many years at his residence in Westminster, near Palace Yard. It was in this house that he formed that magnificent collection of manuscripts and other antiquities which now ranks as one of the principal treasures of the British Museum. The dissolution of the monasteries in the reigns of Henry VIII. and Edward VI. afforded special facilities to Cotton in forming the collection which comprises such valuable manuscripts as the famous *Durham Book* (a copy of the Gospels in Latin, written and illuminated in honour of St. Cuthbert by Eadfrith, Bishop of Lindisfarne, between the years 698 and 720, with an interlinear translation in Northumbrian Saxon), and the copy of the Gospels said to have been used to administer the oath at the coronation of King Athelstan. Other treasures are the original Bull of Pope Leo X. conferring on King Henry VIII. the title of Defender of the Faith; and a contemporary and official copy of Magna Charta, granted by King John, and dated at Runnymede, 15th June, in the seventeenth year of his reign, which was given to Cotton by Sir Edward Dering. Both these precious documents were unfortunately damaged by the fire at Ashburnham House, but have since been very skilfully repaired. More than two hundred volumes of the library consisted of letters of sovereigns and statesmen; but Cotton did not acquire these valuable documents without creating a strong feeling that such a large and important collection of official papers should rather be preserved in the Record Office than left in the possession of a private individual, and his library was twice sequestrated by the Government. On the first occasion his books were given back to him; but on the second, although he repeatedly petitioned the King for their restoration, he died before his applications were answered. His death took place at his house in Westminster on the 6th of May 1631, and he was buried in Connington Church, where a monument was erected to his memory. Cotton was knighted on the accession of James I., and was also one of the baronets created by that sovereign in 1611. Sir Robert Cotton gave directions in his will that his library should not be sold, and bequeathed it to his son, Sir Thomas Cotton, who on the decease of his father made great efforts to obtain its restoration, which were ultimately successful. He died in 1662, leaving the collection to his son, Sir John Cotton, who, having declined an offer for it of sixty thousand pounds from Louis XIV. in 1700, expressed his intention of practically giving it to the nation; and in the same year an Act was passed, enacting that on the death of Sir John (he died in 1702), Cotton House, together with the collection, should be vested in trustees, but at the same time continue in his family and name, and not be sold or otherwise disposed of. It was further ordered that the library should be kept and preserved for public use and advantage, and that a room should be provided for it, with 'a convenient way, passage, and resort to the same, at the will and discretion of the heirs of the family.' Obstacles, however, occurred in carrying out these directions, principally on account of the difficulty of access to the library, and the unsuitableness of the room in which it was deposited, it being described as 'a narrow little room, damp, and improper for preserving the books and papers.' An agreement was therefore made, by virtue of an Act of Parliament (5 Anne, cap. 30), with Sir John Cotton, grandson of the Sir John Cotton who died in 1702, for the purchase of the inheritance of the house where the library was deposited for the sum of four thousand five hundred pounds; and it was further provided that the library should continue to be settled in trustees, and a convenient room built in part of the grounds for its accommodation. This, however, was not done, and the dilapidated condition of Cotton House soon necessitated the removal of the collection, which was taken to Essex House, Essex Street, Strand, where it remained until 1730, when it was conveyed to Ashburnham House in Little Dean's Yard, Westminster, which was purchased by the Crown to receive it, together with the royal MSS. Here, on the 23rd of October 1731, the disastrous fire broke out in which one hundred and fourteen manuscripts were burnt, lost, or entirely spoiled, and ninety-eight damaged, but many of these have been cleverly restored. Those which were saved were placed in a new building designed for the dormitory of Westminster School, where they remained until they were transferred to the British Museum in 1757, having been included in the Act under which the Museum was founded in 1753.

SIR ROBERT COTTON. From an engraving by R. White.

The Cottonian Collection originally consisted of 958 volumes. A catalogue of it was compiled by Dr. Thomas Smith in 1696, and a more ample one by Mr. Joseph Planta, Principal Librarian of the British Museum, in 1802.

'Omnis ab illo
Et Camdene tua, et Seldeni gloria crevit.'[29]

WILLIAM LAUD, ARCHBISHOP OF CANTERBURY, **1573-1645**

William Laud, Archbishop of Canterbury, whose eventful history is well known, was born at Reading on the 7th of October 1573. He was the son of a clothier of that town, and was first educated in the free grammar school of his native place, and afterwards proceeded to St. John's College, Oxford, where he successively obtained a scholarship and a fellowship, and in 1611 became President of the College. In 1616 James I. conferred on him the Deanery of Gloucester, on the 22nd of January 1621 he was installed as a prebendary of Westminster, and on the 29th of June in the same year he obtained the See of St. David's. On the accession of Charles I. to the throne Laud's influence became very great, and in 1626 he was made Bishop of Bath and Wells, and two years later Bishop of London. In 1630 he was elected Chancellor of the University of Oxford, and in 1633 he was appointed Archbishop of Canterbury. Shortly after the meeting of the Long Parliament in 1640 Laud was impeached of treason by the House of Commons, and committed to the Tower. After an imprisonment of three years he was brought to trial before the Lords, but as they showed an inclination to acquit him, the Commons passed an ordinance of attainder, declaring him guilty of treason, to which they compelled the Peers to assent, and on the 10th of January 1645 he was brought to the scaffold on Tower Hill. His body was interred in the chancel of All Hallows, Barking, where it remained until 1663, when it was removed to the Chapel of St. John's College, Oxford.

Archbishop Laud was an ardent collector of books, especially of manuscripts, but Wood in his *Athenæ Oxonienses* says he was 'such a liberal benefactor towards the advancement of learning that he left himself little or nothing for his own use.' The Bodleian Library is indebted to him for a large portion of its choicest treasures, especially of Oriental literature. Between the years 1635 and 1640 he enriched the Library with repeated gifts of valuable manuscripts. In 1635 he presented four hundred and sixty-two volumes and five rolls. Among these were forty-six Latin manuscripts, 'e Collegio Herbipolensi [Würzburg] in Germania sumpti, A.D. 1631, cum

Suecorum Regis exercitus per universam fere Germaniam grassarentur.' This gift was followed, in 1636, by another of one hundred and eighty-one manuscripts. In the next year five hundred and fifty-five additional manuscripts were given by him to the Library, and in 1640 eighty-one more. This splendid donation of nearly thirteen hundred manuscripts comprised works in Oriental and many other languages; a large number of them being of exceptional value and interest. Among them was a manuscript of the Acts of the Apostles in Greek and Latin, of the end of the seventh century, which is believed to have been once in the possession of the Venerable Bede. Other notable manuscripts were an Irish vellum manuscript containing the Psalter of Cashel, Cormac's Glossary, Poems attributed to St. Columb-Kill and St. Patrick, etc., and a copy of the *Anglo-Saxon Chronicle*, which ends at the year 1154, and appears to have been written in, and to have formerly been the property of, the Abbey of Peterborough. In addition to the manuscripts, the Archbishop presented the Library with a collection of coins, and other antiquities and curiosities.[30] Archbishop Laud was also a great benefactor to his own college, St. John's. Sir Kenelm Digby in a letter to Dr. Gerard Langbaine, dated Gothurst, November 7th, 1654, writes: 'As I was one day waiting on the late King, my master, I told him of a collection of choice Arabic Manuscripts I was sending after my Latin ones to the University. My Lord of Canterbury [Laud] that was present, wished that they might go along with a parcel that he was sending to St. John's College: whereupon I sent them to his Grace, as Chancellor of the University, beseeching him to present them in my name to the same place where he sent his. They were in two trunks (made exactly fit for them) that had the first letters of my christian and sirname decyphered upon them with nails; and on the first page of every book was my ordinary motto and name written at length in my own hand. The troubles of the times soon followed my sending these trunks of books to Lambeth-house, and I was banished out of the land, and returned not until my lord was dead; so that I never more heard of them.'[31]

Some curious entries in the Journals of the House of Commons show that the books which the Archbishop retained for his own use fell into the hands of Hugh Peters, the regicide.

'Aº. 1643-4, March 8. Ordered, That a Study of books to the value of one hundred pounds out of such books as are sequestered, be forthwith bestowed upon Mr. Peters.'

'Aº. 1644, 25 April. Whereas this House was formerly pleased to bestow upon Mr. Peters, Books to the Value of an Hundred Pounds, it is this day ordered, that Mr. Recorder, Mr. Whitlock and Mr. Hill, or any Two of them, do cause to be delivered unto Mr. Peters Books of the Value of an Hundred Pounds, out of the particular and private study of the Archbishop of Canterbury, and out of the Books belonging to the said Archbishop, in his own particular.'

'Aº. 1644, 27 Junij. Whereas formerly Books to the Value of an Hundred Pounds were bestowed upon Mr. Peters, out of the Archbishop of Canterbury's particular private Study: And whereas the said Study is appraised at a matter of Forty Pounds more than the said Hundred Pounds; It is this day ordered, That Mr. Peters shall have the whole Study of Books freely bestowed upon him.'

These books, however, appear to have been recovered after the Restoration, for we find an entry in the Journals of the date of May 16, 1660, ordering 'That it be referred to the Committee to whom the Business of Secretary Thurloe is referred, to take Order, that all the Books and Papers, heretofore belonging to the Library of the late Archbishop of Canterbury, and now, or lately, in the Hands of Mr. Hugh Peters, be forthwith secured.'

In addition to his other benefactions to the University of Oxford, Archbishop Laud founded in that university a Professorship of Arabic, and endowed it with lands in the parish of Bray, in the county of Berks.

The works written by Laud are but few in number. They are *Officium Quotidianum, or a Manual of Private Devotions*; *A Summary of Devotions*;

his *Diary*; and *A History of his Troubles and Tryal*; together with some smaller pieces, sermons, and speeches. *A Relation of the Conference between him and Fisher the Jesuit*, by Laud's chaplain John Baily, was printed in 1624. A collected edition of his works, edited by Henry Wharton, was printed in 1695-1700, and a second one in the Library of Anglo-Catholic Theology, in six volumes in 1847-49.

Portraits of him are to be found in St. John's College, Oxford, and at Lambeth Palace. A copy of the last portrait, by Henry Stone, is in the National Portrait Gallery.

FOOTNOTES:

[29] Preface to Weaver's *Funeral Monuments*.

[30] Macray, *Annals of the Bodleian Library*, pp. 61-65.

[31] Walker, *Letters by Eminent Persons*. London, 1813.

ROBERT BURTON, 1576-1640

Robert Burton, the author of *The Anatomy of Melancholy*, who is numbered by Dibdin 'among the most marked bibliomaniacs of the age,' was the second son of Ralph Burton of Lindley in the county of Leicester, and was born on the 8th of February 1576. He received the early part of his education at the grammar schools of Nuneaton and Sutton Coldfield. In 1593 he was admitted a commoner at Brasenose College, Oxford, and in 1599 was elected a student of Christ Church. He took the degree of B.D. in 1614. The last-named college presented him with the vicarage of St. Thomas, in the west suburb of Oxford, in 1616, and some years later George, Lord Berkeley, gave him the rectory of Segrave in Leicestershire. The first edition of his famous work, *The Anatomy of Melancholy*, appeared in 1621. Burton, about whose life little is known, died in his chamber at Christ's Church on the 25th of January 1639-40, 'at, or very near that time,' Anthony à Wood writes, 'which he had some years before foretold from the calculation of his own nativity. Which being exact, several of the students did not forbear to whisper among themselves, that rather than there should be a mistake in the calculation, he sent up his soul to heaven thro' a slip about his neck.' Wood adds that he was buried in the north aisle of Christ Church Cathedral, and over his grave 'was erected a comely monument on the upper pillar of the said isle with his bust painted to the life: on the right hand of which, is the calculation of his nativity, and under the bust this inscription made by himself; all put up by the care of William Burton, his brother.

'Paucis notus, paucioribus ignotus, hic jacet Democritus junior, cui vitam dedit & mortem Melancholia. Obiit viii. Id. Jan. A.C. MDCXXXIX.'

Burton's monument and bust have been engraved for Nichols's *History and Antiquities of Leicestershire*, and his portrait hangs in the hall of Brasenose College.

Wood gives the following character of Burton:—'He was an exact mathematician, a curious calculator of nativities, a general-read scholar, a thorough-paced philologist, and one that understood the surveying of lands well. As he was by many accounted a severe student, a devourer of authors, a melancholy and humourous person, so by others who knew him well, a person of great honesty, plain dealing and charity. I have heard some of the ancients of Christchurch often say that his company was very merry, facete and juvenile; and no man in his time did surpass him for his ready and dexterous interlarding his common discourses among them with verses from the poets, or sentences from classical authors; which, being then all the fashion in the university, made his company more acceptable.'

Burton left behind him a large and curious collection of books, the nature of which he well describes in his Address to the Reader of his *Anatomy of Melancholy*: 'I hear new news every day, and those ordinary rumours of war, plagues, fires, inundations, thefts, murders, massacres, meteors, comets, spectrums, prodigies, apparitions, of towns taken, cities besieged in France, Germany, Turkey, Persia, Poland, etc., daily musters and preparations, and such like, which these tempestuous times afford, battles fought, so many men slain, monomachies, shipwrecks, piracies, and sea-fights; peace, leagues, stratagems, and fresh alarms.... New books every day, pamphlets, currantoes, stories, whole catalogues of volumes of all sorts.... Now come tidings of weddings, maskings, mummeries, entertainments, jubilies, embassies, tilts and tournaments, trophies, triumphs, revels, sports, plays: then again, as in a new shifted scene, treasons, cheating tricks, robberies, enormous villanies in all kinds, funerals, burials, deaths of princes, new discoveries, expeditions, now comical, then tragical matters.' He appears to have purchased indiscriminately almost everything that was published.

In his will, dated August 15th, 1639, he gives directions for the disposal of his books:—

'Now for my goods I thus dispose them. First I give an Cth pounds to Christ Church in Oxford where I have so long lived to buy five pounds Lands per Ann. to be Yearly bestowed on Books for the Library. Item I give an hundreth pound to the University Library of

Oxford to be bestowed to purchase five pound Land per Ann. to be paid out Yearly on Books.... If I have any Books the University Library hath not, let them take them. If I have any Books our own Library hath not, let them take them.' After bequeathing books to various friends, he directs, 'If any books be left let my Executors dispose of them with all such books as are written with my own hands and half my Melancholy Copy for Crips hath the other half. To Mr. Jones Chaplin and Chanter my Surveying Books and Instruments.'

In addition to *The Anatomy of Melancholy*, Burton wrote a Latin comedy, entitled *Philosophaster*, which was acted at Christ Church on Shrove Monday, February the 16th, 1618, and which was first printed in 1862 for the Roxburghe Club at the expense of the late Rev. W.E. Buckley, of Middleton Chaney, the possessor of one of two manuscripts of it which have been preserved.

JAMES USHER, ARCHBISHOP OF ARMAGH, 1581-1656

ARCHBISHOP USHER.

James Usher or Ussher, Archbishop of Armagh, was born in Dublin on the 4th of January 1581. He was the second, but elder surviving son of Arland Usher, one of the six clerks of the Irish Court of Chancery. His mother was a daughter of James Stanyhurst, Recorder of the City of Dublin, who was thrice elected Speaker of the Irish House of Commons. Usher is said to have been taught to read by two aunts who had been blind from their infancy. At the age of eight he was sent to a school in Dublin conducted by Mr. James Fullerton and Mr. James Hamilton, two secret political agents of King James of Scotland, who were afterwards made Sir James Fullerton and Viscount Clandeboye. In 1594 he proceeded to Trinity College, Dublin, being the second scholar admitted in the newly opened University, of which he was made a Fellow in 1599. On the 20th of December 1601 he was ordained by his uncle, the Archbishop of Armagh, having first made over his paternal inheritance to his younger brother and his sisters, reserving only a small portion for his support during his studies. On the 24th of the same month the Spaniards were defeated at the battle of Kinsale by the English and Irish, and the officers of the English army determined to commemorate their success by founding a library in the College at Dublin. They collected among themselves about eighteen hundred pounds for this purpose,[32] and Usher, in conjunction with Dr. Luke Challoner, was requested to select the books. For this object, in 1602, he paid a visit to England, where he made the acquaintance of Sir Thomas Bodley, Sir Robert Cotton, Camden, and other distinguished persons. In 1606 he again made a journey to England, this time to buy books for his own library, as well as for that of his college,[33] and for some time he repeated his visits every three or four years. In 1607 he was made Professor of Divinity in Trinity College, which office he held for thirteen years. He was consecrated Bishop of Meath and Clonmacnoise in 1621, and four years later he was raised to the Archbishopric of Armagh and the Primacy of the Irish Church. Usher came to England on a visit in 1640, but he never returned to his native country, for in the next year his residence at Armagh was attacked and plundered by the rebels, and he lost everything he possessed except his library, and some furniture in his house at Drogheda. In consequence of the unsettled state of the country it was thought useless for him to return to his see, and the king therefore bestowed on him the bishopric of Carlisle, to be held *in commendam*. For some time he resided in Oxford, but that city being threatened with a siege by the Parliamentary forces, in 1645 he proceeded to Cardiff, of which town Sir Timothy Tyrrell, who had married his only child, was governor. Some months later, when Tyrrell was obliged to give up his command, Usher accepted an invitation from

Mary, widow of Sir Edward Stradling, to take up his abode at her residence, St. Donat's Castle, Glamorganshire. On his way thither, in company with his daughter, he unluckily fell into the hands of a party of Welsh insurgents, who plundered him of all his books and papers, but these were afterwards to a great extent recovered by the exertions of the clergy and gentry of the country. In 1646 Usher came to London, and found a home in the house of his friend the Dowager Countess of Peterborough, which was situated in St. Martin's Lane, 'just over against Charing Cross.' From the roof of the building he witnessed the preliminaries of the execution of Charles I., but he nearly fainted when 'the villains in vizards began to put up the king's hair,' and had to be removed. Usher was appointed Preacher to the Society of Lincoln's Inn in 1647, and for nearly eight years preached regularly during term-time in the chapel. He had a suite of furnished apartments provided for him in the Inn, 'with divers rooms for his library.' He retired in 1656 to Lady Peterborough's house at Reigate in Surrey, and died there on the 21st of March in that year. On the 21st of the following month he was buried in Westminster Abbey; a public funeral being given him by order of Cromwell, who is said, however, to have left the relations of the deceased prelate to pay the greater part of the expense. Usher formed a large and valuable library of nearly ten thousand volumes, which cost him many thousand pounds. Dr. Richard Parr, his biographer, states that 'after he became archbishop he laid out a great deal of money in books, laying aside every year a considerable sum for that end, and especially for the procuring of manuscripts, as well as from foreign parts, as near at hand.' His library contained a number of rare Oriental manuscripts, which he obtained through the instrumentality of Mr. Thomas Davis, a merchant at Aleppo. Among them were a copy of the Samaritan Pentateuch, a Syrian Pentateuch, and a Commentary on a great part of the Old and New Testaments. From the Samaritan Pentateuch Usher furnished some extracts for his friend Selden's *Marmora Arundeliana*, and he deposited the manuscript itself in the Cottonian Library. Dr. Walton also found Usher's collection of much use in preparing his Polyglot Bible. Several of the manuscripts which had belonged to Usher were given to the Bodleian Library by James Tyrrell, the historian, who was the Archbishop's grandson. It was Usher's intention to have left his library to Trinity College, but having lost all his other property he thought it right to bequeath it to his daughter, Lady Tyrrell, who had a large family. After his death it was offered for sale, and the King of Denmark and Cardinal Mazarin were both anxious to acquire it; but Cromwell, considering it disgraceful to his administration to allow such a splendid collection of books to be sent out of the kingdom, prohibited the disposal of it without his consent, and it was purchased for the sum of two thousand two hundred pounds, the money being principally contributed by the officers and soldiers of the army in Ireland. It is said that the amount paid for it was much less than what had been previously offered. The books were sent to Dublin and placed in the Castle, with a view that they should form the library of a new College or Hall then projected. They remained in the Castle until the Restoration, when Charles II., in accordance with Usher's first intention, gave them to Trinity College, where they are still preserved. Usher, who is said by Selden to have been 'ad miraculum doctus,' was the author of many works, some of the more important being *Immanuel, or the Mystery of the Incarnation of the Son of God* (Dublin, 1638), 4to; *Britannicarum Ecclesiarum Antiquitates et Primordia* (Dublin, 1639), 4to; *Annales Veteris et Novi Testamenti* (London, 1650-54), folio[34]; *De Græca Septuaginta Interpretum Versione Syntagma* (London, 1654), 4to; and *Chronologia Sacra* (London, 1660), 4to. A complete edition of the Archbishop's works, in seventeen octavo volumes, partly edited by Dr. C.R. Elrington, and partly by Dr. J.H. Todd, with an index volume by Dr. W. Reeves, was published in Dublin in 1847-64.

FOOTNOTES:

[32] Life of Usher, by Dr. C.R. Elrington, prefixed to Usher's works, vol. i. p. 23. Dublin, 1847.

[33] A list of these books, with the prices annexed to several, is still extant in Usher's handwriting, and preserved among the MSS. of Trinity College, Dublin. *Ibid.*, p. 25.

JOHN WILLIAMS, ARCHBISHOP OF YORK, 1582-1650

John Williams, Lord Keeper of the Great Seal and Archbishop of York, was the son of Edmund Williams of Aber-Conway, Caernarvonshire, at which place he was born on the 25th of March 1582. He was first educated at the public school at Ruthin, and later at St. John's College, Cambridge, where he was sent when sixteen years of age. While at the university he appears to have indulged in a somewhat reckless expenditure, and Bishop Hacket, who wrote his biography, informs us that 'from a youth and so upward he had not a fist to hold money, for he did not lay out, but scatter, spending all that he had, and somewhat for which he could be trusted.' He was, however, by no means neglectful of his studies, for we are told by Lloyd in his *State Worthies*, 'that unwearied was his industry, unexpressible his capacity: He never saw the book of worth he read not; he never forgot what he read; he never lost the use of what he remembered: Everything he heard or saw was his own; and what was his own he knew how to use to the utmost.' From the time of Williams's ordination in 1609, his career until the accession of Charles I. was a remarkably rapid and successful one. After holding one or two livings, he was appointed Chaplain to the King and Sub-Dean of Salisbury, and in 1620 Dean of Westminster. On the fall of Bacon, in July 1621, in whose ruin he had taken a large share, he was sworn in as Lord Keeper. Lloyd observes with reference to the manner in which he fulfilled the duties of this post, that 'the lawyers despised him at first, but the judges admired him at last.' Williams was also made Bishop of Lincoln, and allowed to retain the deanery of Westminster and the rectory of Walgrave; in fact the number of preferments he held was so large that Dr. Heylyn remarks that 'he was a perfect diocese within himself, as being bishop, dean, prebend, residentiary, and parson, all at once.' Williams held the post of Lord Keeper until 1626, when he was deprived of his office, and various charges, including one of betraying the King's secrets, were brought against him by Archbishop Laud, his great enemy. He was found guilty of subornation of perjury in defending himself from these charges, suspended from all his dignities and appointments, condemned to suffer imprisonment during the pleasure of the King, and fined ten thousand pounds. Lloyd says 'he suffered for conniving at Puritans, out of hatred to Bishop Laud; and for favouring Papists, out of love to them.' At the meeting of the Long Parliament Williams was released, and having been again received into favour at court, he was translated in 1641 to the Archbishopric of York. During the Civil War he retired to his estate at Aber-Conway, and for some time held Conway Castle for the King. He died of a quinsy on the 25th of March 1650, and was interred in Llandegay church, where a monument was erected to his memory by his nephew and heir Sir Griffyth Williams.

ARCHBISHOP WILLIAMS.

Archbishop Williams was a generous patron of learning, and Lloyd states that 'his pensions to Scholars were more numerous than all the Bishops and Noble-mens besides'; and that he imposed 'Rent-charges on all the Benefices in his Gift as Lord Keeper, or Bishop of Lincoln, to maintain hopeful youth.' He formed a library in his palace at Buckden in Huntingdonshire, which was dispersed or destroyed during his imprisonment,[35] but upon his release he collected another, which he bequeathed to St. John's College, Cambridge, having previously given upwards of two thousand pounds to the college for the purpose of building a new library; and in Bagford and Oldys's *London Libraries* we find an account of the books which he gave to the library of Westminster Abbey. 'In the great cloister of the abbey,' they write, 'is a well-furnished library, considering the time when it was erected by Dr. Williams, Dean of Westminster and Bishop of Lincoln; who was a great promoter of learning. He purchased the books of the heirs of one Baker of Highgate, and founded it for public use every day in Term, from nine to twelve in the forenoon, and from two till four in the afternoon. The MSS. are kept in the inner part, but by an accident many of them were burnt.' Mr. James Yeowell, the editor of the work, adds in a note that 'Dean Williams converted a waste room, situate in the east side of the cloisters, into a library, which he enriched with the valuable works from the collection of Sir Richard Baker, author of *The Chronicles of the Kings of England*, which cost him 500*l*. A catalogue of this library is in Harl. MS. 694. There is also a MS. catalogue, compiled in 1798 by Dr. Dakin, the precentor, arranged alphabetically.'

A portrait of Archbishop Williams is hung in the library of St. John's College, Cambridge.

FOOTNOTES:

[34] The chronology given in this work is still the standard adopted in editions of the English Bible.

[35] 'After this, hearing his Majesty would not abate anything of his fine, he desired that it might be taken up by 1000*l*. yearly as his

estate would bear it, till the whole should be paid. But that was not granted: Kilvert [the solicitor for the prosecution] was ordered to go to Bugden and Lincoln, and there to seize upon all he could and bring it into the Exchequer. Kilvert, glad of the office, made sure of all that could be found, goods of all sorts, plate, books, etc. to the value of 10,000*l.*, of which he never gave account but of 800*l.* The timber he felled, killed the deer in the park, sold an organ which cost 120*l.* for 10*l.*, pictures which cost 400*l.* for 4*l.*, made away with what books he pleased, and continued revelling for three summers in Bugden-house. For four cellars of wine, cyder, ale, and beer, with wood, hay, corn, and the like, stored up for a year or two, he gives no account at all; and thus a large personal estate was squandered away, and not the least part of the King's fine paid all this while, whereas if it had been managed to the best advantage, it would have been sufficient to have discharged the whole.'—*Biographia Britannica,* vol. vi. p. 4288 (note).

JOHN SELDEN, 1584-1654

John Selden, the distinguished legal antiquary, historian, and Oriental scholar, who was styled by his friend Ben Jonson 'a monarch in letters,' and 'vir omni eruditionis genere instructissimus' by Archbishop Laud, was born on the 16th of December 1584 at Salvington, near Worthing, in Sussex. His father was John Selden, a farmer, known as the 'Minstrel' on account of his proficiency in music. Aubrey describes him as 'a yeomanly man of about forty pounds a year, who played well on the violin, in which he took much delight.' Selden was first educated at the free grammar school at Chichester, and afterwards proceeded with an exhibition to Hart Hall, since merged in Magdalen Hall, Oxford. On leaving the university he was admitted a member of Clifford's Inn; but in 1604 removed to the Inner Temple. Wood, in his *Athenæ Oxonienses*, says of him that 'after he had continued there a sedulous student for some time, he did, by the help of a strong body and a vast memory, not only run through the whole body of the law, but became a prodigy in most parts of learning, especially in those which were not common or little frequented or regarded by the generality of students of his time. So that in a few years his name was wonderfully advanced not only at home but in foreign countries, and he was usually styled the great dictator of learning of the English nation.... He was a great philologist, antiquary, herald, linguist, statesman, and what not.' Selden devoted his time rather to chamber practice and to legal researches and the study of history and antiquities than to the more active part of his profession. It is said he wrote his first work, *Analecton Anglo-Britannicon*, as early as 1607, when only twenty-two years of age, but it was not published until eight years later. *The Duello, England's Epinomis*, and *Jani Anglorum Facies Altera* appeared in 1610, *Titles of Honour* in 1614, *De Diis Syris Syntagmata Duo* in 1617, and *The History of Tithes* in 1618, wherein he allows the legal, but denies the divine, right of the clergy to the receiving of tithes. The more important of his later works are *Marmora Arundeliana*, published in 1628, *De Successionibus* in 1631, *Mare Clausum* in 1635, *De Jure Naturali et Gentium juxta Disciplinam Ebræorum Libri VII.* in 1640, and *Fleta, seu Commentarius Juris*

Anglicani, an ancient manuscript which he edited and annotated, in 1647. Among his other literary labours are the notes appended to Drayton's *Polyolbion.* A volume of his *Table Talk* was published after his death in 1689, and his complete works in 1726, in three volumes folio. In 1621 Selden was committed to prison for having advised the House of Commons to assert its right to offer advice to the Crown, but was released after an imprisonment of five weeks. He first entered the House of Commons in 1623 as Member for Lancaster, and for some years took a very prominent part in its proceedings. During the later disputes between Charles and the Parliament he acted with great moderation, and it is said that at one time the King thought of intrusting him with the Great Seal. Selden subscribed the Covenant in 1643, and was made Keeper of the Rolls and Records in the Tower. In 1645 he was appointed a Commissioner of the Admiralty, and in the same year he was elected Master of Trinity Hall, Cambridge, an office he declined to accept. Parliament voted him five thousand pounds in 1647 as compensation for his sufferings during the monarchy; but Wood states that 'some there are that say that he refused and could not out of conscience take it, and add that his mind was as great as his learning, full of generosity and harbouring nothing that seemed base.' Although he remained in Parliament after the execution of the King, he almost entirely withdrew from public affairs, and, it is said, refused to write a reply to the *Eikon Basilike* when requested to do so by Cromwell. Selden died on November 30, 1654, at Friary House, Whitefriars, the residence of Elizabeth, Countess Dowager of Kent, to whom it was reputed he had been married. He was interred in the Temple Church, where a monument was erected to his memory.

Selden collected a very fine library, 'rich in classics and science, theology and history, law and Hebrew literature,' of which about eight thousand volumes were eventually added to the Bodleian Library. Selden had bequeathed his books to the Bodleian; but it is said he was so offended with the University for refusing the loan of a manuscript except upon a bond for one thousand pounds, that he revoked the bequest, and left them to the free disposal of his executors. They offered the collection to the Society of the Inner Temple, but as no building was provided for its reception, they carried out the original intention of Selden, and gave it in 1659 to the Bodleian, stipulating at the same time that all the books should be chained, and £25, 10s. was expended for that purpose. There is no doubt, however, that a considerable number of the manuscripts came into the possession of that library soon after Selden's death, and the entire affair is involved in some obscurity. The Rev. W.D. Macray, who, in his *Annals of the Bodleian Library*, goes very fully into the matter, gives another reason for Selden's displeasure. 'In July 1649,' he writes, 'the new intruded officers and fellows of Magdalene College found in the Muniment-room in the cloister-tower of the College a large sum of money in the old coinage called Spur-royals, or Ryals, amounting to £1400, the equivalent of which had been left by the Founder as a reserve-fund for law expenses, for re-erecting or repairing buildings destroyed by fire, etc., or for other extraordinary charges. This gold had been laid up and counted in Queen Elizabeth's time, and had remained untouched since then; consequently, although some of the old members of the College were aware of its existence, to the new-comers it seemed a welcome and unexpected discovery, especially as the College was at the time heavily in debt. They immediately proceeded to divide it among all the members on the foundation proportionately, not excluding the choristers (who were at that time undergraduates), the Puritan President, Wilkinson, being alone opposed to such an illegal proceeding, and being with difficulty prevailed upon to accept £100 as his share, which, however, upon his death-bed he charged his executors to repay. The Spur-royals were exchanged at the rate of 18s. 6d. to 20s. each, and each fellow had thirty-three of them. But when the fact of this embezzlement of corporate funds became known, the College was called to account by Parliament, and, although they attempted to defend themselves, they individually deemed it wise to refund the greater, or a considerable, part of what had been abstracted. Fuller, whose *Church History* was published in the year following Selden's death, after telling this scandalous story, proceeds thus (Book IX. p. 234):—"Sure I am, a great antiquarie lately deceased (rich as well in his state as learning) at the hearing thereof quitted all his intention of benefaction to Oxford or any place else." ... And Wood (*Hist. and Antiq.*, by Gutch, ii. 942) says that he had been told that this misappropriation was one reason of Selden's distaste at Oxford.'

Besides the books sent to the Bodleian Library, those relating to law were given to Lincoln's Inn, and some medical works were bequeathed by Selden to the College of Physicians. 'Eight chests full of registers of abbeys, and other manuscripts relating to the history of England,' were unfortunately destroyed in a fire at the Temple; and many volumes also were lost during the interval between Selden's death and their arrival at Oxford.

THOMAS HOWARD, EARL OF NORFOLK, 1586-1646

One of the most zealous and successful collectors of the early part of the seventeenth century was Thomas Howard, only son of Philip, Earl of Arundel, and grandson of Thomas, Duke of Norfolk, who was beheaded in 1572. He was born on the 7th of July 1586. In 1595 his father died in the Tower, and by his attainder his son was deprived of his titles and lands. On the accession of James I. the former were restored to him, but the King retained the property. Lord Arundel was created Earl of Norfolk in 1644, and died at Padua on the 4th of October 1646.

ARMS OF THOMAS HOWARD, EARL OF NORFOLK.

After his death his collections were partially dispersed; and in 1666 his printed books were presented, at the instigation of John Evelyn, to the Royal Society by Henry Howard, afterwards sixth Duke of Norfolk, a grandson of the Earl, while the manuscripts were divided between that Society and the College of Arms. In 1831 the principal portion of the manuscripts in possession of the Royal Society were transferred to the British Museum, and the remainder, consisting of Oriental manuscripts, in 1835. They were valued at three thousand five hundred and fifty-nine pounds, and were paid for partly in money, and partly with duplicates of printed books in the Museum collection. A large portion of the Earl's library consisted of the books of Bilibaldus Pirckheimer of Nuremberg, which he acquired during a diplomatic mission into Germany in 1636. Some of the manuscripts, Oldys states, once formed part of the library of Matthias Corvinus, King of Hungary. The Earl of Norfolk's collections also comprised a very large number of antique marbles, paintings, vases, and gems.

RICHARD SMITH, 1590-1675

Richard Smith or Smyth, who was born in 1590 at Lillingston Dayrell, Buckinghamshire, was the son of the Rev. Richard Smith of Abingdon, Berkshire. He was sent to the University of Oxford, but did not matriculate, and after a short stay there was removed by his parents, and articled to a solicitor of the city of London. In 1644 he became Secondary of the Poultry Compter, which was worth about seven hundred pounds a year. This office he held until the death of his eldest son John in 1655, when he sold it, and 'betook himself,' says Anthony à Wood, 'wholly to a private life, two-thirds of which he at least spent in his library.' He died on the 26th of March 1675, and was buried in the Church of St. Giles, Cripplegate, where a monument was erected to his memory.

Smith was an indefatigable collector, and amassed a library of very fine and rare books, many of which had belonged to an earlier collector, Humphrey Dyson. These books came to Smith by marriage.[36] Wood informs us that 'he was constantly known every day to walk his rounds among the booksellers' shops (especially in Little Britain) in London, and by his great skill and experience he made choice of such books that were not obvious to every man's eye.' 'He lived in times,' Wood adds, 'which ministred peculiar opportunities of meeting with books that were not every day brought into public light: and few eminent libraries were bought where he had not the liberty to pick and choose.... He was also a great collector of MSS., whether ancient or modern that were not extant, and delighted much to be poring on them.' Wood also states that after Smith's death, 'there was a design to buy his choice library for a public use, by a collection of moneys to be raised among generous persons, but the work being public, and therefore but little forwarded, it came into the hands of Richard Chiswell, a bookseller living in S. Paul's Ch.-yard, London: who printing a catalogue of, with others added to, them, which came out after Mr. Smith's death, they were exposed to sale by way of auction, to the great reluctancy of public-spirited men, in May and June 1682.' The sale, which commenced on the 15th of May, and was continued day by day the first five days of every week until all the books were sold, took place at 'the Auction House known by the name of the Swan in Great Bartholomew's Close.' It realised one thousand four hundred and fourteen pounds, twelve shillings and eleven pence.[37] A copy of the catalogue, with the prices in manuscript, is preserved in the British Museum. The sums obtained for the Caxtons, of which there were about a dozen, will be interesting to bibliographers. A copy of *Godfrey of Bulloyn*, which it is stated had belonged to King Edward IV., fetched the highest price—eighteen shillings; and the *Game of the Chesse*, the *History of Jason*, and the *Eneydos of Virgil* sold respectively for thirteen shillings, five shillings and a penny, and three shillings; while no more than two shillings could be got for the *Book of Good Manners*. A fine copy of the Coverdale Bible realised only twenty shillings and sixpence, and Captain John Smith's *History of Virginia* went for seven shillings and twopence. The manuscripts also, even for those days, sold at exceedingly low prices.

A very interesting account of the library will be found in an article on English Book-Sales, 1681-86, by Mr. A.W. Pollard, in vol. ii. of *Bibliographica*. Mr. Smith wrote some learned works which he left in manuscript. *A Letter to Dr. Henry Hammond, concerning the Sense of that Article in the Creed, He descended into Hell*, written by Smith in 1659, was printed in 1684; and his *Obituary, being a catalogue of all such persons as he knew in their life; extending from A.D. 1627 to A.D. 1674*, was edited for the Camden Society by Sir H. Ellis, K.H., in 1849.

The manuscript of the *Obituary*, together with the manuscripts of two or three other works by Smith are preserved among the Sloane Manuscripts in the British Museum. A portrait of him was engraved by William Sherwin.

FOOTNOTES:

[36] Hearne in his *Diary* (Oct. 4, 1714) states: 'That Mr. Rich. Smith's rare and curious collection of books was began first by Mr. Humphrey Dyson, a public notary, living in the Poultry. They came to Mr. Smith by marriage. This is the same Humphrey Dyson that

assisted Howes in his continuation of *Stowe's Survey of London,* ed. folio;' and in his preface to Peter Langtoft's *Chronicle* (vol. i. p. xiii.) Hearne describes Dyson as 'a person of a very strange, prying, and inquisitive genius in the matter of books, as may appear from many Libraries; there being Books (chiefly in old English) almost in every Library, that have belong'd to him, with his name upon them.' Some of his books are preserved in the British Museum.

[37] In an entry in his *Diary* (Sep. 4, 1715) Hearne says:—'Mr. Richard Smith's Catalogue that is printed contains a very noble and very extraordinary collection of books. It was begun first in the time of King Hen. VIII., and comeing to Mr. Smith, he was so very diligent and exact in continueing and improving, that hardly anything curious escaped him.'

GEORGE THOMASON, died 1666

George Thomason, who formed the wonderful collection of Civil War tracts, which was given to the British Museum by King George III., was born at the end of the sixteenth or beginning of the seventeenth century. Nothing appears to be known of his parents. He took up his freedom as a member of the Stationers' Company on the 5th of June 1626.[38] His first publication was a new edition of Martyn's *History of the Kings of England*, which he produced in conjunction with James Boler and Robert Young in 1628, and he continued to publish books until 1660. He carried on business at the Rose and Crown, St. Paul's Churchyard, and we learn from the *Obituary* of Richard Smith that he died on April 10, 1666, and was 'buried out of Stationers' Hall (a poore man).' The Rev. George Thomason, who was Canon of Lincoln from 1683 to 1712, is stated to have been his eldest son.

The number of separate printed tracts in the collection which Thomason formed with such unwearied perseverance for twenty years is stated in an Account of it,[39] printed about 1680, to consist of 'near Thirty Thousand several sorts,' together with 'near one hundred several MS. pieces that were never printed, all, or most of them on the King's behalf, which no man durst then venture to publish without endangering his Ruine,' and it is said that these were contained in 'above Two Thousand bound Volumes.' Mr. Falconer Madan, however, in his admirable paper on the Thomason Tracts in *Bibliographica*,[40] informs us that after going carefully through the collection, and looking at every title-page, he has come to the conclusion that the present number of separate pieces is twenty-two thousand seven hundred and sixty-one in print, and seventy-three in manuscript, comprised in about one thousand nine hundred and eighty-three volumes.

All the tracts are arranged in chronological order, and from July 1642 to the end of the collection Thomason has placed the date of issue on every piece when it is not printed on it, and has also endeavoured to supply the place of printing when not given. These notes are sometimes supplemented by others commenting on the opinions of the authors of the tracts. There is a manuscript catalogue in twelve folio volumes, compiled by Marmaduke Foster, and annotated and corrected by Thomason himself.

The collection is not confined to tracts relating to the Civil War and the Commonwealth; it also contains many works on other subjects. Among these is a fine copy of the first edition of Walton's *Compleat Angler*, which at the present time would realise nearly, if not quite, as large a sum as the amount (three hundred pounds) given by King George III. for the entire series.

The collection, which was commenced by Thomason in 1640, and continued until 1661, was made by him under great difficulties. He was a staunch Royalist, and the books appear to have been in constant danger of falling into the hands of the Parliamentary army. We read in the Account to which we have already referred that 'to prevent the Discovery of them, when the Army was Northwards, he pack'd them up in several Trunks, and by one or two in a week sent them to a trusty Friend in Surry, who safely preserv'd them; and when the Army was Westward, and fearing their Return that way, they were sent to London again; but the Collector durst not keep them, but sent them into Essex, and so according as they lay near Danger, still, by timely removing them, at a great charge, secur'd them, but continu'd perfecting the Work.

'And for a further Security to them, there was a Bargain pretended to be made with the University of Oxford and a Receipt of a Thousand Pounds given and acknowledg'd to be in part for them, that if the Usurper had found them out, the University should claim them, who had greater Power to struggle for them than a private Man.

'All these Shifts have been made, and Difficulties encounter'd to keep the Collection from being embezel'd and destroy'd; which with the great Charges of collecting and binding them, cost the Undertaker so much that he refused Four Thousand Pounds for them in his Life time, supposing that Sum not sufficient to reimburse him.'

And in another account, at one time prefixed to the catalogue of the collection, it is stated that 'not thinking them safe anywhere in England, he at last took a resolution to send them into Holland for their more safe preservation. But considering with himself what a treasure it was, upon second thoughts, he durst not venture them at sea, but resolved to place them in his warehouses in form of tables round about the rooms covered over with canvas, continuing still without any intermission his going on; nay, even then, when by the Usurper's power and command he was taken out of his bed, and clapt up close prisoner at Whitehall for seven weeks' space and above,[41] he still hoping and looking for that day, which, thanks be to God, is now come, and there is put a period to that unparallelled labour, charge and pains he had been at.

'Oxford's Library Keeper[42] (that then was) was in hand with them, about them a long time, and did hope the Publick Library might compass them; but that could not be then effected, it rising to so great a sum as had been expended on them for so long a time together.'

After Thomason's death a trust was appointed under his will to take charge of the tracts, and one of the trustees, Dr. Thomas Barlow, Bodley's librarian from 1652 to 1660, afterwards Bishop of Lincoln, had them for a long time in his custody, as appears from a letter addressed by him to the Rev. George Thomason, the son of the collector, dated Oxon, February 6, 1676. He mentions in the letter that he had endeavoured to secure them for the Bodleian Library, and that although he had hitherto failed, he still did not despair of finding a way to do so. He was not, however, successful in his efforts, and King Charles II. appears to have directed Samuel Mearn, the royal stationer and bookbinder, to buy them on his account; it is not known for what sum. It is to be presumed, however, that the King did not find the money for them, for on May 15, 1684, the Privy Council considered and granted a petition from Anne Mearn, widow of Samuel Mearn, that she might dispose of the tracts by sale. She does not seem to have succeeded in doing this, and they appear to have been returned to the Thomason family, for in the year 1745 we find them in possession of Mr. Henry Sisson, a druggist in Ludgate

Street, London, who, Richard Gough, the antiquary, was informed, was a descendant of the collector.[43] After some negotiations with the Duke of Chandos for their purchase, they were brought by Thomas Hollis[44] to the notice of King George III., who, through the Earl of Bute, bought them of Miss Sisson in 1761 for the sum of three hundred pounds, and in the following year they were presented by him to the British Museum.

On one of the volumes of the collection are some mud stains, which have an interesting history. The volume was borrowed from Thomason by King Charles I., who was anxious to read one of the tracts in it, and while journeying to the Isle of Wight let it fall in the dirt. Thomason made a memorandum of the circumstance on a fly-leaf of the book, adding the 'volume hath the marke of honor upon it, which noe other volume in my collection hath.'

In 1647 Thomason published a trade catalogue in quarto, consisting of fifty-eight closely printed pages, entitled *Catalogus Librorum diversis Italiæ locis emptorum Anno Dom. 1647, a Georgio Thomasono Bibliopola Londinensi apud quem in Cæmiterio D. Pauli ad insigne Rosæ Coronatæ prostant venales. Londini, Typis Johannis Legatt*, 1647, and in 1648 a selection of works in oriental languages from this catalogue was purchased by order of the House of Commons,[45] who directed that the sum of five hundred pounds out of the receipts at Goldsmiths' Hall should be paid for the books, in order that they might be bestowed upon the Public Library at Cambridge.

Mr. A.W. Pollard, in a note to Mr. Madan's article in *Bibliographica*, states that Thomason had great difficulty in getting the money for these books: 'On March 28th, 1648,' he tells us, 'the five hundred pounds was ordered to be paid from the arrears of the two months' assessments for the Scots army before Newark; on Sep. 25th it was charged on the composition of Colonel Humphrey Matthews; and on Nov. 16th, Thomason, being still unpaid, was consoled by interest at the rate of eight per cent.

FOOTNOTES:

[38] Arber, *Transcript of the Register*, vol. iii. p. 686.

[39] Copies are preserved in the British Museum and the Bodleian Library, and it is reprinted in Beloe's *Anecdotes* vol. ii. p. 248.

[40] Vol. iii. p. 304.

[41] Thomason was implicated in Christopher Love's plot against the Commonwealth. There are several entries in the *Calendar of State Papers* which refer to his imprisonment. Mr. A.W. Pollard, the editor of *Bibliographica*, has given a list of them in a note (vol. iii. p. 298) to Mr. Madan's paper on the Thomason Collection in that publication.

[42] Probably Dr. Thomas Barlow, librarian of the Bodleian Library.

[43] Gough, *Anecdotes of British Typography*, second edition, p. 699, note.

[44] *Memoirs of Hollis*, vol. i. pp. 121, 192; vol. ii. p. 717.

[45] *Journals of the House of Commons*, 24th March 1648.

SIR SYMONDS D'EWES, Bart., 1602-1650

Book-stamp of Sir Symonds D'Ewes, Bart.

Sir Symonds D'Ewes, one of the most eminent of the antiquaries and collectors of the first half of the seventeenth century, was born in 1602. He was the son of Paul D'Ewes of Milden, Suffolk, and Cecilia, daughter and heiress of Richard Simonds of Coxden, Chardstock, Dorsetshire. In 1618 he was sent to St. John's College, Cambridge, but left in 1620, and entered at the Middle Temple, being called to the Bar in 1623. He soon, however, gave up his legal practice, and devoted himself to the study of history and antiquities. D'Ewes was made a knight in 1626, and created a baronet in 1641. He was twice married, and died in 1650. The baronetcy became extinct in 1731.

D'Ewes possessed a very fine collection of manuscripts, which were sold by his grandson to Sir Robert Harley, afterwards Earl of Oxford, notwithstanding the injunction of D'Ewes, in his will, that his library should not be sold or dispersed. Oldys states that Harley recommended Queen Anne to purchase the manuscripts for a public library, as the richest collection in England next to Sir Robert Cotton's, but that the Queen said, 'It was no virtue for her, a woman, to prefer as she did arts to arms; but while the blood and honour of the nation was at stake in her wars, she could not, till she had secured her living subjects an honourable peace, bestow their money on dead letters.' 'Whereupon,' adds Oldys, 'the Earl stretched his own purse, and gave six thousand pounds for the library.' The manuscripts, together with a list of them, which is believed to have been made by D'Ewes himself, now form part of the Harleian Collection in the British Museum. The manuscript of an Anglo-Saxon Dictionary, compiled by D'Ewes in conjunction with Francis Junius, and several of his diaries are also preserved there. His great work was the *Journals of all the Parliaments during the reign of Queen Elizabeth*, which was not published until 1682.

SIR KENELM DIGBY, 1603-1665

ONE OF SIR KENELM DIGBY'S BOOK-STAMPS.

The celebrated scholar and collector, Sir Kenelm Digby, was born at Gayhurst, near Newport Pagnell, Buckinghamshire, in 1603. He was the son of Sir Everard Digby, who was executed in 1606 for the part he took in the Gunpowder Plot. Sir Kenelm, who was the author of several remarkable works, is described by Lord Clarendon as a man of 'very extraordinary person and presence, with a wonderful graceful behaviour and a flowing courtesy and civility.' He was knighted in 1623. Digby possessed a very fine library, which he formed during his residence in Paris, and he had many of the volumes bound there by Le Gascon and other eminent binders. An earlier library which he collected is said to have been burnt by the Roundheads during the Civil War.[46] When he died in 1665, his library, which was still in France, was claimed as the property of the French king, by virtue of the *droit d'aubaine*, and it is said to have been purchased for ten thousand crowns by the Earl of Bristol, who died in 1676, and whose books, conjointly with those of another collector, were sold in London in April 1680. A priced catalogue of the sale is preserved in the British Museum; and it is stated in it that the books principally belonged 'to the library of the Right Honourable George, late Earl of Bristol, a great part of which were the Curiosities collected by the learned Sir Kenelme Digby.' It is evident, however, that a considerable number of the volumes which belonged to Digby remained in France, as several are to be found in the Bibliothèque Nationale and other libraries. In a communication to the Library Association of the United Kingdom, M. Léopold Delisle, Director of the Bibliothèque Nationale, gives a list of manuscripts and printed books in that library, which were formerly the property of the collector. One volume, with a very beautiful binding by Le Gascon, is preserved in the Bibliothèque Mazarine. Sir Kenelm presented to the Bodleian Library a valuable collection of manuscripts and printed books which Thomas Allen, his former tutor, had bequeathed to him in 1630. He also gave a considerable number of volumes to the library of Harvard College, Cambridge, Mass., and the following notice of the gift occurs in the works of Richard Baxter:—

'I proposed,' he writes, 'to have given almost all my library to Cambridge in New England; but Mr. Thomas Knowles, who knew their library, told me that Sir Kenelm Digby had already given them the Fathers, Councils and Schoolmen, and that it was Histories and Commentators which they wanted. Whereupon I sent them some of my Commentators and some Histories, among which were Freherus, Renherus, and Pistorius's collections.'

Unfortunately, this first Harvard library was destroyed by fire in 1764. At that time it contained about six thousand volumes.

FOOTNOTES:

[46] See Article on English Book-Sales, 1676-1680, by Mr. A.W. Pollard, in *Bibliographica*, vol. i. p. 373.

RALPH SHELDON, 1623-1684

Ralph Sheldon, who was born on the 1st of August 1623, at Beoley in Worcestershire, was the eldest son of William Sheldon of Beoley and Elizabeth, daughter of William, second Lord Petre. He was privately educated, and at the age of nineteen he paid a visit to France and Italy, and resided at Rome for some time, returning home about 1647, after an absence of four years from his native country. Sheldon appears to have been greatly respected, and Nash, in his *Collections for the History of Worcestershire,* says 'he was a person of such rare worth and excellent qualities as deserve particular notice. He was a great patron of learning and learned men, and well skilled in the history and antiquities of his country, sparing no money to set up a standing library at Weston. He was a great friend to Anthony Wood, and left him a legacy of £40. He purchased the valuable MSS. of the ingenious Augustine Vincent, Windsor Herald, and Keeper of the records in the Tower, *temp.* Charles I., which at his death he bequeathed to the Heralds' College, where they are still preserved; and allowed John Vincent his son a yearly pension for many years. He travelled often to Rome, and spent some time there to furnish himself with choice books, coins and medals. In short, he was of such remarkable integrity, charity and hospitality, as gained him the universal esteem of all the gentlemen of the county; insomuch that he usually went by the name of the Great Sheldon.... And for the sufferings which himself and father had undergone in the civil wars, he was nominated by Charles II. one of the gentlemen of Warwickshire, who were to have received the honour of the Order of the Royal Oak, had it been instituted; his estate being then valued at £2000 per annum, the largest of any in the county, except that of the Middlemores of Edgbaston, which was estimated of the same annual value.' The library formed by Sheldon at his manor-house of Weston in the parish of Long Compton, Warwickshire, was a fine one. Among the printed books was a very curious and probably unique copy of the first folio of Shakespeare (now the property of the Baroness Burdett-Coutts), where the concluding passages of *Romeo and Juliet,* and the opening passages of *Troilus and Cressida,* are printed twice over at different parts of the volume. This irregularity was discovered by Mr. Sidney Lee, who read a paper on the subject before the Bibliographical Society on March 21, 1898. The library at Weston was dispersed in 1781.

BOOK-STAMP OF RALPH SHELDON.

In commemoration of Sheldon's gifts to Heralds' College, Mr. Ralph Bigland, who was created Blue Mantle in 1757, and died as Garter in 1784, caused a handsome canvas to be painted, on which are emblazoned Sheldon's arms, impaled with those of his wife, accompanied by the following biographical notice: —'To the Memory of Ralph Sheldon of Beoley in the County of Worcester, Esquire, a great Benefactor to this Office. Who died at his Manor-House of Weston in the Parish of Long-Compton, in the County of Warwick, on Midsu[m]er Day, 1684, aged 61 years wanting 6 weeks: the Day after wards his Heart and Bowels were buried in Long-Compton Chancel, in a Vault by those of his Father, Mother, Grandfather, etc., and on the 10th of July following, his Body in a Vault by his Ancestors under our Lady's Chapel, Joyning on the North Side to St. Leonard's Church of Beoley: He married Henrietta-Maria, Daughter of Thomas Savage, Viscount Rock-Savage by Elizabeth his wife,

Daughter of Thomas, Lord Darcy, of Chich in Essex, Viscount Colchester and Earl Rivers, but by her had no issue.'

This canvas is still preserved in Heralds' College.

Sheldon compiled *A Catalogue of the Nobility of England since the Norman Conquest, according to theire severall Creations by every particular King,* with the arms handsomely emblazoned. This manuscript came into the possession of Sir Thomas Phillipps, and formed one of the lots at the sale of his collection in June 1893.

DR. FRANCIS BERNARD, 1627-1698

Dr. Francis Bernard was born in 1627. He was a Fellow of the College of Physicians, Assistant-Physician to St. Bartholomew's Hospital, and Physician-in-Ordinary to King James II. He died on the 9th of February 1698, and was buried in the parish church of St. Botolph, London, where his wife erected a monument to his memory.

Dr. Bernard formed a very extensive library, which consisted, 'more especially of that sort of Books which are out of the Common Course, which a Man may make the Business of his Life to collect, and at last not be able to accomplish.'[47] It was very rich in works relating to medicine, and it also contained a considerable number of early English books, among which were about a dozen Caxtons. The collection was sold by auction shortly after Bernard's death. The title-page of the sale catalogue reads:—'A Catalogue of the Library of the late learned Dr. Francis Bernard, Fellow of the College of Physicians, and Physician to S. Bartholomew's Hospital. Being a large Collection of the best Theological, Historical, Philological, Medicinal and Mathematical Authors, in the Greek, Latin, Italian, Spanish, French, German, Dutch and English Tongues, in all Volumes, which will be sold by Auction at the Doctor's late Dwelling House in Little Britain; the Sale to begin on Tuesday, Octob. 4, 1698.' A copy of the catalogue, with the prices in manuscript, is in the British Museum. The sale consisted of nearly fifteen thousand lots and thirty-nine bundles of tracts, which realised nineteen hundred and twenty pounds; the expenses of the sale amounting to three hundred and twenty pounds. The Caxtons sold for a little over two guineas. *The Dictes or Sayings of the Philosophers* and the *Knight of the Tower* each fetched five shillings and fourpence, the *History of Jason* three shillings and sixpence, the *Histories of King Arthur* two shillings and tenpence, the *Chastising of God's Children* one shilling and tenpence, and the second edition of the *Game of the Chesse* one shilling and sixpence.

Dibdin says that Dr. Bernard was 'a stoic in bibliography. Neither beautiful binding, nor amplitude of margin, ever delighted his eye or rejoiced his heart: for he was a stiff, hard, and straightforward reader—and learned, in Literary History, beyond all his contemporaries'; and in the preface to the sale catalogue we read that he was 'a person who collected books for use, and not for ostentation or ornament, and he seemed no more solicitous about *their* dress than *his own.*' A memorandum book containing notes of his visits to patients, etc., is in the Sloane collection of manuscripts in the British Museum.

FOOTNOTES:

[47] Address to the reader, prefixed to sale catalogue.

SAMUEL PEPYS, 1633-1703

Samuel Pepys, Secretary to the Admiralty in the reigns of King
Charles II. and King James II., was born either at London or
Brampton in Huntingdonshire on the 23rd of February 1633.

BOOK-PLATE OF SAMUEL PEPYS.

His father, John Pepys, was a citizen of London, where he followed the trade of a tailor, but in 1661 retired to Brampton, at which place he had inherited a property of eighty pounds a year from his eldest brother Robert Pepys. He died there in 1680. Samuel Pepys received his early education at Huntingdon, and afterwards at St. Paul's School, London, where he continued until 1650, in which year he was admitted at Trinity Hall, Cambridge. On the 5th of March 1651 he migrated as a sizar to Magdalene College, Cambridge, where he is entered in the books of the College as 'Samuel Peapys,' and where, two years later, he was elected to a scholarship founded by John Smith. He graduated B.A. in 1653 and M.A. in 1660. In 1659 he accompanied his relative, Sir Edward Montagu, afterwards Earl of Sandwich, on his expedition to the Sound, and on his return became a clerk in the office of Sir G. Downing, one of the Tellers of the Exchequer. In 1660 he was appointed Clerk of the Acts of the Navy, which post he held until 1673, when he was made Secretary for the Affairs of the Navy, and in 1684 he became Secretary of the Admiralty, an office he retained until the accession of William and Mary, when he lost his public appointments, and retired into private life. Pepys was elected a Fellow of the Royal Society in 1665, and in 1684 became President. He died at Clapham on the 26th of May 1703, and was buried in the church of St. Olave, Hart Street, London.

Pepys collected a very interesting library, which is now preserved in a fireproof room in Magdalene College, Cambridge. It consists of about three thousand volumes arranged in eleven mahogany cases in the precise order in which Pepys left them. The cases are the identical ones mentioned in his *Diary*, August 24, 1666:—'Up and dispatched several businesses at home in the morning, and then comes Sympson to set up my other new presses for my books, and so he and I fell in to the furnishing of my new closett, and taking out the things out of my old, and I kept him with me all day, and he dined with me, and so all the afternoon till it was quite dark hanging things, that is my maps and pictures and draughts, and setting up my books, and as much as we could do, to my most extraordinary satisfaction; so I think it will be as noble a closet as any man hath, and light enough—though indeed it would be better to have a little more light.'

This room, Mr. Wheatley tells us in his excellent account of the library in vol. i. of *Bibliographica*, 'was at the Navy Office in Crutched Friars, and the illustration in the ordinary editions of the *Diary* shows the position of the cases when they were transferred to the house in York Buildings (now Buckingham Street, Strand).' 'The presses,' he adds, 'are handsomely carved, and have handles fixed at each end; the doors are formed of little panes of glass, and in the lower divisions the glass windows are made to lift up. The books are all arranged in double rows; but by the ingenious plan of placing small books in front of large ones, the letterings of all can be seen. Neatness was a mania with Pepys, and the volumes were evened on all the shelves; in one instance some short volumes have been raised to the required height by help of wooden stilts, gilt in front.'

The library consists principally of ordinary books, but it also comprises some valuable manuscripts, and many volumes from the presses of the early English printers. It contains as many as nine Caxtons, eight Pynsons, and nineteen Wynkyn de Wordes, several of the last being unique. The books printed by Caxton are the *Game of the Chesse, Polychronicon, Chronicles of England, Description of Britain, Mirrour of the World, Book of the Order of Chivalry*, the first and second editions of the *Canterbury Tales*, and the *Chastising of God's Children*. Among the most interesting collections is one of eighteen hundred ballads in five folio volumes; and another of four duodecimo volumes of garlands and other popular publications, printed for the most part in black letter. The volumes are lettered: Vol. 1 *Penny Merriments*, Vol. 2 *Penny Witticisms*, Vol. 3 *Penny Compliments*, and Vol. 4 *Penny Godlinesses*. In the first volume of the ballads Pepys has written:—'My collection of ballads, begun by Mr. Selden, improv'd by the addition of many pieces elder thereto in time; and the whole continued to the year 1700.' The library also possesses collections of old novels, pieces of wit, chivalry, etc, plays, books on shorthand, tracts on the Popish Plot, liturgical controversies, sea tracts, news-pamphlets, etc.

BOOK-STAMP OF SAMUEL PEPYS.

The most interesting manuscripts are the famous *Diary* in six volumes, the papers collected by Pepys for his proposed *Navalia,* and a collection of Scottish poetry, formed by Sir Richard Maitland of Lethington, Lord Privy Seal and Judge in the Court of Session, who died in 1586. The drawings and prints in the library are numerous and valuable. Among them are portraits of Pepys's friends, and prints and drawings illustrating the city of London; one of the rarest of these is the large plan of London attributed to Agas, of which only one other copy is known. The library also contains some volumes of music with the title, *Songs and other Compositions, Light, Grave and Sacred, for a single voice adjusted to the particular compass of mine; with a thorough base on yᵉ ghitarr by Cesare Morelli.* Several songs composed by Pepys are in this collection, one of which, entitled *Beauty Retire,* was a great success, and the composer was very proud of it. All the books in the library are in excellent condition, and, with the exception of a few in morocco or vellum, are bound in calf. Almost all of them bear Pepys's arms on the lower cover; while on the upper is found a shield with the inscription, SAM. PEPYS CAR. ET IAC. ANGL. REGIB. A SECRETIS ADMIRALIÆ. This shield is surmounted with his helmet and crest, and is surrounded by mantling, in which are introduced two anchors, indicating his office. He also used three bookplates—one with his arms, quartering Talbot of Cottenham; a second with his portrait by Robert White, with his motto, *Mens cujusque is est Quisque*, from the *Somnium Scipionis* of Cicero; and a third bearing his initials, with two anchors crossed, together with his motto.

BOOK-STAMP OF SAMUEL PEPYS.

Pepys left his library, together with his other property, to his nephew, John Jackson; but in a paper of directions respecting it, preserved among the Harleian Manuscripts in the British Museum, he expresses a desire that at his nephew's death it should be placed in either Trinity or Magdalene College, Cambridge, preferably 'in the latter, for the sake of my own and my nephew's education therein.' In addition to Pepys' collection at Magdalene College, the Bodleian Library contains a series of his miscellaneous papers in twenty-five volumes, together with numerous other volumes which belonged to him, including many curious dockyard account-books of the times of King Henry VIII. and Queen Elizabeth.[48] These were bequeathed to the library by Dr. Richard Rawlinson, the nonjuring bishop. Mr. John

Eliot Hodgkin, F.S.A., of Childwall, Weybridge, Surrey, also possesses some papers which once belonged to Pepys.

Pepys published *Memoirs relating to the State of the Royal Navy of England for ten years determined December 1688*, in 1690; and a work entitled *The Portugal History: or a Relation of the Troubles that happened in the Court of Portugal in the years 1667 and 1668 ... by S.P., Esq.*, printed at London in 1677, is also attributed to him. His well-known *Diary*, the manuscript of which fills six small volumes of closely written shorthand, was first deciphered by the Rev. John Smith, Rector of Baldock, Hertfordshire, and was published, with a selection from his private correspondence, by Lord Braybrooke, in two volumes in 1825. It has since been several times reprinted. The last edition, edited by Mr. H.B. Wheatley, F.S.A., published in eight volumes octavo in 1893-96, contains the whole of the *Diary*, with the exception of passages which cannot possibly be printed.

FOOTNOTES:

[48] Macray, *Annals of the Bodleian Library*.

EDWARD STILLINGFLEET, BISHOP OF WORCESTER, 1635-1699

Edward Stillingfleet, Bishop of Worcester, was the seventh son of Samuel Stillingfleet of the family of Stillingfleet of Stillingfleet, Yorkshire. He was born at Cranborne in Dorsetshire on the 17th of April 1635, and received his early education in the grammar schools of Cranborne and Ringwood. In his fifteenth year he was admitted into St. John's College, Cambridge, where he obtained a Fellowship in 1653. For several years after leaving college he was engaged as a private tutor, first in the family of Sir Roger Burgoyne of Wroxall in Warwickshire, and afterwards in that of the Hon. Francis Pierrepoint of Nottingham, during which period he was ordained by Ralph Brownrig, the deprived Bishop of Exeter. In 1657 he was presented by Sir R. Burgoyne to the rectory of Sutton, Bedfordshire, and in 1665 the Earl of Southampton gave him the rectory of St. Andrew's, Holborn. He was also appointed Preacher at the Rolls Chapel, and shortly afterwards Reader of the Temple, and Chaplain in Ordinary to Charles II. In 1667 he was collated to a Canonry in St. Paul's, London; in 1669 he became a Canon 'in the twelfth prebend' in Canterbury Cathedral; in 1677 Archdeacon of London; in 1678 Dean of St. Paul's; and on the 13th of October 1689 he was consecrated Bishop of Worcester. He died at his residence in Park Street, Westminster, on the 27th of March 1699, and was buried in Worcester Cathedral, where a monument was erected to his memory by his son, with a Latin epitaph by Richard Bentley, who had been one of his chaplains.

Bishop Stillingfleet collected 'at a vast expence of time, pains and money' a very choice and valuable library, which contained a considerable number of manuscripts, and upwards of nine thousand five hundred printed volumes, besides many pamphlets. It is stated that there were over two thousand folios in it, and that it cost the Bishop six thousand pounds. Evelyn in a letter to Pepys, dated August 12th, 1689, writes: 'The Bishop of Ely[49] has a well stor'd library; but the very best is what Dr. Stillingfleete, Deane of St. Paule's, has at Twicknam, ten miles out of towne.' After Stillingfleet's death his library was offered for sale. Entries in

Evelyn's diary[50] show that great efforts were made to persuade William III. to buy it, but they evidently failed, as the historical manuscripts were purchased by Robert Harley (afterwards Earl of Oxford), while the remainder of the collection was acquired by Narcissus Marsh, Archbishop of Armagh, who bought the books for a public library in Dublin which he had founded. He is said to have paid two thousand five hundred pounds for them. Stillingfleet, who on account of his handsome person was nicknamed 'the beauty of holiness,' was the author of *Origines Britannicæ, or Antiquities of the British Churches*, and many controversial works. His collected works were printed in 1710 in six volumes folio, and a volume of his miscellaneous works was published in 1735 by his son, the Rev. James Stillingfleet, Canon of Worcester.

FOOTNOTES:

[49] John Moore, Bishop of Ely, whose library was purchased by King George I., and presented by him to the University of Cambridge.

[50] '*April 29, 1699.*—I dined with the Archbishop, but my business was to get him to persuade the King to purchase the late Bishop of Worcester's library, and build a place, for his own library at St. James's, in the Parke, the present one being too small.'

'*May 3, 1699.*—At a meeting of the Royal Society I was nominated to be of the Committee to wait on the Lord Chancellor to move the King to purchase Bp. of Worcester's library.'

JOHN MOORE, BISHOP OF ELY, 1646-1714

John Moore, Bishop successively of Norwich and Ely, who was born at Sutton-juxta-Broughton, Leicestershire, in 1646, was the eldest son of Thomas Moore, an ironmonger at Market Harborough. He was educated at the Free School, Market Harborough, and at Clare College, Cambridge, where he obtained a fellowship in 1667. Having taken holy orders, he was collated in 1676 to the rectory of Blaby in Leicestershire; and in 1679, through the influence of Heneage Finch, Earl of Nottingham, who, in 1670, had appointed him his chaplain, he was installed canon in Ely Cathedral. In 1687 he was presented by the dean and chapter of St. Paul's to the rectory of St. Austin, London, and in 1689 he obtained the rectory of St. Andrew's, Holborn, which he held with his canonry at Ely until 1691, when he was consecrated Bishop of Norwich. He remained in that see until 1707, in which year he was translated to the more valuable bishopric of Ely. Moore died on the 31st of July 1714, from the effects of a cold which he caught while presiding at the trial of Dr. Bentley, Master of Trinity College, Cambridge, who was charged with encroaching on the privileges of the fellows of that institution. He was buried in Ely Cathedral, where a monument was erected to his memory.

Bishop Moore, who is called by Dibdin 'the father of black-letter collectors in this country,' was a great and generous patron of learning, and formed a magnificent library, which at the time of his death contained nearly twenty-nine thousand printed books and seventeen hundred and ninety manuscripts. John Bagford was the principal assistant in its collection, and in return for his services the Bishop procured him a place in the Charterhouse. The library, which was kept in the episcopal residence in Ely Place, Holborn, where it occupied 'eight chambers,' is mentioned in *Notices of London Libraries*, by John Bagford and William Oldys, where it is stated that 'Dr. John Moore, the late Bishop of Ely, had also a prodigious collection of books, written as well as printed on vellum, some very ancient, others finely illuminated. He had a *Capgrave's Chronicle*, books of the first printing at Mentz, and other places abroad, as also at Oxford, St. Alban's, Westminster, etc.' John Evelyn, Bishop Burnet, and Ralph

Thoresby also write in terms of high praise of the excellence and great extent of the collection. Richard Gough, the antiquary, states that 'the Bishop formed his library by plundering those of the clergy in his diocese. Some he paid with sermons or more modern books; others only with quid illiterati cum libris'; but there appears to be little, if any, truth in this accusation. Moore, who was anxious that his library should not be dispersed after his death, offered it, in 1714, to Robert Harley, Earl of Oxford, for the sum of eight thousand pounds; but the negotiation failed in consequence, it is said, of the Bishop 'insisting on being paid the money in his lifetime, though Lord Oxford was not to have the books till the Bishop's death.' After Moore's decease the collection was sold for six thousand guineas to George I., who gave it, on the suggestion of Lord Townsend, to the University of Cambridge. A special book-plate, designed and engraved by John Pine, was placed in the volumes. At the same time that the king sent these books to the University he despatched a troop of horse to Oxford, which occasioned the two well-known epigrams attributed to Dr. Tripp and Sir William Browne—

'Contrary methods justly George applies
To govern his two universities,
To Oxford sent a troop of horse;—for why?
That learned body wanted Loyalty.
To Cambridge he sent books, as well discerning,
How much that loyal body wanted learning.'

The reply by Sir W. Browne runs—

'Contrary methods justly George applies
To govern his two universities,
And so to Oxford sent a troop of horse,
For Tories hold no argument but force;
To Cambridge Ely's learned books are sent,
For Whigs admit no force but argument.'

BOOK-PLATE PLACED IN BOOKS FROM BISHOP MOORE'S LIBRARY GIVEN
BY GEORGE I. TO THE UNIVERSITY OF CAMBRIDGE.

This is not the only version of these epigrams, but the Rev. Cecil
Moore in his Memoir of the Bishop considers it to be the correct one.

Moore's diaries, letters, and private accounts are also preserved in
the Cambridge University Library. A volume containing his printed
sermons was published in 1715, and a second issue in two volumes
in 1724. Both series were edited by the Rev. Samuel Clarke, D.D.

JOHN BAGFORD, 1650?-1716

John Bagford was born about 1650. The exact date of his birth is unknown, and he does not appear to have been acquainted with it himself, for a short time before his death he informed Mr. James Sotheby that he was either sixty-five or sixty-six years of age, he could not tell which. According to the belief of Thomas Hearne, the antiquary, he was born in Fetter Lane, London, and he was no doubt for some time a shoemaker, for in a very curious and entertaining little treatise on the *Art of Shoemaking and Historical Account of Clouthing of ye foot*, which is believed to have been written by him, and is now preserved among the Harleian manuscripts in the British Museum, the writer states that he was brought up to the 'craft of shoemaking.' This trade, however, he soon abandoned for a more congenial occupation, and he became a collector of books on commission for booksellers and amateurs. In pursuance of this work he made several journeys to the Continent, and acquired a great knowledge of books, prints, and literary curiosities. He was specially employed by Robert Harley, Earl of Oxford, Sir Hans Sloane, and John Moore, Bishop of Ely, who appear to have greatly appreciated his judgment, diligence, and honesty; and the last-named collector procured him, as some recompense for his services, admission into the Charterhouse. Nothing is known of Bagford's parents, and little of his domestic life, but he appears to have been married, for on the back of a leaf in one of the volumes of his collections we find the following memorandum in Bagford's writing: 'John, son of John and Elizabeth Bagford, was baptized 31st October 1675, in the parish of St. Anne, Blackfriars.' This son seems to have become a sailor in the Royal Navy, for in another volume in the same collections there is a power of attorney, dated April 6, 1713, signed by John Bagford, Junior, empowering his 'honoured father, John Bagford, Senior, of the parish of St. Sepulchre, in the county of Middlesex, bookseller,' to claim and receive from the Paymaster of Her Majesty's Navy his wages as a seaman in case of his death. Bagford, who took great interest in all descriptions of antiquities, was one of the little group of distinguished men who reconstituted in 1707 the Society of Antiquaries. He died, Dr. Birch informs us, at Islington on the 15th of

May 1716, and was buried in the graveyard belonging to the Charterhouse.

JOHN BAGFORD.

During his researches for his employers Bagford amassed two great collections: one consisting of ballads, now known as the 'Bagford Ballads'; the other being a vast collection of leaves from manuscripts, title-pages and fragments of books, specimens of paper, book-plates, engravings, bindings, catalogues, advertisements, and various interesting and curious pieces. With the aid of these materials Bagford intended to write a history of printing, and in 1707 he published his *Proposals for an Historical Account of that most universally celebrated as well as useful Art of Typography*. The work, which was also to contain a history of bookbinding, paper-making, etc., was, however, never published, and it has been often stated that Bagford was quite incompetent to carry out such an undertaking. This may possibly have been the case, for although he was certainly a man of much ability, and possessed an extensive knowledge of books, he had received but little education. Several of his contemporaries, however, held a different opinion, and among them Hearne, who repeatedly expresses in his works his admiration of both Bagford's genius and his collections.

The method of compiling a history of printing from a collection of title-pages appears to be both a clumsy and a costly one, but it seems probable from entries in the diary of Oldys, and from Gough's memoir of Ames, that that bibliographer wrote his *Typographical Antiquities* with the aid of similar materials.

Bagford has been subjected to very severe censure for mutilating books for the purpose of forming his collection of title-pages. Mr. Blades, in his work *The Enemies of Books*, accuses him of being 'a wicked old biblioclast who went about the country, from library to library, tearing away title-pages from rare books of all sizes'; and Dr. Dibdin in *Bibliomania* states that he 'was the most hungry and rapacious of all book and print collectors.' The testimony of Hearne (who knew Bagford well, and who was also amply qualified to judge both of his merits and demerits), however, is very different. He writes: 'It was very laudable in my Friend, Mr. John Bagford (who I think was born in Fetter Lane, London), to employ so much of his time, as he did, in collecting Remains of Antiquity. Indeed he was a man of very surprising genius, and had his education (for he was first a shoemaker, and afterwards for some time a bookseller) been equal to his natural genius, he would have proved a much greater man than he was. And yet, without this education, he was, certainly, the greatest man in the world in his way.... 'Tis very remarkable, that, in collecting, his care did not extend itself to Books and to the fragments of Books, only, but even to the very Covers, and to the Bosses and Clasps; and all this, that he might, with the greater ease, compile the History of Printing, which he had undertaken, but did not finish. In this noble Work he intended a Discourse about

Binding,... and another about the Art of making paper, in both of which his observations were very accurate.'

A great number of the title-pages and fragments collected by Bagford are evidently taken from books which could be purchased in his day for a few shillings, many of them probably for a few pence; while it is possible that some may have been salvage from the Great Fire of 1666, when we know immense quantities of books were burnt or damaged. The collections, it is true, contain fragments of the Gutenberg Bible, various Caxtons, and other rare books, but there is no reason to think that these were abstracted from complete copies; it is much more likely that they were odd leaves which Bagford had picked up, while the leather stains on some of the most valuable show that they once formed part of the padding of old bindings. Many of the books were probably acquired by Bagford when he took part in the book-hunting expeditions of the Duke of Devonshire, the Earls of Oxford, Sunderland, and other collectors, who amused themselves every Saturday during the winter in rambling through various quarters of the town in search of additions to their libraries. After Bagford's death Hearne was very anxious to obtain his collections, as he wished to publish 'a book from them, for the service of the public, and the honour of Mr. Bagford,' but much to his chagrin he was forestalled by Wanley, Lord Oxford's librarian, who acquired them for his employer's library, and they formed part of the Harleian Manuscripts, etc., purchased in 1753 for the British Museum. Wanley, however, does not appear to have secured the whole of Bagford's papers, as the Sloane collection contains four volumes of manuscripts and printed matter which belonged to him, and the Bodleian Library possesses some Indulgences which he acquired and gave to Hearne.

The Bagford collections in the British Museum consist of one hundred and twenty-nine[51] volumes, including three of ballads. The manuscript pieces are contained in thirty-six folios; the printed pieces in sixty-three folios, twenty-one quartos, and nine octavos. Among the more important manuscripts are Bagford's Commonplace Book; his Book of Accounts; his Account of Public and Private Libraries; Collections in reference to Printing; Names of old English Printers, with lists of the works which passed through their hands; an Account of Paper; Patents granted to Printers in England; Observations on the History of Printing; Lives of famous Engravers, etc. The collection also contains a large number of fragments of early Bibles, Service Books, Decretals, Lives of Saints, etc. These are almost entirely of vellum, and some of them are as early as the eighth century.

Among the printed fragments is a leaf from the Gutenberg Bible,[52] portions of the *Recuyell of the Histories of Troy*, the *Polychronicon*, the *Book of Fame*, and many other books from the presses of Caxton, Machlinia, Rood and Hunte, Pynson, Wynkyn de Worde, and other early printers, both English and foreign.

The maps in the collection are especially important and interesting, including a very rare one sometimes found in Hakluyt's *Navigations and Discoveries of the English Nation*, printed in the years 1599 and 1600, and worth at least two hundred pounds;[53] and the even more valuable celestial and terrestrial planispheres by John Blagrave of Reading, which are believed to be unique. There are also some rare documents relating to the Post Office; a number of early book-plates; some fine specimens of English, French, and German stamped bindings of the sixteenth century; several volumes of Chinese, marbled, and other papers; early almanacks; a quantity of engravings of towns, costumes, trades, furniture, etc.; curious advertisements of tobacco, tea, quack medicines, etc.; specimens of fine writing; and many other miscellaneous papers of much interest.

Bagford was the author of a letter on the antiquities of London, prefixed to the first volume of Hearne's edition of Leland's *Collectanea*; and also of an *Account of London Libraries*, first printed in 1708 in *The Monthly Miscellany, or Memoirs for the Curious*. This little brochure was continued by Oldys, and the complete work published by Mr. James Yeowell in 1862. *The Essay on the Invention of Printing, by Mr. John Bagford*, in vol. XXV. of the *Philosophical Transactions of the Royal Society*, was, Dibdin says, drawn up by Wanley. The collection of ballads has been edited by the Rev. J.W. Ebsworth for the Ballad Society.

FOOTNOTES:

[51] It is somewhat doubtful whether a few of these belonged to Bagford.

[52] Probably given to Bagford by Michael Maittaire, the collector, who possessed a very imperfect copy of the Gutenberg Bible, which sold for fifty shillings at the sale of his library.

[53] This is believed to be the map alluded to by Shakespeare in Act. iii. Sc. 2 of *Twelfth Night,* where he makes Maria say of Malvolio: 'He does smile his face into more lines than there are in the new map, with the augmentation of the Indies.'

THOMAS HERBERT, EIGHTH EARL OF PEMBROKE, 1656-1733

Thomas Herbert, eighth Earl of Pembroke, who was born in 1656, was the third son of Philip, the fifth Earl. By the deaths of his elder brothers, the sixth and seventh Earls, he succeeded to the title in 1683, and from that time to his death in 1733 he held many of the highest appointments in the State. He was one of the representatives of England at the treaty of Ryswick, and he carried the Sword of Justice at the coronations of William and Mary, Anne, George I. and George II. He was also President of the Royal Society in 1689-90.

Many of the Earls of Pembroke were men of culture and patrons of learning. In 1629 William, the third Earl, gave to the University of Oxford, of which he was Chancellor, a very valuable series of Greek manuscripts collected by Giacomo Barocci, a gentleman of Venice; and in 1649 his brother Philip, the fourth Earl, gave to the same University, of which he was also Chancellor, a splendidly bound copy of the Paris Polyglot Bible, printed in 1645 in nine volumes. These two brothers are 'the incomparable pair of brethren' to whom the first folio of Shakespeare is dedicated. There had been for several generations a library at Wilton House, Salisbury, which Dibdin considered to be one of the oldest of private collections existing; but Thomas, the eighth Earl, added to it so large a number of rare books that it 'entitled him to dispute the palm even with the Lords Sunderland and Oxford.' Maittaire, in his *Annales Typographici*, calls the library a 'Bibliotheca exquisitissima,' and styles its owner 'Humanitatis politioris cultor et patronus.' Dibdin also states that Lord Pembroke spared no expense for books, and that he was 'a collector of everything the most precious and rare in the book-way.' The library was still further augmented by his successor Henry.

Dr. Dampier, Bishop of Ely, compiled a list in 1776 of the earlier printed works in the library, which Dibdin has reproduced in his *Decameron*. The books are one hundred and ninety-nine in number, of which one hundred and eighty-eight are of the fifteenth century. The list contains eight Caxtons, eighteen volumes printed by Jenson, and ten by the Spiras. Among the most notable of the incunabula are the *Rationale Divinorum Officiorum* of Durandus, on vellum, printed by Fust and Schoeffer at Mentz in 1459; the *Catholicon* of Balbus, printed at Mentz in 1460; *Cicero de Oratore,* printed by Sweynheym and Pannartz at the Monastery of Subiaco in 1465; Cicero's *Epistolæ ad Familiares,* printed by Joannes de Spira at Venice in 1469; and the *Bokys of Hawkyng and Huntyng,* printed at St. Albans in 1486. The Caxtons are *The Recuyell of the Histories of Troy;* the first and second editions of *The Game of the Chesse;* the first edition of *The Dictes or Sayings of the Philosophers, Tully of Old Age, Chronicles of England,* the *Polychronicon,* and the *Liber Festivalis.*

NARCISSUS LUTTRELL, 1657-1732

Narcissus Luttrell, who was born in 1657, was the son of Francis Luttrell of London, a descendant of the Luttrells of Dunster Castle, in the county of Somerset. He received his early education under Mr. Aldrich at Sheen in Surrey, and in 1674 was admitted a fellow-commoner of St. John's College, Cambridge. In the succeeding year he was created M.A. by royal mandate.[54] While at the University he presented a silver tankard to his college, which was lost, together with a quantity of other plate, on the 9th of October 1693, for the recovery of which a reward of ten pounds was offered.[55] Luttrell, who, Dibdin says, was 'ever ardent in his love of past learning, and not less voracious in his bibliomaniacal appetites,' formed an extensive library at Shaftesbury House, Little Chelsea, where he resided for many years in seclusion. Hearne speaks of it 'as a very extraordinary collection,' and adds that 'in it are many manuscripts, which, however, he had not the spirit to communicate to the world, and 'twas a mortification to him to see the world gratified without his assistance.' A special feature of the library was the large and interesting collection of fugitive pieces issued during the reigns of Charles II., James II., William III., and Anne, which Luttrell purchased day by day as they appeared. Sir Walter Scott found this collection, which in his time was chiefly in the possession of the collectors Mr. Heber and Mr. Bindley, very useful when editing the *Works* of Dryden, published in eighteen volumes at London in 1808. In the preface he remarks that 'the industrious collector seems to have bought every poetical tract, of whatever merit, which was hawked through the streets in his time, marking carefully the price and date of purchase. His collection contains the earliest editions of many of our most excellent poems, bound up, according to the order of time, with the lowest trash of Grub Street.' On Luttrell's death, which took place at his residence in Chelsea on the 27th of June 1732, the collection became the property of Francis Luttrell (presumed to be his son), who died in 1740. It afterwards passed into the possession of Mr. Serjeant Wynne, and from him descended to Edward Wynne, his eldest son, the author of *Eunomus, or Dialogues concerning the Law and Constitution of England; and a Miscellany containing several law tracts,* published at London in 1765. He died a bachelor in 1784, and the library, which had been considerably enlarged by its later possessors, was inherited by his brother, the Rev. Luttrell Wynne, of All Souls' College, Oxford, by whose direction it was sold by auction by Leigh and Sotheby in 1786. The sale, which consisted of two thousand seven hundred and fifty-six lots, commenced on March 6th, and lasted twelve days. It is stated in the catalogue that 'great part of the library was formed by an Eminent and Curious Collector in the last Century, and comprehends a fine Suite of Historical, Classical, Mathematical, Natural History, Poetical and Miscellaneous Books, in all Arts and Sciences ... by the most Eminent Printers, Rob. Steph., Morell, Aldus, Elzevir, Caxton, Wynkyn de Worde, &c. &c. Also a very curious Collection of old English Romances, and old Poetry; with a great number of scarce Pamphlets during the Great Rebellion and the Protectorate.' Various portions of the Luttrell collections were bought by Messrs. Heber and Bindley. The greater part of those purchased by Mr. Bindley were eventually acquired by the British Museum at the Duke of Buckingham's sale in 1849, while those which belonged to Mr. Heber are now to be found on the shelves of the Britwell library. Dibdin informs us that 'a great number of poetical tracts was disposed of, previous to the sale, to Dr. Farmer, who gave not more than forty guineas for them.' Two Caxtons in the sale—the *Mirrour of the World* and *Caton*—fetched respectively five guineas and four guineas, and a collection of plays, in twenty-one volumes, by Gascoigne, Dekker, etc., sold for thirty-eight pounds, seventeen shillings.

Luttrell compiled a chronicle of contemporary events, which was frequently quoted by Lord Macaulay in his *History of England*. This remained in manuscript for many years in the library of All Souls' College, Oxford, but in 1857 it was printed in six volumes by the Delegates of the University Press under the title of *A Brief Historical Relation of State Affairs from September 1678 to April 1714*. He also left a personal diary in English, but whimsically written in Greek characters, consisting principally of entries recording the hours of his rising and going to bed, the manner in which he spent his time, what friends called to see him, the sermons he heard, where and how he dined, and the occasions, which were not infrequent, when he took too much wine. This manuscript is preserved in the British Museum (Add. MS. 10447).

FOOTNOTES:

[54] *Notes and Queries.* Second Series. Vol. xii., page 78.

[55] See *London Gazette*, October 16-19, 1693.

SIR HANS SLOANE, BART., 1660-1753

SIR HANS SLOANE, BART.

Sir Hans Sloane, Bart., was born on the 16th of April 1660 at Killileagh, County Down, Ireland. His father, Alexander Sloane, was a Scotchman, who had settled in Ireland on his appointment to the post of receiver-general of the estates of Lord Claneboy, afterwards Earl of Clanricarde.[56] Hans Sloane gave early indications of unusual ability, and as soon as his health, which was delicate, would permit, he came to London, and devoted himself to the study of medicine, and the kindred sciences of chemistry and botany. In 1683 he went to Paris, which at that time possessed greater facilities for medical education than could be found in London. Having taken the degree of Doctor of Medicine in the University of Orange in July 1683, he made a tour in France, and towards the close of the year 1684 he returned to England and settled in London. In 1685 he was elected a Fellow of the Royal Society, and in 1687 he was admitted a Fellow of the College of Physicians. His love for scientific research led him to accept the offer of the post of physician to the Duke of Albemarle, who had been recently appointed Governor-General of the West India Colonies. He was also appointed physician to the West Indian fleet. He set sail for Jamaica on the 12th of September 1687, and reached Port Royal on the 19th of December; but in consequence of the death of the Duke, which took place towards the end of the following year, Sloane returned to England in May 1689, bringing with him large collections in all branches of natural history, which he had obtained in Madeira, as well as in Jamaica and other West Indian islands. In 1693 Sloane was appointed to the Secretaryship of the Royal Society, and in 1727 he had the honour of succeeding Sir Isaac Newton as President. His professional career was a very successful one. In 1712 he was made Physician-Extraordinary to Queen Anne, whom he attended during her last illness; and in 1716 he was created a baronet by King George I., who also bestowed on him the post of Physician-General to the Forces. On the accession of King George II. in 1727 he was appointed First Physician to the King. He was elected President of the College of Physicians in 1719, and held the office till 1735. In 1741 he removed his museum and library from his residence in Great Russell Street, Bloomsbury, to the fine old manor-house of Chelsea, which he had purchased from the family of Cheyne. Here he spent his time in the society of his friends, and in enriching and arranging the treasures he had collected. He died after a short illness on the 11th of January 1753, in the ninety-third year of his age, and was buried in Chelsea church, where a monument was erected to his memory by his daughters. Sir Hans Sloane married Elizabeth, daughter and heiress of Alderman Langley, and widow of Fulk Rose of Jamaica, by whom he had four children, two of whom died young. Sarah, the elder of the two daughters who survived their father, married George Stanley of Poultons, Hampshire; the younger, Elizabeth, married Colonel Charles Cadogan, afterwards second Baron Cadogan.

A table drawn up by Sloane's trustees immediately after his death shows that, in addition to his splendid natural history museum, his collections comprised between forty and fifty thousand printed books, three thousand five hundred and sixteen manuscripts,[57] and six hundred and fifty-seven pictures and drawings. The coins and medals amounted to thirty-two thousand, and other antiquities to two thousand six hundred and thirty-five. Sir Hans Sloane expressed a desire in his will that his collection in all its branches might be kept and preserved together after his decease, and that an application should be made by his trustees to Parliament for its purchase for twenty thousand pounds, a sum which did not represent more than a fourth of its real value. This application was favourably received, and in June 1753 an Act was passed, 'For the purchase of the Museum, or Collection of Sir Hans Sloane, and of the Harleian Collection of Manuscripts; and for providing one general repository for the better reception and more convenient use of the said Collections; and of the Cottonian Library, and of the additions thereto.' The Act further enacted that a board, consisting of forty-two trustees, be appointed for putting the same into execution; and at a general meeting of this body, held at the Cockpit, at Whitehall, on the 3rd of April 1754, it was resolved to accept of a proposal which had been made to them, of the 'Capital Mansion House, called Montague House, and the freehold ground thereto belonging, for the general repository of the British Museum, on the terms of ten thousand pounds.'[58] Although the Act had been passed, considerable difficulty was experienced in finding the purchase-money. When the matter was brought before George II. he dismissed it with the remark, 'I don't think there are twenty thousand pounds in the Treasury'; and eventually it was proposed that the needful sum should be raised by a public lottery, which should consist of 'a hundred thousand shares, at three pounds a share; that two hundred thousand pounds should be allotted as prizes, and that the remaining hundred thousand—less the expenses of the lottery itself—should be applied to the threefold purposes of the Act, namely, the purchase of the Sloane and Harleian Collections; the providing of a Repository; and the creation of an annual income for future maintenance.'[59] Sir Hans Sloane's principal work was the *Natural History of Jamaica*, 2 vols., London, 1707-25, which occupied him for no less than thirty-eight years.

FOOTNOTES:

[56] Edwards, *Lives of Founders of the British Museum*, p. 274.

[57] There are 4100 volumes of Sloane MSS. in the British Museum. A catalogue of them, compiled by the Rev. S. Ayscough, was printed in 1782.

[58] Sims, *Handbook to the Library of the British Museum*, p. 2.

PETER LE NEVE, 1661-1729

Peter Le Neve was the son of Francis Neve (the *Le* had been dropped for several generations, when Peter resumed the ancient form of his name), a citizen and draper of London. He was born in London in 1661, and was educated at Merchant Taylors' School. From an early age he displayed a great love of antiquarian pursuits, and in 1707, when the Society of Antiquaries was reconstituted, he was chosen the first President, which office he held until 1724. He was also a Fellow of the Royal Society. On the 17th of January 1690, Le Neve was appointed Rouge-Croix Pursuivant; on April the 5th 1704, Richmond Herald; and on the 25th of the succeeding month Norroy King-at-Arms. He died on the 24th of September 1729, and was buried in the chancel of Great Witchingham Church, Norfolk. Oldys states that Le Neve had 'a vast treasure of Historical Antiquities, consisting of about 2000 printed books and above 1200 MSS., interspersed with many notes of his own.' Oldys also mentions that 'it is said that he had some pique with the Heralds' Office a little before his death, so cut them off with a single book, otherwise he had left them the whole of his library.'[60]

'Honest Tom Martin of Palgrave,' the antiquary, who was Le Neve's executor, and who married his widow, appears to have succeeded to the bulk of Le Neve's collections. They were sold by auction in 1731. The title-page of the sale catalogue reads:—'A Catalogue of the valuable library collected by that truly Laborious Antiquary, Peter Le Neve, Esq.; Norroy King of Arms (lately deceas'd), containing most of the Books relating to the History and Antiquities of Great Britain and Ireland, and many other nations. With more than a thousand Manuscripts of Abstracts of Records, etc., Heraldry, and other Sciences, several of which are very antient, and written on Vellum. Also, a great number of Pedigrees of Noble Families, etc. With many other Curiosities. Which will be Sold by Auction the 22nd Day of February 1730-1 at the Bedford Coffee-house, in the Great Piazza, Covent Garden. Beginning every Evening at Five a-Clock. By John Wilcox, Bookseller in Little Britain.'

The sale appears to have lasted about a fortnight, and was followed by a small supplementary one on March the 19th, of 'Some Curiosities and Manuscripts omitted in the previous Catalogue.' A copy of the sale catalogue, with the prices and the names of some of the purchasers in manuscript, is to be found in the British Museum.

Although Le Neve was an ardent collector and compiled a considerable number of works on heraldry and topography, many of which are preserved in the British Museum, the Bodleian Library, Heralds' College, and the Record Office, he does not appear to have printed anything. His list of *Pedigrees of Knights made by King Charles II., King James II., King William III. and Queen Mary, King William alone, and Queen Anne*, was edited by Dr. G.W. Marshall for the Harleian Society in 1873.

FOOTNOTES:

[59] Edwards, *Lives of the Founders of the British Museum*, p. 308.

[60] *Memoir of Oldys*, etc. London, 1862, p. 76.

ROBERT HARLEY, FIRST EARL OF OXFORD, 1661-1724
AND
EDWARD HARLEY, SECOND EARL OF OXFORD, 1689-1741

Robert Harley, Earl of Oxford, who was born in Bow Street, Covent Garden, on the 5th of December 1661, was the eldest son of Sir Edward Harley, K.B., who was Governor of Dunkirk after the Restoration. Entering Parliament in 1689, in 1701 he was elected Speaker of the House of Commons; in 1710 he was appointed Chancellor of the Exchequer, and in 1711 he was created Earl of Oxford and Earl Mortimer, and made Lord High Treasurer, from which post he was dismissed in 1714. In 1713 he received the Order of the Garter. He was impeached by the House of Commons in 1715; acquitted without being brought to a trial in 1717, and died at his house in Albemarle Street, London, on the 21st of May 1724.

ONE OF THE BOOK-PLATES OF ROBERT HARLEY AS A COMMONER.

Harley was the greatest collector of his time, and formed a splendid library, which, at the time of his death, besides the printed books, contained more than six thousand volumes of manuscripts, and an immense number of charters, rolls, and deeds. This noble collection was inherited by Lord Oxford's son Edward, second Earl, by whom it was very considerably augmented in every department; and when he died in June 1741, the volumes of manuscripts amounted to seven thousand six hundred and thirty-nine volumes, exclusive of fourteen thousand two hundred and thirty-six original rolls, deeds, charters, and other legal documents. The printed books were estimated at about fifty thousand volumes, the pamphlets at about three hundred and fifty thousand, and the prints at forty-one thousand. In the *Account of London Libraries*, by Bagford and Oldys, it is stated: —

ROBERT HARLEY'S BOOK-STAMP.

'For libraries in more expressly particular hands, the first and most universal in England, must be reckoned the Harleian, or Earl of Oxford's library, begun by his father and continued by himself. He has the rarest books of all countries, languages, and sciences, and the greatest number of any collector we ever had, in manuscript as well as in print, thousands of fragments, some a thousand years old; vellum books, some written over; all things especially respecting English History, personal as well as local, particular as well as general. He has a great collection of Bibles, etc., in all versions, and editions of all the first printed books, classics, and others of our own country, ecclesiastical as well as civil, by Caxton, Wynkyn de Worde, Pynson, Berthelet, Rastall, Grafton, and the greatest number of pamphlets and prints of English heads of any other person. Abundance of ledgers, chartularies, old deeds, charters, patents, grants, covenants, pedigrees, inscriptions, etc., and original letters of eminent persons, as many as would fill two hundred volumes; all the collections of his librarian Humphrey Wanley, of Stow, Sir Symonds D'Ewes, Prynne, Bishop Stillingfleet, John Bagford, Le Neve, and the flower of a hundred other libraries.'

The library was remarkably rich in early editions of the Greek and Latin classics (there were as many as one hundred and fifteen volumes of various works by Cicero printed in the fifteenth century), English early poetry and romances, and books of prints, sculpture and drawings. The collection of Caxtons was both large and fine, and it comprised the only perfect copy known of the *Book of the Noble Histories of King Arthur*, which, nearly a century and a half after the dispersion of the Harleian library, was purchased for nineteen hundred and fifty pounds, at the sale of the Earl of Jersey's books in 1885, by Mr. Quaritch for a New York collector.

The volumes in the library were all handsomely bound; mostly in red morocco, and tooled with a distinctive kind of ornamentation, which has since been known as the Harleian Style. This commonly consisted of a centrepiece, generally of a lozenge form, surrounded by a broad and elegant border. Eliot and Chapman were the binders of the greater portion of the books, at a cost, it is said, of upwards of eighteen thousand pounds.

Humphrey Wanley was for several years librarian to both the first and the second Earls, and he commenced the compilation of the catalogue of the manuscripts, which was finally completed by the Rev. Thomas Hartwell Horne in 1812. Among the Lansdowne manuscripts in the British Museum is a diary,[61] kept by Wanley, which contains much interesting information respecting the library. Some time after Wanley's decease, William Oldys was appointed librarian at a salary of two hundred pounds per annum.

The second Earl of Oxford had a passion for building and landscape gardening, as well as for collecting books, paintings and curiosities, and some years before his death these expensive tastes involved him in pecuniary difficulties. George Vertue, the eminent engraver, in one of his commonplace-books, now preserved in the British Museum,[62] thus feelingly refers to the embarrassed circumstances of the Earl:—'My good Lord, lately growing heavy and pensive in his affairs, which for some late years have mortify'd his mind.... This lately manifestly appeared in his change of complexion; his face fallen less; his colour and eyes turned yellow to a great degree; his stomach wasted and gone; and a dead weight presses continually, without sign of relief, on his mind.'

A fortnight after this was written Vertue had to lament his loss.

Lord Oxford died in Dover Street, London, on the 16th of June 1741, and on his decease the library became the property of Margaret, Duchess of Portland, the only daughter and heiress of the Earl, who sold the printed books to Mr. Thomas Osborne, the bookseller of Gray's Inn, for about thirteen thousand pounds. The manuscripts were purchased by Parliament in 1753 for the sum of ten thousand pounds, and were placed in the library of the British Museum four years later. The portraits, coins, and miscellaneous curiosities were sold by auction in March 1742.

Osborne bought Lord Oxford's books with a view of disposing of them by sale, and engaged Dr. Johnson and Oldys to compile a catalogue of them, which was printed in four volumes octavo in the years 1743-44. A fifth volume was issued in 1745, but this is nothing more than an enumeration of Osborne's unsold stock. Osborne also published in eight volumes quarto, 'The Harleian Miscellany: or, a Collection of Scarce, Curious, and Entertaining Pamphlets and Tracts, as well as in Manuscript as in Print, found in the late Earl of Oxford's library, interspersed with Historical, Political and Critical notes. London 1744-46.' This work, which was edited by Oldys, was republished by Thomas Park in 1808-12, with two supplemental volumes. A catalogue of the pamphlets contained in the Harleian Miscellany was also prepared by Oldys, and printed in a quarto volume, which appeared in 1746; and a Collection of Voyages and Travels, compiled from the Miscellany, was published in two volumes folio in 1745.

FOOTNOTES:

[61] Lansdowne MSS. 771, 772.

[62] Add. MS. 23,093.

JOHN BRIDGES, 1666-1724

John Bridges, the author of *The History and Antiquities of Northamptonshire*, was born in 1666 at Barton Seagrave, Northamptonshire. He was appointed Solicitor of the Customs in 1695, a Commissioner of the Customs in 1711, and in 1715 a Cashier of the Excise. He was a Bencher of Lincoln's Inn, and a Fellow of the Society of Antiquaries. He died on the 16th of March 1724.

Bridges, who is mentioned with great respect by Hearne and other antiquaries, was, says Dibdin, 'a gentleman, a scholar, and a notorious book-collector.' His library, which consisted of 'above 4000 Books and Manuscripts in all languages and faculties, particularly in Classics and History, and especially the History and Antiquities of Great Britain and Ireland,'[63] was sold at his chambers, No. 6 Lincoln's Inn, by Mr. Cock, on the 7th of February 1726, and twenty-six following days. The number of lots was four thousand three hundred and thirteen, and the total proceeds of the sale were four thousand one hundred and sixty pounds, twelve shillings. The books sold well, and Hearne, in his *Diary*, under February 15th, 1726, writes: 'My late friend John Bridges esqr.'s books being now selling by auction in London (they began to be sold on Monday the 7th inst.). I hear they go very high, being fair books, in good condition, and most of them finely bound. This afternoon I was told of a gentleman of All Souls' College, I suppose Dr. Clarke, that gave a commission of 8s. for an Homer in 2 vols., a small 8° if not 12°. But it went for six guineas. People are in love with good binding more than good reading.' Humphrey Wanley, who was a buyer at the sale for Lord Oxford's library, was much dissatisfied with the large sums which the books fetched, and suspected there was a conspiracy to run up the prices. He writes in his *Diary* (February 9, 1725-26): 'Went to Mr. Bridges's chambers, but could not see the three fine MSS. again, the Doctor his brother having locked them up. He openly bid for his own books, merely to enhance their price, and the auction proves to be, what I thought it would become, very knavish'; and on the 11th of February he adds: 'Yesterday at five I met Mr. Noel and tarried long with him; we settled then the whole affair touching his bidding for my Lord [Oxford] at the roguish auction of Mr. Bridges's books. The Reverend Doctor one of the brothers hath already displayed himself so remarkably as to be both hated and despised, and a combination among the booksellers will soon be against him and his brother-in-law, a lawyer. These are men of the keenest avarice, and their very looks (according to what I am told) dart out harping-irons. I have ordered Mr. Noel to drop every article in my Lord's commissions when they shall be hoisted up to too high a price. Yet I desired that my Lord may have the Russian Bible, which I know full well to be a very rare and a very good book.'

A copy of the sale catalogue, with the prices in manuscript, is preserved in the library of the British Museum.

Bridges expended several thousand pounds in making collections for his *History of Northamptonshire*, which, after many delays, was published under the editorship of the Rev. Peter Whalley in 1791.

FOOTNOTES:

[63] Description of library in sale catalogue.

JOHN MURRAY, 1670-1748

John Murray of Sacombe in Hertfordshire, who was born on the 24th of January 1670, and died on September 13, 1748, was an indefatigable collector of books. In the *Account of London Libraries*, by Bagford and Oldys, we read that he 'made scarce publications of English authors his inquiry all his life,' and that he had been 'a collector above forty years at all sales, auctions, shops, and stalls, partly for his own curiosity, and partly to oblige such authors and gentry as have commissioned him.' He was a friend of Hearne, who frequently mentions him in his works and *Diary*. Hearne states that Murray told him he began to collect books at thirteen years of age. Dr. Rawlinson possessed a painting of him, which was engraved by Vertue. He is leaning on three books, inscribed 'T. Hearne, V. III., Sessions Papers, and Tryals of Witches,' and holding a fourth under his coat. Underneath are the following lines, signed G.N.:—

> 'Hoh Maister John Murray of Sacomb!
> The Works of old Time to collect was his pride,
>   Till Oblivion dreaded his Care:
> Regardless of Friends, intestate he dy'd,
>   So the Rooks and the Crows were his Heir.'

DR. MEAD, 1673-1754

Dr. Richard Mead, the eminent physician and collector, was born at Stepney, Middlesex, on the 11th of August 1673. His father, Matthew Mead, was a divine of some eminence among the dissenters, and during the Commonwealth was minister of Stepney, but was ejected for nonconformity in 1662. Richard Mead was first educated at home, and at a private school kept by Mr. Thomas Singleton, who was at one time second master at Eton. At the age of sixteen he entered the University of Utrecht, where he remained three years, and then proceeded to the University of Leyden for the purpose of qualifying himself for the medical profession. In 1695 he made a tour in Italy, and after taking the degree of doctor of philosophy and physic at Padua, he visited Naples and Rome. In 1696 he returned to England, and began to practise at Stepney, in the house in which he was born. In 1703 he was elected a Fellow of the Royal Society, and in the same year he was chosen Physician to St. Thomas's Hospital, and took a house in Crutched Friars, in the City of London, where he resided until 1711, when he removed to one in Austin Friars, which had formerly been inhabited by Dr. Howe. In 1707 the University of Oxford conferred on him the degree of Doctor of Medicine, and in the following year he was admitted a member of the College of Physicians, of which institution he was elected a Fellow in 1716. On the death of Dr. Radcliffe in 1714, Mead removed to the residence which had been occupied by that distinguished physician in Bloomsbury Square, and in 1720 he took a house in Great Ormond Street, which he filled with books, pictures and antiquities, and where he lived until his death on the 16th of January 1754. In 1727 he was appointed Physician-in-Ordinary to King George II., and in 1734 he was offered the post of President of the College of Physicians, but this he declined, being desirous of retirement. He was twice married. Dr. Mead was the foremost medical man of his time, and his professional income was a very large one. The greater part of his wealth he devoted to the patronage of science and literature, and to the acquisition of his valuable collections, which were always open to students who wished to consult them. He had a very large circle of attached friends, amongst whom were Newton, Halley, Pope,

Bentley, and Freind; and Dr. Johnson said of him that he 'lived more in the broad sunshine of life than almost any other man.' Pope refers to his love of books in his epistle to Richard Boyle, Earl of Burlington, *Of the Use of Riches*:—

> 'Rare monkish manuscripts for Hearne alone,
> And books for Mead and butterflies for Sloane.'

DR. MEAD.

Dr. Mead's library consisted of upwards of ten thousand printed volumes, and many rare and valuable manuscripts. The collection was especially rich in medical works, and in early editions of the classics. Among the latter were to be found the Spira Virgil of 1470 on vellum, and the 1469 and 1472 editions of the *Historia Naturalis* of Pliny; the former of which was bought at the sale of his books by the King of France for eleven guineas, and the latter by a bookseller named Willock for eighteen guineas. One of the choicest manuscripts was a missal said to have been illuminated by Raphael and his pupils for Claude, wife of Francis I., King of France. This was acquired by Horace Walpole for forty-eight pounds, six shillings. It was bought at the Strawberry Hill sale in 1842 by Earl Waldegrave for one hundred and fifteen pounds, ten shillings. The books were generally very fine copies and handsomely bound. After Mead's death they were sold by auction by Samuel Baker of Covent Garden, in two parts, and realised five thousand five hundred and eighteen pounds, ten shillings and elevenpence, including nineteen pounds, six shillings and sixpence for fifteen bookcases. The sale of the first part commenced on the 18th November 1754, and lasted twenty-eight days; that of the second part began on the 7th of April 1755, and lasted twenty-nine days. The pictures, prints and drawings, antiquities and coins and medals, were sold in the early part of 1755 for ten thousand five hundred and fifty pounds, eighteen shillings; the pictures fetching three thousand four hundred and seventeen pounds, eleven shillings—about six or seven hundred pounds more than Mead gave for them. Some portions of his collections were sold during his lifetime.

Dr. Mead was the author of several medical works, of which his *Discourse on the Plague*, published in 1720, was the best. The magnificent edition of De Thou's *Historia Sui Temporis*, in seven folio volumes, London, 1733, edited by Samuel Buckley; and the *Opus Majus* of Roger Bacon, London, 1733, edited by Dr. Samuel Jebb, were produced partly at his expense. Collected editions of his medical works were published in London in 1762, and in Edinburgh in 1765. His life has been written by Dr. Maty, the second Principal Librarian of the British Museum; and a very interesting account of his library, by Mr. Austin Dobson, will be found in the first volume of *Bibliographica*. A portrait of him by Allan Ramsay, painted in 1740, is in the National Portrait Gallery, and a bust of him by Roubillac is preserved in the College of Physicians. His gold-headed cane, given him by Dr. Radcliffe, is also kept in that institution.

CHARLES SPENCER, THIRD EARL OF SUNDERLAND, 1674-1722

EARL OF SUNDERLAND.

Charles Spencer, third Earl of Sunderland, who was born in 1674, was the second son of Robert, second Earl, by Anne, daughter of George Digby, second Earl of Bristol. He appears, even when a boy, to have displayed much ability, for as early as 1688, Evelyn, who was on very intimate terms with the Spencer family, mentions him as 'a youth of extraordinary hopes, very learned for his age, and ingenious, and under a governor of great merit.' This governor appears to have been Dr. Trimnell, afterwards Bishop of Winchester. When quite young, Lord Spencer manifested a great love for books, and already possessed a considerable collection of them, for he was but twenty years of age when Evelyn wrote to him: 'I was with great appetite coming to take a repast in the noble library which I hear you have lately purchased.' Evelyn's Diary also contains several notices of the collection, and particularly mentions the purchase of the books of Sir Charles Scarborough, an eminent physician, which were at one time destined for the Royal Library.

At the general election in 1695 Lord Spencer was returned both for Tiverton in Devonshire, and for Heydon in Yorkshire. He elected to sit for Tiverton, which he represented in Parliament until the death of his father in 1702, when he succeeded to the title, his elder brother having died in 1688. While a member of the House of Commons he appears to have held opinions of a somewhat republican nature; and Swift tells us, 'he would often, among his familiar friends, refuse the title of Lord (as he had done to myself), swear he would never be called otherwise than Charles Spencer, and hoped to see the day when there should not be a peer in England.' These views, however, were very considerably modified on his succession to the title. In 1705 he was appointed envoy extraordinary and plenipotentiary to the Court of Vienna, to congratulate the Emperor Joseph on his accession to the crown. Shortly after his return to England, Sunderland, notwithstanding the opposition of Queen Anne, who always entertained a great antipathy for him, was made one of the Secretaries of State, an office which he held until June 1710, when he was dismissed by the Queen, who wished, however, to bestow on him a pension of three thousand pounds a year. This he refused, with the remark, 'I am glad your Majesty is satisfied I have done my duty. But if I cannot have the honour to serve my country, I will not plunder it.' He remained out of office during the remainder of Anne's reign, but on the accession of George I. to the throne he was made Lord-Lieutenant of Ireland. This post, however, was by no means agreeable to him, for he regarded it as a kind of banishment, and during the short time he held it he never crossed the Channel. In 1715 he was appointed Lord Privy Seal, Vice-Treasurer of Ireland in 1716, and in April 1717 he was a second time made a Secretary of

State, his friend Addison receiving a like appointment. On the 16th of March 1718 he became Lord-President of the Council, and on the 21st of the same month First Lord Commissioner of the Treasury, which office he resigned on the 3rd of April 1721. He died, after a short illness, on the 19th of April 1722.

Lord Sunderland was thrice married, and had children by all his wives. By his second wife, Anne, daughter of the great Duke of Marlborough, he had four sons and a daughter. The eldest son died in infancy; Robert, the second, succeeded to the earldom, and died unmarried on the 15th of September 1729; Charles, the third, became Earl of Sunderland on the death of his elder brother, and in 1733 second Duke of Marlborough, but he did not obtain the Marlborough estates until the demise of the Dowager Duchess in 1744; John, the youngest son, who, by a family arrangement, then succeeded to the Spencer estates, was the father of the first Earl Spencer.

Lord Sunderland was a most liberal patron of literature, and the splendid library which he commenced in his early youth, and sedulously augmented till the time of his death, bore witness for several generations to his love of books. This noble collection was kept in his town house, which stood between Sackville Street and Burlington House, where it occupied five large rooms, and at the time of the Earl's death in 1722 consisted of about twenty thousand printed volumes, together with some choice manuscripts, and was valued at upwards of thirty thousand pounds; the King of Denmark being anxious to purchase it of his heirs for that sum. Charles, the fifth Earl, also took great interest in the library, and added a considerable number of books to it, among which was a copy on vellum of the Livy of 1470, printed at Venice by Vendelin de Spira. Only one other perfect copy on vellum of this edition is known to exist. In 1749 the library was removed to Blenheim, where it remained until 1881. It was sold by Puttick and Simpson in five portions in 1881, 1882 and 1883, and the entire sale, which consisted of thirteen thousand eight hundred and fifty-eight lots, realised fifty-six thousand five hundred and eighty-one pounds, six shillings.

Lord Sunderland was always very liberal in his dealings with booksellers, and the prices which he gave for his books frequently gave umbrage to other collectors. Humphrey Wanley, Lord Oxford's librarian, when giving in his Diary an account of a book-sale which took place in 1721, mentions that: 'Some books went for unaccountably high prices, which were bought by Mr. Vaillant, the bookseller, who had an unlimited commission from the Earl of Sunderland. The booksellers upon this sale intend to raise the prices of philological books of the first editions, and indeed of all old editions, accordingly. Thus Mr. Noel told me that he has actually agreed to sell the Earl of Sunderland six ... printed books, now coming up the river, for fifty pounds per book, although my Lord gives no such prices.' And on the demise of the Earl, Wanley wrote: 'This day died the Earl of Sunderland, which I the rather note here, because I believe by reason of his decease some benefit may accrue to this Library, even in case his relatives will part with none of his books. I mean, by his raising the price of books no higher now; so that, in probability, this commodity may fall in the market, and any gentleman be permitted to buy an uncommon old book for less than forty or fifty pounds.'

BRIAN FAIRFAX, 1676-1749

Brian Fairfax, who was the eldest son of Brian Fairfax, author of the *Life of the Duke of Buckingham* and other works, was born on the 11th of April 1676. He received his early education at Westminster School, where he entered as a Queen's Scholar, and from whence he went to Trinity College, Cambridge, taking the degrees of B.A. in 1697 and M.A. in 1700. He became a Fellow of his College in 1698. In 1723 he was appointed a Commissioner of the Customs, a post he held until his death on the 9th of January 1749.

Fairfax collected in his house in Panton Square a very valuable library, which, together with a considerable fortune, a gallery of pictures, a fine collection of Greek, Roman, and English coins and medals, and other curiosities, he bequeathed to his relative, the Hon. Robert Fairfax, of Leeds Castle, Kent, afterwards seventh Lord Fairfax. Robert Fairfax intended to sell the library by auction on the 26th of April 1756, and the seventeen following days; but after having advertised it, he privately disposed of it for two thousand pounds to his kinsman, Mr. Francis Child,[64] of Osterley Park, Isleworth, Middlesex, and the printed catalogues, with the exception of twenty, were suppressed.[65] The title to the catalogue of the intended sale reads: 'A Catalogue of the Entire and Valuable Library of the Honourable Bryan Fairfax, Esq., one of the Commissioners of His Majesty's Customs, Deceased: which will be sold by Auction, by Mr. Prestage, at his great room the end of Savile Row, next Conduit Street, Hanover Square. To begin selling on Monday, April 26, 1756, and to continue for seventeen days successively. Catalogues to be had at the Place of Sale, and at Mr. Barthoe's, Bookseller in Exeter Exchange in the Strand. Price Six-pence, pp. 68. 8°.' In a copy of the catalogue mentioned by Dibdin in his *Bibliographical Decameron*, the price at which each article was valued is given for the express purpose of the purchase of the whole by Mr. Child. Among the prices thus noted are those of the nine Caxtons which the library contained, which altogether amounted to thirty-three pounds, four shillings. *The Recuyell of the Histories of Troye* was valued at eight guineas, the *Confessio Amantis* at three pounds, and the *Histories of*

King Arthur at two pounds, twelve shillings and sixpence. The prices obtained for these books at the sale of the Osterley library in 1885 were eighteen hundred and twenty pounds, eight hundred and ten pounds, and nineteen hundred and fifty pounds, respectively. The collection became part of the Osterley library, of which a catalogue was made in 1771 by Dr. Thomas Morell, assisted by the preceding labours of the Rev. Dr. Winchester. Only twenty-five copies of this catalogue were printed.

Brian Fairfax's pictures, statues, urns, and other antiquities were sold by auction on April the 6th and 7th, and the prints and drawings on May the 4th and 5th, 1756.

In 1819 the library passed by marriage into the family of the Earls of Jersey, and on the 6th of May 1885 and seven following days it was sold by Sotheby, Wilkinson and Hodge. The sale consisted of one thousand nine hundred and thirty-seven lots, which realised the large sum of thirteen thousand and seven pounds, nine shillings.

FOOTNOTES:

[64] The first wife of the Hon. Robert Fairfax was Martha Collins, niece to Sir Francis Child, Bart.

[65] Nichols, *Literary Anecdotes of the Eighteenth Century*, vol. v. p. 326.

THOMAS HEARNE, 1678-1735

Thomas Hearne, the eminent antiquary, was born in July 1678 at Littlefield Green in the parish of White Waltham, Berkshire, where his father, George Hearne, was the parish clerk. At a very early age he showed such marked ability that Francis Cherry, the nonjuror, who resided at Shottesbrooke in the same neighbourhood, undertook to defray the cost of his education, and first sent him to the free school of Bray, and afterwards, in 1695, to St. Edmund Hall, Oxford. This kindness is frequently referred to by Hearne, who speaks of his benefactor as 'my best friend and patron.' He took the degrees of B.A. in 1679, and M.A. four years later. While an undergraduate, Dr. John Mill, the Principal of St. Edmund Hall, and Dr. Grabe employed him in the collation of manuscripts; and Hearne tells us in his *Autobiography* that, after taking his B.A. degree, 'he constantly went to the Bodleian Library every day, and studied there as long as the time allowed by the Statutes would admit.' His industry and learning attracted the notice of Dr. Hudson, who had been recently elected Keeper of the Bodleian Library, and, in 1701, by his influence Hearne was made Janitor, or Assistant, in the Library, succeeding to the post of Second Librarian in 1712. The duties of this appointment he continued to perform until the 23rd of January 1716, the last day fixed by the Act for taking the oaths to the Hanoverian dynasty. These oaths as a nonjuror he could not conscientiously take, and he was in consequence deprived of his office on the ground of 'neglect of duty'; but the Rev. W.D. Macray, in his *Annals of the Bodleian Library*, tells us that 'to the end of his life he maintained that he was still, *de jure*, Sub-librarian, and with a quaint pertinacity, regularly at the end of each term and half-year, up to March 30, 1735, continued to set down, in one of the volumes of his Diary, that no fees had been paid him, and that his half-year's salary was due.' Hearne continued a staunch nonjuror to the end of his days, and refused many University appointments, including the Keepership of the Bodleian Library, which he might have had, had he been willing to take the oath of allegiance to the government; but he preferred, to use his own words, 'a good conscience before all manner of preferment and worldly honour.' The Earl of Oxford offered to make him his librarian on Wanley's death, but this post he also declined, and continued to reside to the end of his life at St. Edmund Hall, engaged in preparing and publishing his various antiquarian and historical works. He died on the 10th of June 1735, and was buried in the churchyard of St. Peter's-in-the-East at Oxford. Hearne, who was a man of unwearied industry, and a most devoted antiquary, is described by Pope in the *Dunciad*, under the title of Wormius—

> 'But who is he, in closet close ypent,
> Of sober face, with learned dust besprent?
> Right well mine eyes arede the myster wight,
> On parchment scraps y-fed, and Wormius hight.'

Hearne amassed a considerable collection of manuscripts and printed books, of which he made a catalogue, with the prices he gave for them. This manuscript came into the possession of Mr. Beriah Botfield, M.P., of Norton Hall, Northamptonshire, who privately printed some extracts from it in 1848.

Hearne left all his manuscripts and books with manuscript notes to Mr. William Bedford, son of the nonjuring bishop, Hilkiah Bedford, whose widow sold them to Dr. Richard Rawlinson for one hundred guineas, and by him they were bequeathed to the Bodleian Library. Hearne's diary and note-books, in about one hundred and fifty small duodecimo volumes, were among them.[66] His printed books were sold by Thomas Osborne on the 16th of February 1736, and following days. The title-page of the catalogue reads: 'A Catalogue of the Valuable Library of that great Antiquarian Mr. Th°. Hearne of Oxford: and of another Gentleman of Note. Consisting of a very great Variety of Uncommon Books, and scarce ever to be met withal.

Which will begin to be sold very cheap, the lowest Price mark'd in each Book, at T. Osborne's Shop in Gray's Inn, on Monday the 16th day of February 1735-36.'

THOMAS HEARNE M.A. OF EDMUND HALL OXON.

The title-page has also a small portrait of Hearne, with the following lines below it: —

'Pox on't quoth time to Thomas Hearne,
Whatever I forget, you learn.'

The catalogue contains six thousand seven hundred and seventy-six lots.

Hearne's publications, which were almost all printed by subscription at Oxford, are very numerous. Among the most valuable are an edition of Livy in 6 vols., 1708; the *Life of Alfred the Great*, from Sir John Spelman's manuscript in the Bodleian Library, 1710; Leland's *Itinerary*, 9 vols., 1710; Leland's *Collectanea*, 6 vols., 1715; Roper's *Life of Sir Thomas More*, 1716; Camden's *Annals*, 3 vols., 1717; *Curious Discourses by Eminent Antiquaries*, 1720; Robert of Gloucester's *Chronicle*, 2 vols., 1724; Peter of Langtoft's *Chronicle*, 2 vols., 1725; *Liber Niger Scaccarii*, 2 vols., 1728; and Walter of Hemingford's *History*, 2 vols., 1731.

FOOTNOTES:

[66] Extracts from these volumes were published by Dr. Bliss in 1857, and again in 1869, under the title of *Reliquiæ Hearnianæ*; and Hearne's *Remarks and Collections* are now being printed by the Oxford Historical Society.

THOMAS RAWLINSON, 1681-1725

Thomas Rawlinson, who, Dibdin says, 'may be called the Leviathan of book-collectors during nearly the first thirty years of the eighteenth century,' was born in the Old Bailey on the 25th of March 1681. He was the eldest son of Sir Thomas Rawlinson, Lord Mayor of London in 1705-6, by Mary, eldest daughter of Richard Tayler, of Turnham Green, Middlesex, who kept the Devil Tavern near Temple Bar. He was also an elder brother of Dr. Richard Rawlinson, the nonjuring bishop, who was himself an ardent collector. In 1699 he matriculated at the University of Oxford from St. John's College, having been previously educated at Cheam under William Day, and at Eton. He was called to the bar in 1705, and applied himself to the study of municipal law; but three years later, on the death of his father in 1708, who left him a large estate, he devoted himself to the collection of books, manuscripts and pictures. His love for books appears to have been early fostered by his grandfather, Richard Tayler, who settled upon him, while a schoolboy at Eton, an annuity of fourteen pounds per annum for his life to buy books with; 'which,' Hearne informs us in his Diary, 'he not only fully expended, and nobly answered the end of the donor, but indeed laid out his whole fortune this way, so as to acquire a collection of books, both for number and value, hardly to be equalled by any one study in England.' For some years Rawlinson resided in Gray's Inn, but in 1716, having filled his four rooms so completely with books that he was obliged to sleep in the passage, he was compelled to move, and he took lodgings at London House, in Aldersgate Street, an ancient palace of the bishops of London, but at that time the residence of Mr. Samuel May, a wealthy druggist. Here he lived, says Oldys, 'in his bundles, piles, and bulwarks of paper, in dust and cobwebs,' until the 6th of August 1725, when he died, and was buried in St. Botolph's Church, Aldersgate Street.

Rawlinson was a Fellow of the Royal Society, and of the Society of Antiquaries. He was also a Governor of Bridewell and Bethlehem Hospitals. About a year before his decease he married his servant, Amy Frewin, but left no issue.

Towards the end of his life Rawlinson became involved in pecuniary difficulties, and he sold a portion of his collection by auction to meet his liabilities. Prior to his death there were five sales, the first of which took place on the 4th of December 1721, which realised two thousand four hundred and nine pounds. But when he died an enormous number of books were still left, and it required eleven additional sales, which extended to March 1734, to dispose of them and the manuscripts, of which there were upwards of a thousand. These sales lasted on an average for more than twenty-one days each, but it should be observed that they took place in the evening, generally commencing at five o'clock. All Rawlinson's books were sold by Thomas Ballard, the bookseller, at the St. Paul's Coffee House, with the exception of those disposed of at the seventh and eighth sales, which were sold by Charles Davis, the bookseller; the former at London House, and the latter at the Bedford Coffee House, in the great Piazza, Covent Garden. In addition to the printed books and manuscripts, Rawlinson's gallery of paintings was sold at the Two Golden Bulls in Hart Street, Covent Garden, on April the 4th and 5th 1734, in one hundred and seventeen lots. Among the portraits was one in crayons of Rawlinson by his brother Richard.

Copies of the sale catalogues of Thomas Rawlinson's books are very rare, but the Bodleian Library possesses an entire set of them, almost all of which are marked with the prices which the books fetched, while two or three have also the names of the purchasers. A fairly correct list of them is given by Dibdin in his *Bibliomania*, which he made from a complete collection of them in the Heber library. The catalogue of the manuscripts was compiled by Rawlinson's brother Richard.

Rawlinson's books appear to have realised but poor prices, for Hearne writes in his Diary (Nov. 10th, 1734), that 'Dr. Rawlinson by the sale of his brother's books hath not rais'd near the money expected. For, it seems, they have ill answer'd, however good books; the MSS. worse, and what the prints will do is as yet undetermin'd.' No doubt the low prices were caused by the immense number of books thrown upon the market by Rawlinson's sales; for, as early as April 1723, Hearne tells us in his Diary that 'the editions of classicks of the first print (commonly called *Editiones Principes*), that used to go at prodigious prices, are now strangely lowered; occasioned, in good measure, by Mr. Tho. Rawlinson, my friend's, being forced to sell many of his books, in whose auction these books went cheap, tho' English history and antiquities went dear: and yet this gentleman was the chief man that raised many curious and classical books so high, by his generous and couragious way of bidding.' It is quite possible too that Rawlinson's books were not always in the finest condition, and had suffered from the dust and cobwebs of which Oldys speaks.

The Caxtons, of which there were upwards of five and twenty (perfect and imperfect), realised but very moderate prices. *The Recuyell of the Histories of Troy* sold for two pounds, seven shillings; Gower's *Confessio Amantis* for two pounds, fourteen shillings and sixpence; *The Golden Legend* for three pounds, twelve shillings; and Lydgate's *Life of Our Lady* for two pounds, thirteen shillings. *The Histories of King Arthur and his Knights*, for which Mr. Quaritch, at the Earl of Jersey's sale in 1885, gave as much as nineteen hundred and fifty pounds, fetched no more than two pounds, four shillings and sixpence. These were the highest prices obtained. Many of the volumes went for a few shillings — the first edition of *The Dictes or Sayings* for fifteen shillings, Chaucer's *Book of Fame* for nine shillings and twopence, and *The Moral Proverbs of Christine de Pisan* for four shillings and tenpence. Mr. Blades does not make any mention of Thomas Rawlinson's Caxtons in his life of the printer.

Rawlinson appears to have greatly increased the number of separate works in his library by breaking up the volumes of tracts; for Oldys complains, 'that out of one volume he made many, and all the tracts or pamphlets that came to his hands in volumes and bound together, he separated to sell them singly, so that what some curious men had been pairing and sorting half their lives to have a topic or argument complete, he by this means confused and dispersed again.'

Dr. Richard Rawlinson said of his brother that he collected in almost all faculties, but more particularly old and beautiful editions of the classical authors, and whatever directly or indirectly related to

English history. As early as 1712 Rawlinson told Hearne that his library had cost him two thousand pounds, and that it was worth five thousand. Among many other choice and rare books in the collection were three copies of Archbishop Parker's *De Antiquitate Britannicæ Ecclesiæ*. Two of them are now in the Bodleian Library, and the Rev. W.D. Macray, in his *Annals of the Bodleian Library*, states that 'one of these is the identical copy described by Strype in his Life of Parker, and which was then in possession of Bp. Fleetwood of Ely.'

Rawlinson's passion for collecting books was evidently well known to his contemporaries, for Addison, who disliked and despised bibliomaniacs, gives a satirical account of him, under the name of 'Tom Folio,' in No. 158 of *The Tatler*. Hearne, who was greatly indebted to Rawlinson for assistance in his antiquarian labours, warmly defends his friend:—'Some gave out,' he writes, 'and published it too in printed papers, that Mr. Rawlinson understood the editions and title-pages of books only, without any other skill in them, and thereupon they styled him TOM FOLIO. But these were only buffoons, and persons of very shallow learning. 'Tis certain that Mr. Rawlinson understood the titles and editions of books better than any man I ever knew (for he had a very great memory), but besides this, he was a great reader, and had read abundantly of the best writers, ancient and modern, throughout, and was entirely master of the learning contained in them. He had digested the classicks so well as to be able readily and upon all occasions (what I have very often admired) to make use of passages from them very pertinently, what I never knew in so great perfection in any other person whatsoever.'[67]

A poem of twenty-six lines by Rawlinson on the death of the Duke of Gloucester in 1700 was printed in a collection of verses written by members of the University of Oxford on that event. This appears to be his only publication with his name attached. The pretty edition of the *Satires of Juvenal and Persius*, published at London in 1716, and edited by Michael Maittaire, was dedicated by him to Rawlinson.

It is stated in Nichols's *Literary Anecdotes of the Eighteenth Century* (vol. v. p. 704) that the following inscription was found among the papers of Rawlinson, written with his own hand, and in all probability designed by him for part of an epitaph on himself:—

> 'Hic jacet——Vir liberrimi Spiritûs
> qui omnes Mortales pari ratione habuit;
> tacuisse de Criminibus non auro vendidit.
> Qui, Rege dempto, neminem agnovit superiorem;
> illum vero, O infortunium! nunquam potuit
> inspicere.'

FOOTNOTES:

[67] *Diary*, Sept. 4, 1725.

JOSEPH SMITH, 1682-1770

Joseph Smith, a portion of whose collection formed the foundation of King George III.'s library, now in the British Museum, was born in 1682. Nothing appears to be known about his parents and his early years, but at the age of nineteen he took up his residence at Venice, where he spent his life, apparently engaged in commerce.[68] In 1740 he was appointed British Consul in that city, and he died there on the 6th of November 1770, aged eighty-eight.

BOOK-PLATE OF JOSEPH SMITH.

Smith was well known as a collector of books, manuscripts, and works of art. In 1762 George III. purchased all the books Smith had amassed up to that time for about ten thousand pounds, and at a later period the king also bought his pictures, coins, and gems for the sum of twenty thousand pounds. After the sale of his library Smith still continued to collect, and the books which he subsequently acquired were sold after his death, partly by auction by Baker and Leigh at their house in York Street, Covent Garden, on Monday, January 25th, 1773, and the thirteen following days, and partly in the shop of James Robson, bookseller, in New Bond Street. Those sold by Baker and Leigh realised two thousand two hundred and forty-five pounds. A portion of his manuscripts was purchased by the Earl of Sunderland for one thousand five hundred pounds. Smith's library was rich in the best and scarcest editions of Latin, Italian and French authors. It also contained a considerable number of fine manuscripts, some of them beautifully illuminated, and many valuable books of prints and antiquities.

About 1727 Smith compiled a catalogue, which was limited to twenty-five copies, of some of the rarest books in his collection, of which a second edition with additions was published in 1737. A catalogue of his entire library was printed at Venice in 1755, and in 1767 an account of his antique gems in two volumes folio, written by Antonio Francesco Gori, was published in the same city under the title of *Dactyliotheca Smithiana*. An edition of Boccaccio's *Decamerone* was brought out by Smith in 1729.

FOOTNOTES:

[68] *Dictionary of National Biography.*

DR. RICHARD RAWLINSON, 1690-1755

Richard Rawlinson was the fourth son of Sir Thomas Rawlinson, Lord Mayor of London in 1705-6, and younger brother of Thomas Rawlinson the collector. He was born in the Old Bailey on the 3rd of January 1690, and, after having received his early education at St. Paul's School and Eton, matriculated as a commoner of St. John's College, Oxford, in 1708; but, in consequence of the death of his father, he became a gentleman-commoner in the following year. He took the degrees of B.A. in 1711, M.A. in 1713, and in 1719 he was created D.C.L. On the 21st of September 1716 he was ordained deacon, and two days later, priest among the nonjurors by Bishop Jeremy Collier, in Mr. Laurence's chapel on College Hill, London.[69] After his ordination he travelled through a great part of England, and in 1719 paid a visit to France, and afterwards to the Low Countries, where he was admitted into the Universities of Utrecht and Leyden. Towards the end of the year he returned home, but in 1720 he again left England, and spent several years in France, Germany, Italy, and other parts of the Continent. In April 1726 he again came home, in consequence of the death of his brother, which took place in the preceding year. During his travels he kept a series of note-books, some of which are preserved among his miscellaneous manuscripts in the Bodleian Library. In 1728 he was consecrated bishop by the nonjuring bishops Gandy, Doughty and Blackbourne in Gandy's chapel, but he appears to have been always desirous of concealing both his clerical and episcopal character, for in a letter written in 1736 to Mr. T. Rawlins of Pophills, Warwickshire, he requests him not to address him as 'Rev.'[70] Dr. Rawlinson was elected a Fellow of the Royal Society in 1714, and a Fellow of the Society of Antiquaries in 1727, but later he quarrelled with both these Societies, and stipulated in his will that the recipients of his bequests should not be Fellows. He was also a Governor of Bridewell, Bethlehem, and St. Bartholomew's Hospitals.

Dr. Rawlinson lived for some time in Gray's Inn, but shortly after the death of his brother Thomas he took up his abode in the rooms which had been occupied by him in London House in Aldersgate

Street. He died at Islington on the 6th of April 1755, and was buried, in accordance with a direction in a codicil to his will, in St. Giles's Church, Oxford. His heart, which he bequeathed as a token of affection to St. John's College, Oxford, is preserved in a marble urn in the chapel of that College, inscribed with the text 'Ubi thesaurus, ibi cor,' and with his name and the date of his death. It is said that Rawlinson also left instructions that a head, which he believed to be that of Counsellor Christopher Layer, the Jacobite conspirator, who was executed in 1723, should be buried with him, placed in his right hand; but this injunction, if really made, does not appear to have been complied with.[71]

Rawlinson devoted himself to antiquarian pursuits, and, like his brother Thomas, was an enthusiastic collector of manuscripts and books. The Rev. W.D. Macray, in his *Annals of the Bodleian Library*, says that his collections were 'formed abroad and at home, the choice of book-auctions, the pickings of chandlers' and grocers' waste-paper, everything, especially, in the shape of a MS., from early copies of Classics and Fathers to the well-nigh most recent log-books of sailors' voyages. Not a sale of MSS. occurred, apparently, in London, during his time, at which he was not an omnigenous purchaser; so that students of every subject now bury themselves in his stores with great content and profit. But history in all its branches, heraldry and genealogy, biography and topography, are his especially strong points.'

Rawlinson bequeathed all his manuscripts, with the exception of private papers and letters, 'to the chancellor, masters and scholars of the University of Oxford, to be placed in the Bodleian Library, or in such other place as they should deem proper'; and he further directed that they should be 'kept separate and apart from any other collection.' All his deeds and charters, his books printed on vellum or silk, and those containing MS. notes, together with some antiquities and curiosities, were also left by him to the University. His manuscript and printed music he bequeathed to the Music School. The number of manuscripts left by him exceeded four thousand eight hundred in number, together with a large collection of charters and deeds. A catalogue of them has been made by the

Rev. W.D. Macray, the author of the *Annals of the Bodleian Library*. The printed books which he selected from his library for the University amounted to between eighteen and nineteen hundred.[72] Other books and manuscripts, together with some valuable pictures and coins, were given by him to the Bodleian Library during his lifetime. The remainder of his printed books, with the exception of a few which he bequeathed to St. John's College, were sold by auction by Samuel Baker, of York Street, Covent Garden, at two sales. The first commenced on the 29th of March 1756, and lasted fifty days. It consisted of nine thousand four hundred and five lots, which fetched one thousand one hundred and sixty-one pounds, eighteen shillings and sixpence. The second sale, which, as the preface to the catalogue informs us, consisted of 'upwards of Twenty Thousand Pamphlets ... and his most Uncommon, Rare and Old Books,' began on Thursday, March 3rd, 1757, and was continued on the nine following evenings. It realised but two hundred and three pounds, thirteen shillings and sixpence. These were followed by a sale of prints, books of prints and drawings, upwards of ten thousand in number. One hundred and sixty-three pounds, ten shillings and threepence, however, was all that could be obtained for them. Marked catalogues of the three sales are preserved in the Library of King George III. in the British Museum. The prices at all the sales were very low. There were three Caxtons in the first sale — *Tully of Old Age, Curia Sapientiæ*, and the *Order of Chivalry*, which fetched respectively one pound five shillings, six shillings, and eleven shillings. The prints and drawings fared even worse than the printed books. One hundred and three prints by Albert Dürer, in two lots, sold for one pound, ten shillings and sixpence, and a large collection of woodcuts by the same artist for half a crown. Twenty-four etchings by Rembrandt, in four lots, realised but three pounds, five shillings; while eleven shillings and sixpence was all that could be got for thirty-four heads and thirty-five views by Hollar.

DR. RICHARD RAWLINSON.

The collection of manuscripts which Dr. Rawlinson bequeathed to the University of Oxford is a magnificent one, and Mr. Macray gives a long and very interesting account of it in his *Annals of the Bodleian Library*. It contains some fine Biblical manuscripts, and about one hundred and thirty Missals, Horæ, and other Service-books, many of them from the library of the celebrated collector Nicolas Joseph Foucault. It is rich in early copies of the classics, and there are upwards of two hundred volumes of poetry, including the works of Chaucer, Hoccleve, Lydgate, etc. English history is remarkably well represented. Among the manuscripts of this division of the collection are the *Thurloe State Papers* in sixty-seven volumes, which were published by Dr. Birch in 1742, and the *Miscellaneous Papers* of Samuel Pepys in twenty-five volumes. The Pepys papers, among other very interesting matter, comprise many curious dockyard account-books of the reigns of King Henry VIII. and Queen Elizabeth. This division also contains some important letters of King Charles II., King James II., and the Duke of Monmouth, together with an acknowledgment by Monmouth that Charles II. had declared that he was never married to Lucy Walters, the Duke's mother. This was written and signed by him on the day of his execution, and witnessed by Bishops Turner and Ken, and also by Tenison and Hooper. As might be expected, the number of works relating to topography, heraldry and genealogy is very large. The collection also comprises many Irish manuscripts, a considerable number of Italian papers bearing on English history, and the valuable collections made by Rawlinson for a continuation of Wood's *Athenæ Oxonienses*, and for a History of Eton College. There are one hundred volumes of letters, two hundred volumes of sermons, and the immense quantity of ancient charters and deeds already mentioned.

Rawlinson also bequeathed to the University Hearne's daily diary and note-books in about one hundred and fifty small duodecimo volumes, which he had bought of the widow of Mr. William Bedford.

Among the printed books is a magnificent collection of the original broadside proclamations issued during the reign of Elizabeth, and a set of almanacs extending from 1607 to 1747, bound in one hundred and seventy-five volumes.[73]

To St. John's College, Rawlinson bequeathed a large portion of his estate, amounting to about seven hundred pounds a year, a few of his printed books, a collection of coins, etc.; and to the College of

Surgeons he gave some anatomical specimens. He also left property to endow a professorship of Anglo-Saxon at Oxford, and to provide a salary for the Keeper of the Ashmolean Museum. But all his endowments were accompanied by eccentric restrictions, which remained in force until a few years ago, when they were annulled by statute. He directed 'that no native of Scotland or Ireland, or of any of the plantations abroad, or any of their sons, or any present or future member of the Royal or Antiquary societies,' should hold these endowments; and in the case of the Ashmolean Museum, he further enjoined that the Keeper 'is not to be a doctor in divinity or in holy orders ... neither born nor educated in Scotland, neither a married man nor a widower, but one who hath regularly proceeded in Oxford to the degrees of master of arts or bachelor of law.'

Rawlinson wrote a considerable number of works, chiefly of an antiquarian or topographical nature. Among the more important are *The English Topographer, The History and Antiquities of the City and Cathedral Church of Hereford, The History and Antiquities of the Cathedral Church of Rochester, The History and Antiquities of Glastonbury*; and a *Life of Anthony à Wood*. He also edited Aubrey's *Natural History and Antiquities of Surrey*, and other books.

Although Dr. Rawlinson, like his father and his brother, was a warm Jacobite, he does not appear to have taken part in any of the movements for the restoration of the Stuart family to the throne. He entirely occupied himself with antiquarian and literary pursuits, and the formation of his noble collections. In order that he might devote as much as possible of his income to the purchase of books and antiquities, he denied himself the luxuries, and even the comforts of life; and he went about so meanly clad, that the coachman of his late father happening to meet him one day, and judging from his appearance that he was in a destitute condition, begged his acceptance of half a crown to relieve his distress. The story is told by Dr. Rawlinson himself.

FOOTNOTES:

[69] Rev. W.D. Macray, *Annals of the Bodleian Library*. London, etc., 1868, p. 168.

[70] *Ibid.* p. 168.

[71] When the head of Layer was blown off from Temple Bar (where it had been placed after his execution), it was picked up by a gentleman in that neighbourhood, who showed it to some friends at a public-house; under the floor of which house, I have been assured, it was buried. Dr. Rawlinson, mean-time, having made enquiry after the head, with a wish to purchase it, was imposed on with another instead of Layer's, which he preserved as a valuable relique, and directed it to be buried in his hand.—Nichols, *Literary Anecdotes of the Eighteenth Century*, vol. v. p. 497.

[72] Macray, *Annals of the Bodleian Library*, p. 170.

[73] Rawlinson also left to the University some autograph writings of King James I. The existence of these had been forgotten, and has only been recently discovered.

MARTIN FOLKES, 1690-1754

Martin Folkes, the eminent antiquary and scientist, was the eldest son of Martin Folkes, a Bencher of Gray's Inn. He was born in Lincoln's Inn Fields, London, on the 29th of October 1690, and after receiving his early education at the University of Saumur, was sent, in 1707, to Clare Hall, Cambridge, where he so greatly distinguished himself in all branches of learning, and more particularly in mathematics and philosophy, that in 1714, when only twenty-three years of age, he was elected a Fellow of the Royal Society, and two years later was chosen one of its Council. In 1723 he was appointed a Vice-President of the Society, and on the retirement of Sir Hans Sloane in 1741 he became President, a post he held until 1753, when he resigned it on account of his health. Folkes was also elected a Fellow of the Society of Antiquaries in 1720, and in 1750 he succeeded the Duke of Somerset as President, an office he filled during the remainder of his life. His attainments were also recognised by the French Academy, which elected him in 1742 one of its members. He was a D.C.L. of the University of Oxford, and LL.D. of the University of Cambridge. He died on the 28th of June 1754, and was buried in the chancel of Hillington Church, Norfolk. In 1792 a monument was erected to his memory in Westminster Abbey.

Folkes, who was the author of two works on English coins, and several papers in the *Philosophical Transactions* of the Royal Society and the *Archæologia* of the Society of Antiquaries, formed a fine collection of books, prints, drawings, pictures, gems, coins, etc., a considerable portion of which he acquired during his travels in Italy and Germany. His library, which was very rich in works on natural history, coins, medals, inscriptions, and the fine arts, was sold by Samuel Baker, York Street, Covent Garden, on Monday, February the 2nd 1756, and forty following days. The sale consisted of five thousand one hundred and twenty-six lots, which produced three thousand and ninety-one pounds, six shillings. A catalogue, marked with the prices, is preserved in the Library of King George III. in the British Museum. A copy of the first Shakespeare folio fetched but three guineas. The sale of Folkes's prints and drawings occupied eight days, and that of his pictures, gems, coins, and mathematical instruments five days. Dibdin says that 'the MSS. of his own composition, not being quite perfect, were, to the great loss of the learned world, ordered by him to be destroyed.'

WILLIAM OLDYS, 1696-1761

William Oldys, Norroy King-at-Arms, was born on the 14th of July 1696. There is some obscurity respecting his parentage, but there is little doubt he was the natural son of Dr. William Oldys, Chancellor of Lincoln, and Advocate of the Admiralty Court. His father left him some property, which he appears to have lost in the South Sea Bubble. From the year 1724 to 1730 Oldys resided in Yorkshire, but in the latter year he returned to London, and became acquainted with Edward Harley, the second Earl of Oxford, to whom he sold his collection of manuscripts for forty pounds. In 1738 the Earl appointed him his literary secretary and librarian, first at a salary of one hundred and fifty pounds, and afterwards of two hundred pounds, a year. Unfortunately the Earl died in 1741, and Oldys was obliged to earn a precarious livelihood by working for booksellers, and was soon involved in pecuniary difficulties. He was confined in the Fleet prison from 1751 to 1753, when he was released by the kindness of the Duke of Norfolk, who not only paid his debts, but in 1755 procured for him the office of Norroy King-at-Arms, which congenial post he held for six years. He died at his rooms in Heralds' College on the 15th of April 1761, and was buried in the church of St. Benet, Paul's Wharf. A portrait of him will be found in the *European Magazine* for November 1796. The principal works by Oldys are a *Life of Sir Walter Raleigh*, prefixed to an edition of his *History of the World*, printed in 1736; *The British Librarian*, published anonymously in 1738; and *The Harleian Miscellany*, published in 1744-46. He also annotated *England's Parnassus*, and two copies of Langbaine's *Account of the early Dramatick Poets*. One of these copies was purchased by Dr. Birch at the sale of Oldys's books for one guinea, and was bequeathed by him to the British Museum. Twenty-two of the lives in *Biographia Britannica* were from his pen, and in addition to the works already mentioned he wrote a few minor ones on bibliographical and medical subjects. Oldys's library was not a large one, but it contained some very interesting and scarce books. After his death it was purchased by Thomas Davies, the bookseller, author of *Memoirs of the Life of Garrick*, and was sold by him in 1762. The title of the sale catalogue reads: 'A Catalogue of the Libraries of the late William

Oldys, Esq., Norroy King-at-Arms (author of *The Life of Sir Walter Raleigh*); the Rev. Mr. Emms of Yarmouth, and Mr. Wm. Rush, which will begin to be sold on Monday, April 12 [1762] by Thomas Davies.' The books were disposed of for extremely low prices.

JOHN RATCLIFFE, -1776

Nothing appears to be known of the parentage and birth of John Ratcliffe, the collector, who for some years kept a chandler's shop in Southwark, where he seems to have amassed a sufficient competency to enable him to retire from business and devote the remainder of his life to the acquisition of old books. It is said that his passion for collecting them arose from the perusal of some of the volumes which were purchased by him for the purpose of wrapping his wares in. Ratcliffe kept his library at his house in East Lane, Bermondsey, where, Nichols informs us in his *Literary Anecdotes*, 'he used to give Coffee and Chocolate every Thursday morning to Book and Print Collectors; Dr. Askew, Messrs. Beauclerk, Bull, Croft, Samuel Gillam, West, etc., used to attend, when he would produce some of his fine purchases.' Nichols adds, 'he generally used to spend whole days in the Booksellers' warehouses; and, that he might not lose time, would get them to procure him a chop or a steak.' An amusing letter respecting him appeared in the *Gentleman's Magazine* for 1812. The writer states that 'Mr. John Radcliffe was neither a man of science or learning. He lived in East Lane, Bermondsey; was a very corpulent man, and his legs were remarkably thick, probably from an anasarcous complaint. The writer of this remembers him perfectly well; he was a very stately man, and, when he walked, literally went at a snail's pace. He was a Dissenter, and every Sunday attended the meeting of Dr. Flaxman in the lower road to Deptford. He generally wore a fine coat, either red or brown, with gold lace buttons, and a fine silk embroidered waistcoat, of scarlet with gold lace, and a large and well-powdered wig. With his hat in one hand, and a gold-headed cane in the other, he marched royally along, and not unfrequently followed by a parcel of children, wondering who the stately man could be. A few years before his death, a fire happened in the neighbourhood where he lived; and it became necessary to remove part of his household furniture and books. He was incapable of assisting himself; but he stood in the street lamenting and deploring the loss of his Caxtons, when a sailor, who lived within a few doors of him attempted to console him: "Bless you, Sir, I have got them perfectly safe!" While Ratcliffe was expressing his thanks, the sailor produced two of his fine curled periwigs, which he had saved from the devouring element; and who had no idea that Ratcliffe could make such a fuss for a few books.' He died in 1776.

Ratcliffe's collection, though not large, was marvellously rich in the productions of the early English printers; and the volumes were generally in fine condition, and handsomely bound, though not always in good taste. It contained no less than forty-eight Caxtons, among which were the *Game of the Chesse*, the *Dictes or Sayings of the Philosophers*, the *History of Jason*, and Chaucer's *Canterbury Tales*. It comprised also numerous books from the presses of the Schoolmaster of St. Albans, Lettou, Machlinia, Pynson, Wynkyn de Worde, etc., and a few manuscripts. Dibdin in his *Bibliomania* remarks: 'If ever there was a unique collection, this was one — the very essence of Old Divinity, Poetry, Romances and Chronicles.' Ratcliffe compiled a manuscript catalogue of his library in four volumes, which was disposed of at the sale of his collection for seven pounds, fifteen shillings. It is said that he always wrote on the first fly-leaf of his books 'Perfect' — or otherwise, as the case might be.

After his death his library was sold by auction by Mr. Christie of Pall Mall. The sale, which commenced on the 27th of March 1776 and lasted till April 6th, consisted of one thousand six hundred and seventy-five lots. It does not appear to have been well managed, for Nichols says, 'there were many hundred most rare Black-letter books and Tracts, unbound, with curious cuts. They were sold I remember in large bundles, and were piled under the tables in the Auction Room, on which the other books were exposed to view, and were not seen by the Booksellers who were the purchasers.' A priced copy of the catalogue is preserved in the British Museum, which shows that the Caxtons fetched but two hundred and thirty-six pounds, five shillings and sixpence; the highest prices obtained being sixteen pounds for the *Game of the Chesse*, fifteen guineas for the *Dictes or Sayings of the Philosophers*, and nine pounds, fifteen shillings for the *Golden Legende*. King George III. bought twenty of the Caxtons at an aggregate cost of about eighty-five pounds. Among them were the *De Consolatione Philosophiæ* of Boethius, *Reynard the Foxe*, the *Golden*

Legende, the *Curial*, and the *Speculum Vitæ Christi*. The Boethius, which was a fine copy, was acquired for four pounds, six shillings. A copy of the *Bokys of Hawkyng and Huntyng, etc.*, ascribed to Dame Juliana Bernes, printed at St. Albans in 1486, sold for nine pounds, twelve shillings, and a manuscript Bible on vellum, finely illuminated, for two pounds, ten shillings.

JAMES WEST, 1704?-1772

James West, who is described by Dibdin as 'a Non-Pareil Collector: the first who, after the days of Richard Smith, succeeded in reviving the love of black-letter lore and of Caxtonian typography,' was born about 1704. He was the son of Richard West of Priors Marston in Warwickshire, said to be descended from Leonard, a younger son of Thomas West, Lord de la Warr, who died in 1525. James West was educated at Balliol College, Oxford, whence he took the degrees of B.A. in 1723 and M.A. in 1726. In 1721 he was admitted as a student at the Inner Temple, and was called to the Bar in 1728. On the 4th of January 1737, while residing in the Temple, he lost a large portion of his collections, valued at nearly three thousand pounds, through a fire in his chambers.[74] In 1741 he was elected one of the representatives in Parliament for St. Albans, and was appointed one of the Joint Secretaries of the Treasury, which post he held until 1762. Three or four years later his patron the Duke of Newcastle obtained for him a pension of two thousand a year. He sat for St. Albans until 1768, and afterwards represented the constituency of Boroughbridge in Yorkshire until his death on July the 2nd, 1772. He was Recorder of Poole for many years, and also High Steward of St. Albans. He married the daughter of Sir Thomas Stephens, timber merchant in Southwark, with whom he had a large fortune in houses in Rotherhithe.

West had a great love for scientific and antiquarian pursuits, and as early as 1726 he was elected a Fellow of the Royal Society, and in the following year a Fellow of the Society of Antiquaries, of which he became a Vice-President. Of the first-named Society he was chosen Treasurer in 1736 and President in 1768, which office he held during the remainder of his life. In addition to his extensive and valuable library of manuscripts and printed books, West collected paintings, prints, and drawings, coins and medals, plate, and miscellaneous curiosities. His collection of printed books was exceedingly rich in early English ones. It contained no fewer than thirty-four Caxtons, and a large number of works from the presses of Lettou, Machlinia, the anonymous 'Scole mayster' of St. Albans, Wynkyn de Worde,

Pynson, and the rest of the old English typographers, many of which were unique copies. His manuscripts were exceptionally interesting and valuable. These, with some exceptions, were bought by William, Earl of Shelburne, afterwards Marquis of Lansdowne, and were subsequently purchased by Parliament, together with the other manuscripts of the Marquis, for the British Museum. Many of the manuscripts had previously belonged to Bishop Kennet.

West's coins, pictures, prints, drawings, and museum of curiosities were disposed of at various sales in the early part of 1773,[75] and on the 29th of March and twenty-three following days in the same year his library was sold by Messrs. Langford[76] at his late dwelling-house in King Street, Covent Garden.[77] There were four thousand six hundred and fifty-three lots, which realised two thousand nine hundred and twenty-seven pounds, one shilling. A copy of the catalogue with the prices and the names of the purchasers is preserved in the Library of King George III. in the British Museum. Many of the more valuable books were purchased by Gough, the antiquary, the greater part of which were bequeathed by him to the Bodleian Library. Although Horace Walpole, in a letter to the Rev. W. Cole, dated April 7th, 1773, writes that he considered 'the books were selling outrageously,' the prices were only fairly good for the time, and not high. The thirty-four Caxtons realised no more than three hundred and sixty-one pounds, four shillings and sixpence. The highest prices obtained were forty-seven pounds, fifteen shillings and sixpence for the first edition of Chaucer's *Canterbury Tales*, thirty-two pounds, eleven shillings for the *Recuyell of the Histories of Troy*, thirty-two pounds and sixpence for the first edition of the *Game of the Chesse*, and twenty-one pounds for the second edition of the *Dictes or Sayings of the Philosophers*. These four works were purchased for King George III., who bought largely at the sale. Among many other rare English books a fine example of the *Bokys of Hawkyng and Huntyng*, printed at St. Albans in 1486, fetched thirteen pounds, and unique copies of two works from the press of Wynkyn de Worde—*The Passe Tyme of Pleasure*, 1517, and the *Historye of Olyver of Castille*, 1518—three guineas, and one pound, twelve shillings respectively. The latter book was reprinted in 1898 by Mr. Christie-Miller for the Roxburghe Club. It was edited by Mr. R.E.

Graves, late Assistant-Keeper, Department of Printed Books, British Museum. West's famous collection of ballads, which was begun by Robert Harley, Earl of Oxford, was bought for twenty pounds by Major Pearson, who made many additions to it. It afterwards came into the possession of the Duke of Roxburghe, by whom it was also greatly enlarged. After passing through the library of Mr. Bright, it was finally acquired in 1845 by the trustees of the British Museum.

Among the manuscripts a beautifully illuminated Missal, made by order of King Henry VII. for his daughter Margaret, afterwards Queen Consort of James IV., King of Scotland, was bought by the Duke of Northumberland for thirty-two pounds, eleven shillings; a Book of Hours sold for forty-three pounds, one shilling; and a manuscript of Boccaccio for twenty-five pounds, four shillings. Both of these manuscripts had exceedingly fine illuminations.

FOOTNOTES:

[74] Oldys, *Diary*, London, 1862, p. 3.

[75] Horace Walpole says that the prints sold for the 'frantic sum of £1495, 10s.'—*Letters*, London, 1857-59, vol. v. p. 439.

[76] Nichols states that the books were sold by auction under the name of Messrs. Langford, but actually by Mr. Samuel Paterson, who compiled the catalogue.—*Anecdotes of literature*, vol. vi. p. 345.

[77] West's country residence was Alscot Park, Preston-on-Stour, Gloucestershire.

BENJAMIN HEATH, 1704-1766

Benjamin Heath, who was born at Exeter on the 20th of April 1704, was the eldest son of Benjamin Heath, a fuller and merchant of that city.[78] He was educated at the Exeter Grammar School, and afterwards studied law, with a view of being called to the Bar; but having inherited a handsome fortune on the death of his father, he abandoned his intention, and devoted himself to literature, and also to the formation of a library, which he had commenced at a very early age. In 1752 Heath was elected town-clerk of Exeter, an appointment he held until his death on the 13th of September 1766. In 1762 the University of Oxford conferred on him the degree of D.C.L. He was the author of several works, principally on the Greek and Latin classics and the text of Shakespeare. Heath in his lifetime divided a portion of his fine library between two of his sons, but retained a large part of it. Dibdin in *Bibliomania* prints an interesting letter, dated Exeter, March 21st, 1738, from Heath to Mr. John Mann of the Hand in Hand Fire Office, London, asking him to superintend the purchase of some books at a sale which was shortly to take place, and appending a list of those he desired, and the prices he was willing to pay for them.

FOOTNOTES:

[78] Drake, *Heathiana*. London, 1882.

HORACE WALPOLE, FOURTH EARL OF ORFORD, 1717-1797

Horatio or Horace Walpole, fourth Earl of Orford (he disliked the name Horatio, and wrote himself Horace), was the fourth and youngest son of Sir Robert Walpole, first Earl of Orford, by his first wife, Catherine Shorter, eldest daughter of John Shorter of Bybrook, near Ashford in Kent. He was born, as he himself tells us, on the 24th of September 1717 O.S. In 1727 he was sent to Eton, where he had for his schoolfellows the future poets Thomas Gray and Richard West; and eight years later he proceeded to King's College, Cambridge. Walpole entered the House of Commons in 1741 as Member for Callington in Cornwall, and afterwards sat for the family boroughs of Castle Rising and King's Lynn, but although he took a considerable interest in politics, public life was not congenial to his pursuits and tastes, and in 1767 he resigned his seat in Parliament. In his earlier days he was a Whig with a strong leaning to republicanism, but the public events of his later years greatly modified his views. It has been well said of him that 'he was an aristocrat by instinct and a republican by caprice.' On the death of his nephew, George, the third Earl, in 1791, he succeeded to the earldom, but he never took his seat in the House of Lords, and seldom signed his name as Orford. He died at his house in Berkeley Square on the 2nd of March 1797, and was buried at Houghton, the family seat in Norfolk.

In 1747 Walpole purchased the remainder of the lease of a small house which stood near the Thames 'just out of Twickenham,' popularly called Chopped-Straw Hall, on account of its having been the residence of a retired coachman of an Earl of Bradford, who was supposed to have made his money by starving his master's horses. On the 5th of June 1747 Walpole writes to Sir Horace Mann, that although 'the house is so small that I can send it to you in a letter to look at, the prospect is as delightful as possible, commanding the river, the town (Twickenham), and Richmond Park, and being situated on a hill descends to the Thames through two or three little meadows, where I have some Turkish sheep and two cows, all studied in their colours for becoming the view.' This cottage grew into the Gothic mansion of Strawberry Hill, the erection and embellishment of which formed for so many years the principal occupation and amusement of Walpole's life. Here he collected works of art and curiosities of every kind—pictures, miniatures, prints and drawings, armour, coins, and china, together with a fine library of about fifteen thousand volumes, chiefly of antiquarian and historical subjects. These he acquired with the emoluments of three sinecure offices which his father had obtained for him.

VIGNETTE OF STRAWBERRY HILL.
Used in books printed at Walpole's Press.

In 1757 Walpole set up a printing-press in a small cottage adjoining his residence, and this continued in use until his death in 1797. Gray's *Odes*, in a handsome quarto, was the first of a large number of works and fugitive pieces, many from his own pen, which issued from it. An excellent account of the press, by Mr. H.B. Wheatley, F.S.A., will be found in *Bibliographica*, vol. iii., pp. 83-98. Walpole was the author of many works, but his literary reputation now rests mainly on his letters. Mr. Austin Dobson, in his delightful Memoir of Walpole, says of them that 'for diversity of interest and perpetual entertainment, for the constant surprises of an unique species of wit, for happy and unexpected turns of phrase, for graphic characterisation and clever anecdote, for playfulness, pungency, irony, persiflage, there is nothing like his letters in English.' A collected edition of his works, edited by Mary Berry, under the name of her father, Robert Berry, was published in 1798 in five volumes.

Although the library formed by Walpole at Strawberry Hill consisted principally of works 'which no gentleman's library should be without,' it also contained some beautiful manuscripts, a goodly number of rare books of the Elizabethan and Jacobean times, and an immense collection of interesting papers and letters, prints and portraits. Many of the prints were by the great engravers of the fifteenth, sixteenth, and seventeenth centuries. The most notable of the manuscripts were a copy of the Psalms of David on vellum, with twenty-one illuminations attributed to Giulio Clovio; a magnificent 'Missal,' executed for Claude, Queen Consort of Francis I., King of France; and a folio volume of old English poetry, written on vellum, from the library of Ralph Thoresby, the antiquary. Among the more important of the collections of papers and letters were those of Sir Julius Cæsar, which contained letters of James I., Henry, Prince of Wales, the King and Queen of Bohemia, and most of the leading nobility and gentry of the time of Elizabeth and James I.; Sir Sackville Crowe's Book of Accounts of the Privy Purse of the Duke of Buckingham in his different journeys into France, Spain, and the Low Countries with Prince Charles; the manuscripts bequeathed to Walpole by Madame du Deffand, together with upwards of eight hundred letters addressed by her to him; and Vertue's manuscripts in twenty-eight volumes. Sir Julius Cæsar's travelling library, consisting of forty-four duodecimo volumes, bound in white vellum, and enclosed in an oak case covered with light olive morocco, elegantly tooled, and made to resemble a folio volume (now in the British Museum); and the identical copy of Homer used by Pope for his translation, with the inscription, 'Finished ye translation in Feb. 1719-20—A. Pope,' and containing a pencil sketch of Twickenham Church by the poet, were among the most interesting printed books in the library. A remarkable and beautiful collection of about forty original drawings, being portraits of Francis the First and Second of France, and the members of their Courts, taken from life in pencil, tinted with red chalk, by Janet; Callot's Pocket Book, with drawings by this master; and fine collections of the works of Vertue and Hogarth also deserve to be mentioned.

After Walpole's death Strawberry Hill and its contents passed to the Hon. Mrs. Damer, the sculptress, daughter of his cousin, Field-Marshal Conway, together with two thousand a year for its maintenance. After residing in it for some time Mrs. Damer found the situation lonely, and gave up the house and property to the Countess Dowager Waldegrave, in whom the fee was vested under Walpole's will. In 1842, George, seventh Earl Waldegrave, to whom Strawberry Hill had descended, ordered the contents to be sold by George Robins, the well-known auctioneer. The sale was advertised to occupy twenty-four days, from April 25th to May 21st. The catalogue was badly compiled, and so much dissatisfaction was expressed at the intention of selling some of the collections *en masse*, that the contents of the seventh and eighth days' sale, which consisted of prints, drawings, and illustrated books, were withdrawn, re-catalogued, and disposed of at a sale at Robins's rooms at Covent Garden, which lasted from the 13th to the 23rd of June. The amount realised at the sale at Strawberry Hill was twenty-nine thousand six hundred and twelve pounds, sixteen shillings and threepence; and at that in London, three thousand eight hundred and thirty-seven pounds, fifteen shillings and sixpence. The library, consisting of books, manuscripts, prints, etc., sold for about seven thousand seven hundred and forty pounds. The copy of the Psalms, with illuminations ascribed to Giulio Clovio, fetched four hundred and forty-one pounds; the volume of English poetry, two hundred and twenty pounds, ten shillings; the 'Missal' executed for Queen Claude, one hundred and fifteen pounds, ten shillings; and the manuscripts and letters of Madame du Deffand, one hundred and fifty-seven pounds, ten shillings.

RALPH WILLETT, 1719-1795

Ralph Willett, the collector of the famous Merly Library, was born in 1719. He was the elder son of Henry Willett, of the island of St. Christopher in the West Indies. In 1736 he matriculated at the University of Oxford from Oriel College, but did not take a degree; and in 1739 he was admitted a student at Lincoln's Inn. Willett early developed a taste for books and pictures, and his inheritance of the family estates in the West Indies, on the death of his father in 1740, enabled him to form splendid collections of them. In 1751 he purchased a property at Merly, near Wimborne, Dorsetshire, where in 1752 he built a noble mansion, which later he enlarged by adding two wings, in one of which he constructed a handsome room for a library, which he ornamented with frescoes and arabesque designs. A description of this library, written by Willett in English and French, was printed in 1776 in octavo, and reprinted in 1785 by John Nichols in a large folio volume, with twenty-five illustrations of the designs. His London house was in Dean Street, Soho. Willett was elected a Fellow of the Society of Antiquaries in 1763, and contributed two papers on *The Origin of Printing* to the *Archæologia*, which were reprinted at Newcastle in 1818-20; and a third on *British Naval Architecture*. In 1764 he was also elected a Fellow of the Royal Society. He died on the 13th of January 1795. Willett, who was twice married, but left no issue, bequeathed his property to his cousin John Willett Adye, who took the name of Willett, and was M.P. for New Romney from 1796 to 1806. This gentleman, shortly before his death, which occurred on 26th of September 1815, parted with the collections which had been left to him. The pictures were sold by Peter Coxe and Co. on May 31st, 1813, and two following days, and the books by Leigh and Sotheby on December 6th, and sixteen following days. The same auctioneers also sold the botanical drawings, of which there was a large number, on the 20th and 21st of December; and the books of prints on the 20th of February in the succeeding year. The books were disposed of in two thousand seven hundred and twenty lots, and realised thirteen thousand five hundred and eight pounds, four shillings. The sale catalogue states that the library consisted of 'a most rare assemblage of the early printers, fine specimens of block-printing, old English chronicles, etc., in the finest preservation, likewise an extensive and magnificent collection of books in every department of literature, from the earliest period to the present time. All the books are in the finest condition, many printed on vellum and on large paper, and bound in morocco and russia leathers. Likewise a most splendid missal; and a very choice selection of botanical drawings, by Van Huysum, Taylor, Brown, Lee, etc.'

The block-books in the collection comprised a *Biblia Pauperum*, which realised two hundred and fifty-seven pounds, five shillings; the first and another edition of the *Speculum Humanæ Salvationis*, which sold for three hundred and fifteen pounds and two hundred and fifty-two pounds; and the *Apocalypse of St. John*, which fetched forty-two pounds. There were seven Caxtons—the first edition of the *Dictes or Sayings of the Philosophers, Tully of Old Age*, the *Polychronicon*, the second edition of the *Game of the Chesse*, the *Confessio Amantis*, the second edition of the *Mirrour of the World*, and *Diverse Ghostly Matters*. These realised altogether one thousand three hundred and eighteen pounds, sixteen shillings; the *Dictes* and the *Confessio Amantis* fetching the highest prices—three hundred and fifteen pounds, and two hundred and sixty-two pounds, ten shillings.

Some of the many other notable books in the library, and the prices obtained for them, were a copy of the Mentz Psalter of 1459 on vellum, sixty-three pounds; *Rationale Divinorum Officiorum* of Durandus (Mentz, 1459), one hundred and five pounds; the *Catholicon* of Joannes Balbus (Mentz, 1460), sixty pounds, eighteen shillings; the *Constitutiones* of Pope Clement V. (Mentz, 1460), sixty-six pounds, three shillings; Latin Bible (Mentz, 1462), one hundred and five pounds; the *Officia* of Cicero (Mentz, 1465), seventy-three pounds, ten shillings; Latin Bible on vellum (Venice, 1476), one hundred and sixty-eight pounds; *Rhetorica Nova*, by Laurentius de Saona (St. Albans, 1480), seventy-nine pounds, sixteen shillings; a vellum copy of the first edition of Homer (Florence, 1488), eighty-eight pounds, four shillings; a nearly complete set of De Bry's collections in seven volumes, one hundred and twenty-six pounds; and a large paper copy of Prynne's *Records* in three volumes,

London, 1665-70, one hundred and fifty-two pounds, five shillings. The 'splendid' manuscript missal, specially mentioned in the sale catalogue, sold for one hundred and five pounds.

DR. ANTHONY ASKEW, 1722-1774

Dr. Anthony Askew, M.D., was born at Kendal, Westmoreland, in the year 1722. His father was Dr. Adam Askew, an eminent physician of Newcastle-upon-Tyne. He received his education at Sedbergh School, the Grammar School of Newcastle, and Emmanuel College, Cambridge. He took the degree of M.B. in 1745, and that of M.D. five years later. After leaving the University he went to Leyden, where he remained twelve months studying medicine, and then undertook an extensive tour on the Continent, during which he purchased a large number of valuable books and manuscripts. Dibdin says he was well known as a collector in most parts of Europe. In 1750, having finished his travels, Askew returned to Cambridge, where he practised for some time as a physician. He afterwards removed to London, where, aided by the patronage and support of his friend Dr. Mead, he soon acquired a considerable reputation, but he is better known as a scholar than a physician. Dr. Parr entertained a very high opinion of his attainments in Greek and Roman literature. Askew was a Fellow and Registrar of the College of Physicians, and also a Fellow of the Royal Society. He died at Hampstead on the 27th of February 1774.

Dr. Askew was an indefatigable collector, and filled his house from the ground floor to the attics with rare and handsomely bound books. The library, which numbered about seven thousand volumes, was extremely rich in early editions of the Greek and Latin classics, and its owner was ambitious that it should contain every edition of a Greek author. It comprised the first editions of the *De Officiis* of Cicero, the Natural History of Pliny, Cornelius Nepos, the History of Ammianus Marcellinus, the Fables of Æsop, the Works of Plato, and of many other Greek and Latin writers; the greater number of them being printed on vellum. A vellum copy of the *Rationale* of Durandus, printed by Fust and Schoeffer at Mentz in 1459; a first edition of the *Teseide* of Boccaccio, printed on vellum at Ferrara in 1475; a copy of the *Greek Anthology*, also on vellum, printed at Florence in 1494; *Tully of Old Age*, printed by Caxton, and a fine vellum copy of the *Tewrdannck*, were a few of the other notable books in the collection.

The printed books in the library were sold by Baker and Leigh at their auction rooms in York Street, Covent Garden, on the 13th of February 1775, and the nineteen following days. The lots were three thousand five hundred and seventy in number, and realised three thousand nine hundred and ninety-three pounds and sixpence. Among the purchasers at the sale were King George III., Louis XVI., King of France, Dr. Hunter and the Rev. C.M. Cracherode. The British Museum also acquired a considerable number of the books. The manuscripts, and the printed books with manuscript notes, were sold by Leigh and Sotheby in 1785. The sale took place on March the 7th and the eight subsequent days. There were six hundred and thirty-three lots, which produced eighteen hundred and twenty-seven pounds.

Askew was the author of a manuscript volume of Greek and Latin Inscriptions, copied by him during his travels in Greece and the Levant. The collection is preserved among the Burney Manuscripts in the British Museum.

REV. C.M. CRACHERODE, 1730-1799

REV. C.M. CRACHERODE.

The Rev. Clayton Mordaunt Cracherode, to whom the British Museum is indebted for some of its most precious collections, was the son of Colonel Mordaunt Cracherode, who commanded the Marines in Anson's voyage round the world. He was born at Taplow in 1730, and was educated at Westminster and Christ Church, Oxford, taking the degree of B.A. in 1750, and that of M.A. in 1753.

After leaving the University he took holy orders, and for some time was curate of Binsey, near Oxford, but he did not seek any preferment in the Church. On the death of his father he inherited a fortune of about three thousand pounds a year, which enabled him to acquire a library of not less than four thousand five hundred volumes, remarkable for their rarity and beauty; seven portfolios of drawings by the great masters, and a hundred portfolios of prints, many of which were almost priceless; and in addition to these a splendid collection of coins and gems, and a cabinet of minerals. Mr. Cracherode, who never married, was a shy, retiring man, who lived entirely among his collections, and it is said that he never mounted a horse, nor travelled a greater distance than from London to Oxford. One great drawback to the happiness of his quiet life was the dread that he might possibly be called upon to officiate at a coronation as the King's cupbearer, as his manor of Great Wymondley was held from the Crown subject to the performance of this duty. Dibdin, in his *Bibliographical Decameron*, says of him that he had 'a dash of the primitiveness of the old school about him, and that his manners were easy, polished and engaging. He was a thorough gentleman, and no mean scholar.' He devoted his life to his favourite pursuit, the formation of his collections; and Edwards, in his *Lives of the Founders of the British Museum*, tells us that—'For almost forty years it was his daily practice to walk from his house in Queen Square, Westminster, to the shop of Elmsly, a bookseller in the Strand, and thence to the still more noted shop of Tom Payne, by the "Mews-Gate." Once a week, he varied the daily walk by calling on Mudge, a chronometer-maker, to get his watch regulated. His excursions had, indeed, one other and not infrequent variety—dictated by the calls of Christian benevolence—but of these he took care to have no note taken.... The ruling passion kept its strength to the last. An agent was buying prints, for addition to the store, when the Collector was dying. About four days before his death, Mr. Cracherode mustered strength to pay a farewell visit to the old shop at the Mews-Gate. He put a finely printed *Terence* (from the press of Foulis) into one pocket, and a large paper *Cebes* into another; and then with a longing look at a certain choice *Homer*, in the course of which he mentally, and somewhat doubtingly, balanced its charms with those of its twin brother in Queen Square—parted finally from the daily haunt of forty peripatetic and studious years.' Mr. Cracherode is also mentioned in the *Pursuits of Literature*, by T.J. Mathias:—

'Or must I, as a wit, with learned air,
Like Doctor Dibdin, to Tom Payne's repair,
Meet Cyril Jackson and mild Cracherode there?
"Hold!" cries Tom Payne, "that margin let me measure,
And rate the separate value of the treasure."
Eager they gaze. "Well, Sirs, the feat is done.
Cracherode's *Poetæ Principes* have won."'

Mr. Cracherode, who was a Fellow of the Royal Society and of the Society of Antiquaries, and a Trustee of the British Museum, died at Queen Square on the 5th of April 1799, and was buried in Westminster Abbey. He bequeathed the whole of his collections to the nation, with the exception of two books. A copy of the Complutensian Polyglot Bible was given to Shute Barrington, Bishop of Durham, and a *princeps* Homer, once the property of De Thou, to Cyril Jackson, Dean of Christ Church; but these volumes ultimately rejoined their former companions in the British Museum.

The library formed by Mr. Cracherode is marvellously rich in choice copies of rare and early editions of the classics; a large proportion of them being printed on vellum. The volumes are almost always in faultless condition, and beautifully bound. Many of them were once to be found in such renowned collections as those of Grolier, Maioli, Henry II. of France and Diana of Poitiers, Katharine de' Medici, De Thou, Longepierre, Count von Hoym, etc.; and have bindings by Nicolas and Clovis Eve, Le Gascon, Padeloup, Derome, and Roger Payne. Among them are magnificent copies of the editions of *Pliny* printed at Venice by Joannes de Spira in 1469, and by Nicolas Jenson in 1476. The latter formerly belonged to Grolier, and the binding bears his well-known motto. A copy of the first edition of *Æsop's Fables*, printed at Milan about 1480, and a very beautiful example of the first edition of the *Greek Anthology*, on vellum, printed in capitals by Laurentius de Alopa at Florence in 1494, in the original binding, are also deserving of special notice. Other remarkable and interesting books are the *Greek Grammar* of Lascaris, printed at Milan in 1476; the

Liber Psalmorum, printed at Milan in 1481; Maioli's copy of the *Hypnerotomachia Poliphili*, printed at Venice by Aldus in 1499; and a fine copy of Petrarch's *Sonetti e Canzoni*, on vellum, printed by Aldus in 1501, which formerly belonged to Isabella d'Este, wife of Gian-Francesco Gonzaga, Marquis of Mantua. This was the first Italian book printed in italic type.

ARMORIAL BOOK-STAMP OF THE REV. C.M. CRACHERODE.

The library contains three Caxtons: *Boethius de Consolatione Philosophiæ*, the *Mirrour of the World*, and the *Boke of Eneydos*.

A copy of Tyndale's New Testament on vellum, which once belonged to Queen Anne Boleyn, with her arms emblazoned on the title-page, and the words 'Anna Regina Angliæ' painted in gold on the edges of the leaves, and a handsome Shakespeare first folio, ought also to be mentioned.

Mr. Cracherode's classical attainments were by no means inconsiderable, but his only writings were a Latin poem printed in the *Carmina Quadragesimalia* of 1748, and some Latin verses in the collection of the University of Oxford on the death of Frederick, Prince of Wales, in 1751.

A portrait of Mr. Cracherode appears in Clarke's *Repertorium Bibliographicum*, and in Dibdin's *Bibliographical Decameron*. This was engraved, contrary to his express wishes, from a drawing made by

Edridge for Lady Spencer. An explanation is given by Dr. Dibdin of the circumstances under which the likeness was reproduced.

JOHN TOWNELEY, 1731-1813

John Towneley, who was born on the 15th of June 1731, and died on the 13th of May 1813, was the younger son of Richard Towneley of Towneley, in the county of Lancaster, and Mary, daughter of William, Lord Widdrington. He married Barbara, fourth daughter of Edward Dicconson of Wrightington, in the county of Lancaster, by whom he had a daughter, Barbara, who married Sir William Stanley, Bart., of Hooton, and a son, Peregrine Edward, who succeeded to the estates. Dibdin, in his *Bibliographical Decameron*, informs us that 'Mr. Towneley had one of the finest figures, as an elderly gentleman (for he died at 82), that could possibly be seen. His stature was tall and frame robust; his gait was firm; his countenance was Roman-like; his manners were conciliatory, and his language was unassuming. His habits were simple and perhaps severe. He generally rose at five, and lighted his own library fire—and his health was manifest in his person and countenance. He was entirely an unpretending man—and may be said to have collected rather from the pleasure and reputation attached to such pursuits than from a thorough and keen relish of the kind of taste which it imparts. He had an ample purse, and it was most liberally unstrung when there was occasion for effectual aid. This observation may equally apply to matters out of the *bibliomaniacal* record; but as a book-purchaser he was considered among the most heavy-metalled and determined champions in the field.'

The library formed by Mr. Towneley was a particularly good one, and it was remarkable for the large number of rare and fine examples it possessed of books from the presses of Caxton, Pynson, Wynkyn de Worde, Julian Notary, and other early English printers. No fewer than nine Caxtons were to be found on its shelves, and Pynson and Wynkyn de Worde were especially well represented. Among the Caxtons were the first edition of the *Dictes or Sayings of the Philosophers*, the *Fayts of Arms*, and *Troilus and Creside*, together with the *Life of St. Katherine*, published by Caxton's executors. Perhaps the most important of the other early English books were Boccaccio's *Falle of Princis*, translated by Lydgate, and Froissart's *Cronycle*, both printed by Pynson; and the *Vitas Patrum* and the *Kalender of Shepeherdes* by Wynkyn de Worde. The library also contained some exceedingly rare and valuable manuscripts, of which some of the most notable were a famous copy of the *Iliad*, a *Pontificale* of Pope Innocent IV., and a very interesting and curious collection of English Miracle-Plays acted at Wakefield in the fourteenth and fifteenth centuries.[79] Of the copy of the *Iliad*, Clarke in his *Repertorium Bibliographicum* remarks:—'This is the identical manuscript which was formerly in the possession of Victorius and Salviati at Florence, the supposed loss of which had been deplored for more than two centuries. Critics have unanimously assigned to it a very remote period of antiquity. It is written upon vellum in a very fair and legible hand, and the margins are replete with most valuable and important scholia. Heyne has given a facsimile of it in his Homer. It was purchased by the late Rev. Dr. Burney, whose entire collection is now deposited in the British Museum.'

Towneley's books were sold after his death, in three portions, by Evans of Pall Mall. The first sale took place on June 8th, 1814, and six following days. It comprised nine hundred and five lots, which realised five thousand eight hundred and fifty-seven pounds, four shillings. The second sale occurred on June 19th, 1815, and nine following days, and the seventeen hundred and three lots in it fetched two thousand seven hundred and seven pounds, sixteen shillings. The third sale consisted only of a few remaining books, which were disposed of in conjunction with the library of Mr. Auditor Harley on May 22nd, 1817, and six following days. Eleven hundred and twenty-seven pounds, two shillings were obtained for the nine Caxtons; the *Troilus and Creside*, the *Life of St. Katherine*, and the *Dictes or Sayings of the Philosophers* fetching the highest prices, viz. two hundred and fifty-two pounds, two shillings, two hundred and thirty-one pounds, and one hundred and eighty-nine pounds. Bochas's *Falle of Princis* and Froissart's *Cronycle* realised twenty-seven pounds, sixteen shillings and sixpence, and forty-two pounds; and the *Vitas Patrum* and the *Kalender of Shepeherdes* fifty-three pounds, eleven shillings and nineteen pounds. Eighty-five pounds were obtained for Henry Boece's *Hystory and Croniklis of Scotland*, translated by Bellenden, and printed by Davidson at Edinburgh in 1536; thirty-three pounds, sixteen shillings for Ricraft's *Survey of England's Champions*, etc., London, 1647; and forty-eight pounds, six shillings for a Book of Hours printed on vellum by Julian Notary in

1503. Among the manuscripts the *Iliad* sold for six hundred and twenty pounds, the Wakefield Miracle-Plays for one hundred and forty-seven pounds, and the *Pontificale Innocentii IV.* for one hundred and twenty-seven pounds, one shilling. The drawings, prints, etc., belonging to Towneley were sold by King of 38 King Street, Covent Garden, in May 1816 for fourteen hundred and fourteen pounds, five shillings and sixpence; and his magnificent collection of Hollar's works was disposed of by the same auctioneer for two thousand one hundred and eight pounds, eleven shillings and sixpence in May 1818. John Towneley was not the only collector of his family. Charles Towneley, his nephew, formed a celebrated collection of marbles, coins, gems, and drawings, now in the British Museum; and Christopher Towneley, who was born in 1604 and died in 1674, was the collector of many of the old manuscripts disposed of in the second sale of the Towneley library which occurred in 1883 after the death of Colonel John Towneley, when in default of a male heir the estates devolved on his daughters and those of his elder brother, Colonel Charles Towneley.

The second sale of the Towneley library took place in June 1883. The printed books were sold on the 18th and seven following days, and the manuscripts on the 27th and following day, by Sotheby, Wilkinson and Hodge. There were two thousand eight hundred and fifteen lots of printed books, which realised four thousand six hundred and sixteen pounds, three shillings; and two hundred and fifty-one lots of manuscripts, for which the sum of four thousand and fifty-four pounds, six shillings and sixpence was obtained. Among the printed books the very rare *York Manual*, printed by Wynkyn de Worde in 1509; the *Pilgrymage of Perfection* of 1531, by the same printer, with the Towneley arms worked in silver on the covers of the binding; and a large paper copy of Nichols's *History and Antiquities of the County of Leicester*, in eight volumes, were the most deserving of special notice. These sold respectively for fifty-nine pounds, twenty-seven pounds, ten shillings, and two hundred and thirty-five pounds. The two principal manuscripts in the sale were a *Vita Christi*, beautifully illuminated by Giulio Clovio for Alexander, Cardinal Farnese, for which Mr. Quaritch gave two thousand and fifty pounds, and the collection of Wakefield Plays, which was also purchased by the same great bookseller for six hundred and twenty pounds.[80]

FOOTNOTES:

[79] These plays were printed for the Surtees Society in 1836, and re-edited by George England, with side-notes and introduction by Alfred W. Pollard, M.A., in 1897, for the Early English Text Society.

[80] This collection was re-purchased for the Towneley library at the sale of Mr. North's books in May 1819 for ninety-four pounds, ten shillings.

SIR JOHN THOROLD, BART., 1734-1815

Sir John Thorold, Bart., of Syston Park, Grantham, Lincolnshire, who was born in 1734, and succeeded his father, Sir John Thorold, eighth baronet, in 1775, was one of the most ardent collectors of his time. The magnificent library which he and his son Sir John Hayford Thorold formed at Syston Park contained some of the rarest incunabula in existence. Among them were copies of the Gutenberg Bible; the Second Mentz Psalter on vellum; the *Catholicon* of 1460; the Latin Bible of 1462, with the arms and cypher of Prince Eugene on the binding; and the *Mirrour of the World*, printed by Caxton in 1481. It also possessed one of the earliest of the block-books, the *Apocalypse*. The library was extremely rich in first editions of the Greek and Latin classics, some of them on vellum. Other choice and rare books in the collection were a copy of the Greek Bible, printed 'in ædibus Aldi' in 1518, described by Dibdin as 'the largest and finest copy I ever saw'; the Polyglot Bible of Cardinal Ximenez; the first edition of the *Tewrdannck*; the four Shakespeare folios; *Purchas his Pilgrimmes*; and the *Pastissier François*, printed by L. and D. Elzevier at Amsterdam in 1655. There were also many editions of *Horæ* and *Officia* of the Virgin Mary, mostly printed on vellum. Several of the Syston Park books once formed part of the famous libraries of Grolier, Maioli, Diana of Poitiers, Katharine de' Medicis, Count von Hoym, Prince Eugene, and Sir Kenelm Digby. The collection also possessed a number of the beautiful little volumes bound by Clovis Eve, which were once thought to have formed part of the library of Marguerite de Valois, but are now believed to have belonged to that of Marie Marguerite de Valois de Saint-Remy, daughter of a natural son of Henry III., King of France. After the death of Sir John Thorold on the 25th of February 1815, his son and successor Sir John Hayford Thorold, having first sold the duplicates in the library, made many additions to it. He died on the 7th of July 1831, and fifty-three years later a portion of the books was sold by auction by Sotheby, Wilkinson and Hodge. The sale, which took place on December 12th, 1884, and seven following days, consisted of two thousand one hundred and ten lots, which realised the large sum of twenty-eight thousand and one pounds, fifteen shillings and sixpence. For some of the rarest of the books very large prices were obtained. Mr. Quaritch acquired the Gutenberg Bible for three thousand nine hundred pounds, and the Mentz Psalter for four thousand nine hundred and fifty. *The Catholicon* sold for four hundred pounds, the 1462 Latin Bible for one thousand pounds, *The Mirrour of the World* for three hundred and thirty-five pounds, the Aldine Greek Bible for fifty-one pounds, and the first Shakespeare folio for five hundred and ninety pounds.

REV. RICHARD FARMER, D.D., 1735-1797

The Rev. Richard Farmer, D.D., was born at Leicester on the 28th of August 1735. He was the second son of Richard Farmer, a wealthy maltster of that town. After receiving his early education in the Free Grammar School of his native place, he was entered in 1753 as a pensioner of Emmanuel College, Cambridge, where he graduated B.A. in 1757 and M.A. in 1760. In the latter year he was appointed classical tutor of his College; which post he held until his election to the Mastership in 1775, when he took the degree of D.D. He served the office of Vice-Chancellor of the University in 1775-76 and again in 1787-88, and on the 27th of June 1778 was chosen the Chief Librarian of the University. In 1780 he was collated to a prebendal stall at Lichfield, and two years later became Prebendary of Canterbury, which he resigned in 1788 on being preferred to a residentiary canonry of St. Paul's Cathedral, London. It is said that he twice refused a bishopric which was offered to him rather than forgo the pleasure of witnessing dramatic performances on the stage. He died on the 8th of September 1797, at the Lodge, Emmanuel College, and was buried in the chapel. A monument, with an epitaph by Dr. Parr, was erected to his memory in the cloisters.

Dr. Farmer, who was an elegant scholar and a zealous antiquary, was somewhat eccentric both in his appearance and manners. It is said of him 'that there were three things he loved above all others, namely, old port, old clothes, and old books; and three things which nobody could persuade him to do, namely, to rise in the morning, to go to bed at night, and to settle an account.[81] His reluctance to settle his accounts, however, was not caused by avarice, but indolence, for he spent a considerable portion of his large income in the relief of distress, and in assisting in the publication of literary works; while his pupils frequently borrowed of him sums of money, well knowing there would be but little chance of a demand for repayment. Dr. Parr, who was one of Farmer's intimate friends, remarked of him 'that his munificence was without ostentation, his wit without acrimony, and his learning without pedantry.' Farmer was a Fellow of the Royal Society, and of the Society of Antiquaries. His only published work was an *Essay on the Learning of Shakespeare*, which appeared in 1767 and went through four editions, besides being prefixed to several issues of Shakespeare's plays.

Dr. Farmer possessed a well-chosen library, which was rich in old English poetry and plays. He himself said of it 'that not many private collections contain a greater number of really curious and scarce books; and perhaps no one is so rich in the ancient philological English literature; but Dibdin tells us that the volumes 'were, in general, in sorry condition; the possessor caring little for large margins and splendid binding.' The collection was sold by auction by Mr. King, of King Street, Covent Garden, on May 7th, 1798, and the thirty-five following days. The catalogue, of which a priced copy is in the British Museum, contains three hundred and seventy-nine pages, and the lots, including a few pictures, number eight thousand one hundred and fifty-five. The sale realised two thousand two hundred and ten pounds, a sum said to be greatly in excess of that which Farmer gave for his books.

There is a portrait of Dr. Farmer by Romney in Emmanuel College, which has been engraved by J. Jones.

FOOTNOTES:

[81] *Dictionary of National Biography.*

RICHARD GOUGH, 1735-1809

Richard Gough, the eminent antiquary, was the only son of Harry Gough, of Perry Hall, Staffordshire. He was born in Winchester Street, London, on the 21st of October 1735, and was privately educated until about seventeen years of age, when he was admitted a fellow-commoner of Benet (now Corpus Christi) College, Cambridge. He left the University in 1756 without taking a degree, and commenced a series of antiquarian excursions into various parts of the kingdom for the purpose of obtaining information for an enlarged edition of Camden's *Britannia*, which he published in London in 1789. In 1767 Gough was elected a Fellow of the Society of Antiquaries, and in 1771, on the death of Dr. Gregory Sharpe, Master of the Temple, was nominated Director, a post he held until 1797, when he left the Society altogether. He was also chosen a Fellow of the Royal Society in 1775, but resigned in 1795. He died at Enfield on the 20th of February 1809, and was buried in the churchyard of Wormley, Hertfordshire.

Gough wrote, and assisted in the production of numerous topographical and antiquarian works, and contributed many articles to the *Archæologia* and the *Vetusta Monumenta* of the Society of Antiquaries. A history of that institution by him is prefixed to the first volume of the first-named publication. The *Gentleman's Magazine* also contains many papers and reviews from his pen. In addition to his edition of Camden's *Britannia*, which occupied seven years in translating and in printing, his more important works are *Anecdotes of British Topography*, published at London in 1768, which was afterwards enlarged and reprinted in 1780 under the title of *British Topography: or an historical Account of what has been done for illustrating the Topographical Antiquities of Great Britain and Ireland*; and *The Sepulchral Monuments of Great Britain*, London, 1786-99.

Gough possessed a considerable fortune, which enabled him to form an extensive library, as well as a fine collection of maps, drawings, prints, coins, and other antiquities. He left to the Bodleian Library 'all his topographical collections, together with all his books relating to Saxon and Northern literature, for the use of the Saxon Professor, his maps and engravings, and all the copper-plates used in the illustration of the various works published by himself.[82] This collection, which numbered upwards of three thousand seven hundred volumes, was placed, in accordance with the wish expressed in his will, in 'The Antiquaries' Closet,' with the collections of Dodsworth, Tanner, Willis, and other antiquaries. Gough also gave to the library a splendid series of early printed Service-books of the English Church, among which is a beautiful vellum copy of the *Hereford Missal*, printed at Rouen in 1502, and which is believed to be unique. A catalogue of the collection was published by Dr. Bandinel in 1814. Gough bequeathed to Mr. John Nichols his interleaved set of the *Gentleman's Magazine*, and of the *Anecdotes of Mr. Bowyer*.

The remainder of his books, prints, and drawings, together with his coins, medals, and other antiquities, were sold, according to his directions, by auction by Leigh and Sotheby in 1810. The books realised three thousand five hundred and fifty-two pounds, and the prints, drawings, coins, medals, etc., five hundred and seventeen pounds more.

FOOTNOTES:

[82] Macray, *Annals of the Bodleian Library*.

GEORGE STEEVENS, 1736-1800

George Steevens, the Shakesperian commentator, who was born on the 10th of May 1736, was the only son of George Steevens of Stepney, for many years an East India captain, and afterwards a Director of the East India Company. He received his early education at a school at Kingston-on-Thames and at Eton. In 1753 he was admitted a fellow-commoner of King's College, Cambridge, but left the University without taking a degree. In 1766 he published a reprint in four octavo volumes of *Twenty of the Plays of Shakespeare, being the whole number printed in quarto during his Lifetime, etc.*; and in 1773 he brought out, in association with Dr. Johnson, an edition of the whole of Shakespeare's dramatic works. Steevens, who was a Fellow of the Royal Society, and of the Society of Antiquaries, died unmarried at Hampstead on the 22nd of January 1800, and was buried in the chapel at Poplar, where a monument by Flaxman was erected to his memory.

Steevens collected a fine library, which was very rich in early English poetry and in the plays and poems of Shakespeare. It contained the first and second folios of the great dramatist, and upwards of forty copies of the separate plays in quarto, many of them being first editions. The second folio formerly belonged to King Charles I., and was given by him on the night before his execution to Sir Thomas Herbert, his Groom of the Bedchamber. This very interesting volume, in which the King has written 'Dum spiro spero C.R.,' was bought at the sale of Steevens's books for King George III. for eighteen guineas, and is now preserved in the Royal Library at Windsor. The collection also comprised some rare plays of Peele, Marlowe, and Nash; Barnabe Googe's *Eglogs, Epytaphes and Sonnettes*; Puttenham's *Arte of English Poesie*, London, 1589; Skelton's *Lyttle Workes and Merie Tales*; Watson's *Passionate Centurie of Love*; *England's Helicon*, collected by John Bodenham, London, 1600; Breton's *Workes of a young Wyt*; *The Paradice of Dainty Devises*, London, 1595; *XII Mery fests of the Wyddow Edyth*, London, 1573; and many other scarce and choice books.

Steevens's library was sold by auction by Mr. King at his great room, King Street, Covent Garden, on May 13th, 1800, and ten following days. The catalogue contained nineteen hundred and forty-three lots, which realised two thousand seven hundred and forty pounds, fifteen shillings. A copy of the catalogue marked with the prices of the books and the names of the purchasers is preserved in the British Museum.

Although Dibdin considered that 'enormous sums were given for some volumes that cost Steevens not a twentieth part of their produce,' the prices were very small compared with those which could be obtained for the same books at the present time. The first folio of Shakespeare's works fetched only twenty-two pounds, and Charles I.'s copy of the second folio, as already mentioned, but eighteen guineas. Of the first editions of the separate quarto plays, *Othello* sold for twenty-nine pounds, eight shillings; *King Lear* and the *Merry Wives of Windsor* for twenty-eight pounds each; *Henry the Fifth* for twenty-seven pounds, six shillings; *A Midsummer Night's Dream* for twenty-five pounds, ten shillings; and *Much Ado about Nothing* for the same sum. The first edition of Shakespeare's *Sonnets* went for three pounds, nineteen shillings. Steevens's copies of the *Merry Wives of Windsor* and the *Sonnets* fetched respectively three hundred and thirty guineas and two hundred and fifteen guineas at the sale of the library of George Daniel in 1864. Other prices obtained for some of the rare books were eleven pounds, fifteen shillings for *England's Helicon*; ten pounds, fifteen shillings for Barnabe Googe's *Eglogs, Epytaphes and Sonnettes*; and seven pounds, ten shillings for Puttenham's *Arte of English Poesie*.

Steevens, who led a very retired life in his house at Hampstead Heath, was the reverse of an amiable man; and while he was very polite and courteous to his literary friends in private, he made bitter attacks upon them in print. Dibdin says of him that 'his habits were indeed peculiar: not much to be envied or imitated; as they sometimes betrayed the flights of a madman, and sometimes the asperities of a cynic. His attachments were warm, but fickle both in choice and duration. He would frequently part from one, with whom he had lived on terms of close intimacy, without any assignable cause; and his enmities, once fixed, were immovable.' Dr. Parr said of him that 'he was one of the wisest, most learned, but most spiteful of men.' Dr. Johnson, however, thought 'he was mischievous, but not malignant.'

JAMES BINDLEY, 1737-1818

Mr. James Bindley was the second son of Mr. John Bindley, distiller, of St. John's Street, Smithfield. He was born in London on the 16th of January 1737, and was educated at the Charterhouse, from whence he proceeded to Peterhouse, Cambridge, taking the degree of B.A. in 1759, and that of M.A. in 1762. Later he became a Fellow of his College. In 1765, through the interest of his elder brother John, he was appointed one of the Commissioners of the Stamp Duties, and in 1781 rose to be the Senior Commissioner, a post he held until his death, which occurred at his apartments in Somerset House on the 11th of September 1818. He was a Fellow of the Society of Antiquaries for upwards of fifty-three years. A handsome monument to his memory was erected in the church of St. Mary-le-Strand. Bindley formed a very large and valuable collection of rare books, engravings, and medals, which he commenced at a very early age, and to which he devoted all his spare time and money. When only fifteen years of age he constantly frequented the book-shops, where he bought everything which he considered rare or curious. He was a man of very regular and retired habits, and it is said of him, that during the long period he held the appointment of Commissioner of the Stamp Duties, 'he never once failed in his daily attendance at the Board, or once slept out of his own apartments since he left his house at Finchley to reside in Somerset House.'[83] Bindley published in 1775 *A Collection of the Statutes now in force relating to the Stamp Duties*; and he read all the proof-sheets of Nichols's *Anecdotes of the Eighteenth Century*, which are dedicated to him, and also of the early volumes of *The Illustrations of the Literary History of the Eighteenth Century*, by the same author. He performed the same work for the *Memoirs of John Evelyn*, edited by William Bray in 1818.

Bindley's library was a remarkably fine one, and few collections have contained a larger number of works of early English literature, especially of those of the time of Elizabeth and James I. Many of these books were excessively rare, and some of them unique. Among them were the *Venus and Adonis* of Shakespeare, printed in 1602; his

Poems printed in 1640, and several of the first editions of his separate plays in quarto. The library also comprised a large portion of the extraordinary collection of poetical sheets, consisting of ballads, satires, elegies, etc., formed by Narcissus Luttrell, who, Sir Walter Scott says, 'seems to have bought every poetical tract, of whatever merit, which was hawked about the streets in his time, marking carefully the price and date of the purchase.'

After Bindley's death his books were sent to Evans of Pall Mall for sale. They were disposed of in five portions. The first sale took place in December 1818, and the fifth, which consisted of omissions, in January 1821. There were nine thousand three hundred and eighty-three lots in the five sales, which occupied forty-six days, and realised upwards of seventeen thousand five hundred pounds. The following are a few of the more notable books, and the prices they fetched in the sales:—*The Temple of Glasse*, printed by Berthelet, forty-six pounds, four shillings; Chute's *Beawtie Dishonoured* (London, 1529)—Steevens's copy, thirty-four pounds; Lewicke's *Titus and Gisippus* (London, 1562), twenty-four pounds, thirteen shillings and sixpence; Parker, *De Antiquitate Britannicæ Ecclesiæ* (London, 1572), forty-five pounds, three shillings; Nicolas Breton's *Floorish upon*

Fancie (London, 1577), forty-two pounds; Hunnis's *Hyve full of Hunnye* (London, 1578), eighteen guineas; *The Forrest of Fancy* (London, 1579), thirty-eight pounds, six shillings and sixpence; Markham's *Tragedie of Sir Richard Grinvile* (London, 1595), forty pounds, nineteen shillings; Robert Fletcher's *Nine English Worthies* (London, 1606), thirty-seven pounds, sixteen shillings; Dolarny's *Primerose* (London, 1606), twenty-six pounds, ten shillings; and Purchas's *Pilgrimes*, five volumes (London, 1625), thirty-four pounds, thirteen shillings. The first edition of *Othello* sold for fifty-six pounds, fourteen shillings; of *Love's Labour Lost* for forty pounds, ten shillings; and the *Venus and Adonis* of 1602 for forty-two pounds. Seven hundred and eighty-one pounds, one shilling were obtained for the Luttrell collection of poetical sheets; and fifty-two pounds, ten shillings for a little *Manual of Devotions*, one inch and seven-eighths long, and one inch and three-eighths broad, written on vellum, and bound in gold, said to have been given by Anne Boleyn on the scaffold to her Maid of Honour, Mistress Wyatt.

Bindley's portraits, prints, drawings, and medals were sold by Leigh and Sotheby in 1819, and realised seven thousand six hundred and ninety-two pounds.

FOOTNOTES:

[83] *Gentleman's Magazine*, vol. lxxviii. part ii. p. 631.

WILLIAM PETTY FITZMAURICE, FIRST MARQUIS OF
LANSDOWNE, 1737-1805

William Petty Fitzmaurice, third Earl of Shelburne and first Marquis of Lansdowne, was born in Dublin on the 2nd of May 1737. He was first privately educated, and afterwards at Christ Church, Oxford, which he left early to take a commission in the Guards. He served with the British troops under Prince Ferdinand in Germany, and was present at the battles of Kampen and Minden, where he distinguished himself by his personal valour. He became a Major-General in 1765. In May 1760, and again in April 1761, he was elected member for Wycombe, but he sat for a short time only in the House of Commons, as the death of his father on the 10th of May 1761 called him to the House of Lords. In April 1763 he was placed at the head of the Board of Trade and Plantations, a post which he held only till September in the same year; but in 1766, when Pitt, Earl of Chatham, formed his second administration, he included Lord Shelburne in it as Secretary of State for the Southern Department, to which, at that time, the Colonial business was attached. From this post, however, he was dismissed in October 1768 by the Duke of Grafton, whose influence in the Cabinet became paramount when the Earl of Chatham's illness prevented him taking an active share in the government. Lord Shelburne remained out of office until March 1782, when on the formation of the Rockingham administration he became Secretary of State for Foreign Affairs. This ministry was dissolved on the death of Lord Rockingham on the 1st of July in the same year, and the King entrusted Lord Shelburne with the construction of a new one, which lasted but little over seven months, as it was defeated in February 1783 by the vote of the Fox and North coalition. Shortly after his retirement he was created Earl Wycombe and Marquis of Lansdowne. Lord Lansdowne did not again accept office, but devoted himself to the augmentation of his fine library, the formation of which had occupied his attention for many years. It was especially rich in historical and political manuscripts, and comprised, among other collections, one hundred and twenty-one volumes of the papers and miscellaneous correspondence of Lord Burghley, including his private note-book and journal, which had formerly been in the hands of Strype the historian. The library also contained a considerable portion of the important collection of State papers amassed by Sir Julius Cæsar, Master of the Rolls in the reign of James I.; the historical collections of White Kennet, Bishop of Peterborough, which amounted to a hundred and seven volumes, many of them being in the bishop's handwriting; the heraldic and genealogical collections of Segar, St. George, Dugdale, Le Neve, and other heralds; and some valuable legal, topographical, musical, biblical and classical manuscripts. The collection of manuscripts, which amounted to one thousand two hundred and forty-five volumes, was acquired in 1807 by the Trustees of the British Museum for the sum of four thousand nine hundred and twenty-five pounds. The printed books, among which were many valuable topographical works and some rare volumes of English literature, numbered about twenty thousand. They were sold by Leigh and Sotheby in 1806, and together with the maps, charts, books of prints, etc., realised over eight thousand three hundred and fifty pounds. The Marquis, who collected pictures and sculpture as well as books, died on the 7th of May 1805, at the age of sixty-eight, and was succeeded by his son John Henry.

TOPHAM BEAUCLERK, 1739-1780

The Honourable Topham Beauclerk was the only son of Lord Sydney Beauclerk, and a grandson of the first Duke of St. Albans. He was born in 1739, and on the death of his father in 1744 succeeded to the estates which Lord Sydney had inherited from Mr. Richard Topham, M.P. for Windsor. In 1757 Beauclerk matriculated at Trinity College, Oxford, but seems to have left the University without taking a degree. While he was at Oxford he made the acquaintance of Dr. Johnson, who appears to have been greatly attracted to him on account of his wit and conversation. This intimacy surprised many of Johnson's friends, for although Beauclerk valued science and literature, he was also gay and dissipated. 'What a coalition,' said Garrick, when he heard of it, 'I shall have my old friend to bail out of the Round-house.' Notwithstanding somewhat frequent squabbles, the friendship lasted for upwards of twenty years, and on Beauclerk's death Johnson remarked of him—'that Beauclerk's talents were those which he had felt himself more disposed to envy, than those of any whom he had known.'[84] His conversational powers were evidently of a very high order, for Dr. Barnard, Bishop of Limerick, in his well-known lines on Dr. Johnson, writes of him:

> 'If I have thoughts, and can't express 'em,
> Gibbon shall teach me how to dress 'em
> In terms select and terse;
> Jones teach me modesty and Greek;
> Smith, how to think; Burke, how to speak;
> And Beauclerk to converse.'

Beauclerk married on the 12th of March 1768 Lady Diana Spencer, eldest daughter of the second Duke of Marlborough, two days after her divorce from Lord Bolingbroke and St. John. He died at Great Russell Street, Bloomsbury, on the 11th of March 1780, leaving one son and two daughters.

Beauclerk possessed a fine library of upwards of thirty thousand volumes, which he kept at his residence at Muswell Hill, near

London, stored, as Horace Walpole informs us, 'in a building that reaches half-way to Highgate.' It did not contain many rare books, but it was rich in works relating to natural history, voyages and travels, and English and French plays; and Dibdin says that it was also valuable to the general scholar, and to the collector of English antiquities and history. It also possessed a few curious and choice manuscripts. Some of the books appear to have belonged to Mr. Topham, but most of them were collected by Beauclerk. After his death they were sold by auction by Mr. Paterson 'at the Great Room, heretofore held by the Society for the Encouragement of Arts and Manufactures, opposite Beaufort Buildings, in the Strand, London,' on Monday, April 9th, 1781, and the forty-nine following days. A priced copy of the catalogue is in the British Museum.

Beauclerk, who was a Fellow of the Royal Society, was a collector of natural curiosities, as well as books, and botany was one of his favourite studies. He had also an observatory at Muswell Hill.

FOOTNOTES:

[84] Boswell, *Life of Johnson* (London, 1811), vol. iii. p. 460.

REV. BENJAMIN HEATH, D.D., 1739-1817

REV. BENJAMIN HEATH, D.D.

The Rev. Benjamin Heath, D.D., one of the sons to whom Mr. Benjamin Heath gave a part of his books, was born on the 29th of September 1739. He was educated at Eton and at King's College, Cambridge, of which College he became a Fellow. After leaving the University he was appointed an assistant master at Eton, and in 1771 succeeded Dr. Sumner as headmaster of Harrow, a post he held for fourteen years.[85] He died on the 31st of May 1817, at the rectory of

Walkerne in the county of Hertford, a living given to him by his College, which he held with the rectory of Farnham in Buckinghamshire. He was buried at Exeter. Dr. Heath, who was 'a scholar and a bibliomaniac,' added greatly to the library given to him by his father, for which he built a large room at Walkerne, where, says Dibdin, 'he saw, entertained, and caressed his friends, with Alduses in the forenoon, and with a cheerful glass towards evening, hospitable, temperate, kind-hearted, with a well furnished mind and purse, and with a larder and cellar which might have supplied materials for a new edition of Pynson's *Royal Boke of Cookery and Kervinge*, 1500, 4to.'[86] Some years before his death Heath offered his books to King's College, Cambridge, for half the sum they had cost him; but the College authorities declined the purchase, and he then sold the principal portion of them to some private individuals, who, Dibdin believes, were Messrs. Cuthell and Martin, for three thousand pounds beneath the sum they ultimately produced,[87] and they instructed Mr. Jeffery of 11 Pall Mall to sell the books by auction. The sale took place on Thursday, the 5th of April 1810, and twelve following days and Wednesday, May 2nd, and eighteen following days. It consisted of four thousand seven hundred and eighty-six lots, which realised eight thousand eight hundred and ninety-nine pounds. The sale catalogue states that the library consisted of 'rare, useful and valuable publications in every department of literature, from the first invention of printing to the present time, all of which are in the most perfect condition.' Another catalogue, with the prices and purchasers' names, of which it is said only two hundred and fifty copies were printed, was published later in the year by Constable of Edinburgh. Both the catalogues are to be found in the Library of King George III. in the British Museum. Dibdin describes this sale in enthusiastic terms in his *Bibliomania*:— 'Never,' he writes, 'did the bibliomaniac's eye alight upon "sweeter copies"—as the phrase is; and never did the bibliomaniacal barometer rise higher than at this sale! The most marked phrensy characterized it. A copy of the Editio Princeps of Homer (by no means a first-rate one) brought £92:[88] and all the ALDINE CLASSICS produced such an electricity of sensation that buyers stuck at nothing to embrace them!'[89]

FOOTNOTES:

[85] Dibdin, *Bibliographical Decameron*, vol. iii. p. 368.

[86] Dibdin, *Bibliographical Decameron*, vol. iii. p. 369.

[87] *Ibid.*, iii. 370.

MAJOR THOMAS PEARSON, 1740?-1781

Major Thomas Pearson was born about the year 1740 at Cote Green, near Burton-in-Kendal, Westmoreland. He was educated at Burton, and came to London about 1756 to fill a post in the Navy Office, which he resigned in 1760. In the course of the following year he left England, having obtained a cadetship on the Bengal Establishment, in which he rose to the rank of Major. He distinguished himself on several occasions, and was particularly noticed by Lord Clive, to whom he adhered during the mutiny fomented by Sir Robert Fletcher, at whose trial he held the office of Judge Advocate. In 1767 Pearson married a sister of Eyles Irwin, the traveller and writer. This lady died in the following year, and an epitaph inscribed to her memory may be found, together with other poetical pieces by Pearson, in vol. iv. of Pearch's *Collection of Poems*. Pearson returned to England in August 1770 with Governor Verelst, under whom he had acted as Military Secretary, and built a house for himself at Burton, in which he collected a very extensive library, consisting of works on the history, antiquities, topography, and heraldry of Great Britain and Ireland, foreign history, voyages and travels, natural history, etc., but it was principally remarkable for the large number of books in all branches of old English literature, and it was especially rich in the works of the early poets and dramatists. In 1776 Pearson again went to India, but after a residence there of five years he fell a victim to the effects of the climate, and died at Calcutta on the 5th of August 1781. Some years after his death his library was brought from Westmoreland, and sold on April 14th, 1788, and twenty-two following days, by T. and J. Egerton at their room in Scotland Yard. The prices obtained at the sale, in which there were five thousand five hundred and twenty-five lots, were very small:— Boccaccio's *The Falle of Princis and Princesses and other Nobles*, translated by Lydgate, and printed by Pynson in 1494, fetched but one pound, twelve shillings; *The Castell of Laboure*, also printed by Pynson, two guineas; two books printed by Wynkyn de Worde — Hawes's *Example of Virtu*, and *The Lyf of Saynt Ursula*, translated by Hatfield—seven pounds, ten shillings and one pound, ten shillings; Skelton's *Ryght Delectable Traytise upon a goodly Garlande, or Chapelet of Laurell*, printed by Richard Faukes in 1523—an excessively rare, if not unique book—seven pounds, seventeen shillings and sixpence; Peele's *Polyhymnia*, London, 1590, three guineas; Lyly's *Midas*, London, 1592, seven pounds; and *England's Helicon*, collected by John Bodenham, London, 1600, five pounds, ten shillings. Two volumes of ballads, chiefly collected by the Earl of Oxford, and purchased by Major Pearson at Mr. West's sale, were bought by the Duke of Roxburghe for thirty-six pounds, four shillings and sixpence, and are now, with additions by the Duke, preserved in the British Museum. Books bound for Pearson may be recognised by the device of a bird surmounting a vase, stamped on the panels of the back.

FOOTNOTES:

[88] The marked catalogue says £94, 10s.

[89] *Bibliomania*, London, 1811, p. 617.

JOHN KER, DUKE OF ROXBURGHE, 1740-1804

John Ker, third Duke of Roxburghe, was born on the 23rd of April 1740 in Hanover Square, London. He was the elder son of Robert Ker, second Duke, and on the death of his father in 1755 succeeded to the title and estates. While on a tour on the Continent he became greatly attached to Christiana, eldest daughter of the Duke of Mecklenburg-Strelitz, and there is little doubt that she would have become his wife had not King George III. soon afterwards sought the hand of the Princess's younger sister in marriage, when it was considered necessary to break off the match, partly for political reasons, and partly because 'it was deemed indecorous that the elder sister should be the subject of the younger.' This was a great disappointment to both the Duke and the Princess, who evinced the strength of their affection by remaining single during their lives. George III., probably feeling that he had done the Duke an injury, always manifested a warm friendship for him, and bestowed upon him various appointments in the royal household. In 1768 he was made a Knight of the Thistle, and in 1801 was invested with the Order of the Garter. He died on the 19th of March 1804.

The Duke, who was remarkable both for his fine presence and his mental accomplishments, collected a magnificent library at his residence in St. James's Square, London. It contained among numerous other treasures the famous Valdarfer Boccaccio, upwards of a dozen volumes printed by Caxton, and many from the presses of Pynson, Wynkyn de Worde, Julian Notary, and other early English printers. The first, second, and third Shakespeare folios were in the collection, as well as a large number of early quarto plays. The library was especially rich in choice editions of the French romances, and in the works of the English dramatists who flourished during the reigns of Elizabeth and James I. Some rare books printed in Scotland were also to be found in it. The collection of broadside ballads in three thick folio volumes, now in the British Museum, is perhaps the most extensive and interesting ever brought together. It was begun by Robert Harley, Earl of Oxford, from whose library it passed successively to those of Mr. James West and Major Thomas

Pearson, and at the sale of the books of the last-named collector it was purchased for thirty-six pounds, four shillings and sixpence by the Duke, who made many additions to it while in his possession. The collection has been admirably edited by Mr. William Chappell and the Rev. J.W. Ebsworth for the Ballad Society. Other books deserving special notice were the first edition of Pliny, printed by J. de Spira at Venice in 1469; Cicero's *Epistolæ ad Atticum*, etc., printed at Rome in 1470; the 1580 edition of the *Paradyse of Daintie Devises*, and the first edition of Shakespeare's *Sonnets*.

DUKE OF ROXBURGHE.

Among the manuscripts the most valuable were Chaucer's *Canterbury Tales*, bound with Lydgate's *Life of St. Margarete*, on vellum, with illuminations, and the *Mystere de la Vengeance de Nostre Seigneur*, also on vellum.

The library was sold in 1812 by Mr. Evans of Pall Mall in the dining-room of the Duke's house in St. James's Square, and the total amount realised was twenty-three thousand three hundred and ninety-seven pounds, ten shillings and sixpence. The sale, which consisted of nine thousand three hundred and fifty-three lots, lasted forty-two days, commencing on the 18th of May, and ending on the 4th of July. It was followed by a supplementary one of seven hundred and sixty-seven lots, which began on the 13th of July, and lasted till the 16th of the same month. The catalogue was compiled by Mr. George Nicol, bookseller to the King. The sale excited very great interest; and Dibdin, who gives an account of it in his *Bibliographical Decameron*, tells us 'the room was so crowded that nothing but standing upon a contiguous bench saved the writer of *The Bibliographical Decameron* from suffocation.' The prices obtained for the books were very high. That 'most notorious volume in existence,' the Valdarfer Boccaccio, which cost the Duke of Roxburghe but one hundred guineas, was acquired by the Marquis of Blandford, after a severe struggle with Lord Spencer, for two thousand two hundred and sixty pounds, and Dibdin says that the Marquis declared that it was his intention to have gone as far as five thousand guineas for it. A copy of the *Recuyell of the Histories of Troye*, which once belonged to Elizabeth Grey, wife of Edward IV., was purchased by the Duke of Devonshire for one thousand and sixty pounds, ten shillings; while three other books from the press of Caxton, *The Mirrour of the World*, the *Fayts of Arms*, and Gower's *Confessio Amantis*, sold respectively for three hundred and fifty-one pounds, ten shillings, three hundred and thirty-six pounds, and three hundred and thirty-six pounds. The collection of ballads fell to Mr. J. Harding for four hundred and seventy-seven pounds, fifteen shillings. At the sale of Mr. B.H. Bright's books in 1845 it was secured for the British Museum for the sum of five hundred and thirty-five pounds. The first folio of Shakespeare's Plays fetched one hundred pounds, and his Sonnets twenty-one pounds. The two manuscripts mentioned realised three hundred and fifty-seven pounds and four hundred and ninety-three pounds, ten shillings.

A dinner was given, at the suggestion of Dr. Dibdin, to commemorate the sale of the Boccaccio; and Earl Spencer, Dr. Dibdin, and other bibliophiles met on the day of the sale at St. Alban's Tavern, St. Alban's Street—now Waterloo Place—and then and there formed the Roxburghe Club; Earl Spencer being the first President.

MICHAEL WODHULL, 1740-1816

Michael Wodhull, the translator of the tragedies of Euripides, was born at Thenford, Northamptonshire, on the 15th of August 1740. His father was John Wodhull, a descendant of Walter Flandrensis, who held the estates of Pateshull and Thenford in the time of William I. He received his early education under the Rev. William Cleaver of Twyford, Bucks. He was afterwards sent to Winchester, and at the age of seventeen proceeded to the University of Oxford, matriculating from Brazenose College. While still young Wodhull inherited a considerable fortune from his father, and he built a fine mansion on the family estate at Thenford, in which he kept his library. He was High Sheriff of Northamptonshire in 1783. Wodhull married a daughter of the Rev. J. Ingram of Wolford, Warwickshire, by whom he had three children, who all predeceased him. He died on the 10th of November 1816. In addition to his translations of the tragedies of Euripides, Wodhull was the author of several poems. From 1764 to his death Wodhull was an indefatigable collector of rare and curious books, and Dibdin says of him that 'a better informed or more finished bibliographer existed not either in France or England.'

His splendid library, which was a great consolation and pleasure to him in the solitude of the last years of his life, was particularly rich in early editions of the Greek and Latin classics, and in works printed in the fifteenth century. All the books—many of which were bound by Roger Payne—were in fine condition, and some of them had once formed part of the libraries of Francis I., Grolier, Henry II. and Diana of Poitiers, Longepierre, and other famous French collectors, and were bound by such fine craftsmen as Boyet, Derome, Monnier, etc. The covers of the volumes bound for Wodhull are mostly impressed with a stamp of his arms, impaled with those of his wife. A portion of Wodhull's books, principally duplicates, was sold by Leigh, Sotheby and Son, of York Street, Covent Garden, at two sales in 1801 and 1803. The first sale consisted of a thousand and fifty-nine lots, which realised three hundred and sixty-one pounds, ten shillings; and the second of one thousand six hundred and thirty-nine lots, for which the sum of eight hundred and fifteen pounds was obtained. The remainder of the library appears to have been kept at Thenford until 1886, when Mr. J.E. Severne, M.P., to whom it had descended, determined to part with it, and it was sold by Wilkinson, Sotheby and Hodge on January 11th, 1886, and nine following days. There were two thousand eight hundred and four lots in the sale, which produced the large sum of eleven thousand nine hundred and seventy-two pounds, fourteen shillings and sixpence.

BOOK-STAMP OF MICHAEL WODHULL.

The following are a few of the rarest and most interesting books in this splendid collection, with the prices they fetched:—the *Catholicon* of Joannes Balbus, printed at Mentz in 1460, three hundred and ten pounds; *Cicero de Officiis*, printed at Mentz in 1466, seventy-one pounds; *Tullius de Senectute et Amicitia*, printed by Caxton in 1481, two hundred and fifty pounds; (a perfect copy of Caxton's *Mirrour of the World* was sold in the 1803 sale for thirty-eight pounds, seventeen shillings); the first edition of Homer, printed at Florence in 1488, two hundred pounds; *Poliphili Hypnerotomachia*, printed by Aldus in 1499, fifty-three pounds; the Aldine Virgil of 1501, one hundred and forty-five pounds; *Roman de Guy de Warwick*, Paris, 1525, one hundred and thirty pounds; the *New Actes and Constitucionis of Parliament maid by James V., Kyng of Scottis*, printed on vellum at Edinburgh in 1541, one hundred and fifty-one pounds; the *Contes* of La Fontaine, Amsterdam (Paris), 1762, in two small 8vo volumes, bound in red morocco, ninety-three pounds; Molière's Works, with plates by Moreau, six volumes, 1773, seventy-seven pounds.

Among the books with historical or fine bindings were Alcyonius, *Medices Legatus de Exsilio*, in ædib. Aldi, Venetiis, 1522, bound for Francis I., with the arms of France, the crowned initial of the king, and the salamander stamped on the covers, fifty-eight pounds; Aristotle, *De Arte Poetica*, Florentiæ, 1548, bound for Henry II. of France and Diana of Poitiers, with the devices of the king and his mistress on the covers, two hundred and five pounds; Crinitus, *De Poetis Latinis*, Florentiæ, 1505, bound for Grolier, seventy-four pounds; *Irenici Germania*, Hagenoæ, 1518, also bound for Grolier, sixty-two pounds; and two works by Giordano Bruno—*Spaccio de la Bestia Trionfante*, Parigi, 1584, and *La Cena de la Ceneri*, 1584; the former bound in citron morocco, with a red doublé by Boyet, and the latter in a beautiful mosaic binding by Monnier, realised respectively the large sums of three hundred and sixty pounds and three hundred and sixty-five pounds.

The principal manuscripts were a copy of Dante, with a commentary by Joannes de Sarravalle, written in the years 1416-17, which sold for one hundred and fifty-one pounds; and a very beautiful Roman Breviary of the beginning of the sixteenth century, on vellum, illuminated for François de Castelnau, Archbishop of Narbonne, for which five hundred and fifteen pounds was obtained.

FRANCIS HARGRAVE, 1741?-1821

Francis Hargrave, the eminent law writer, who was born about 1741, was the son of Christopher Hargrave of Chancery Lane. He entered as a student at Lincoln's Inn in 1760, and in 1772 he greatly distinguished himself in the Habeas Corpus case of James Sommersett, a negro. Soon afterwards he was appointed one of the king's counsel, and in 1797 he was made Recorder of Liverpool. He was also for many years Treasurer of Lincoln's Inn. In 1813, in consequence of the impaired state of Hargrave's health, his wife petitioned Parliament to purchase the fine law library which he had amassed, consisting of a considerable number of printed books and about five hundred manuscripts; and on the recommendation of a Committee of the House of Commons the collection was acquired by the Government for the sum of eight thousand pounds, and deposited in the British Museum. Edwards, in his *Lives of the Founders of the British Museum*, says that 'the peculiar importance of the Hargrave Collection consisted in its manuscripts and its annotated printed books. The former were about five hundred in number, and were works of great juridical weight and authority, not merely the curiosities of black-letter law. Their collector was the most eminent parliamentary lawyer of his day, but his devotion to the science of law had, to some degree, impeded his enjoyment of its sweets. During some of the best years of his life he had been more intent on increasing his legal lore than on swelling his legal profits. And thus the same legislative act which enriched the Museum Library, in both of its departments, helped to smooth the declining years of a man who had won uncommon distinction in his special pursuit.' A catalogue of the manuscripts was compiled by Sir Henry Ellis, and published in 1818. Hargrave, among other important legal works, published a new edition of *State Trials from the eleventh year of Richard II. to the sixteenth of George III.*, in eleven volumes folio, in 1776-81; *Juridical Arguments and Collections*, in two volumes, in 1797-99; and *Jurisconsult Exercitations*, in three volumes, in 1811-13. He died on the 16th of August 1821, and was buried in Lincoln's Inn Chapel. Lord Lyndhurst, in speaking of Hargrave's great legal knowledge, declared that 'no man ever lived who was more conversant with the law of his country.'

ISAAC REED, 1742-1807

Isaac Reed, the editor of Shakespeare, was born in London on the 1st of January 1742. He was a conveyancer, and had chambers, first in Gray's Inn and afterwards in Staple Inn, where he died on the 5th of January 1807. He was buried at Amwell in Hertfordshire. Reed, who was a Fellow of the Society of Antiquaries, collected books for upwards of forty years, and Dibdin says that 'he would appear to have adopted the cobbler's well-known example of applying one room to almost every domestic purpose: for Reed made his library his parlour, kitchen, and hall.' His extensive collection of books, which was rich in works relating to the English drama and poetry, was sold by King and Lochée, 38 King Street, Covent Garden, on Monday, November 2nd, 1807, and thirty-eight following days. The sale consisted of eight thousand nine hundred and fifty-seven lots, including prints and a few miscellaneous articles, and realised four thousand three hundred and eighty-six pounds, nineteen shillings and sixpence. A copy of the catalogue, with the prices added in manuscript, is preserved in the Library of King George III. in the British Museum.

SIR JOSEPH BANKS, BART., 1744-1820

The Right Hon. Sir Joseph Banks, Bart., to whom the British Museum, in addition to other bequests, is indebted for one of the finest libraries of books on natural history ever collected, was born in Argyle Street, London, on the 13th of February 1744. He was the only son of William Banks, of Revesby Abbey, Lincolnshire, by his wife Sarah, daughter of William Bate. Banks was first educated at Harrow and Eton, and proceeded afterwards to Christ Church, Oxford, which college he entered as a gentleman-commoner in 1760. In 1761 his father died, leaving him a large estate. He left the University in 1763, after having taken an honorary degree, and in 1766 he set out on a scientific voyage to Newfoundland with his friend Lieutenant Phipps, afterwards Lord Mulgrave, and brought back a large collection of plants and insects. In 1768 he accompanied Captain Cook's expedition round the world in *The Endeavour*, a vessel which he equipped at his own expense, taking with him his friend and librarian Dr. Solander, two draughtsmen, and several servants. This voyage, which was attended by many dangers and privations, occupied nearly three years, and the specimens which the enterprising collectors brought home with them excited very great and general interest. Banks was anxious to join Captain Cook's second expedition, but owing to some difficulties respecting the fittings of the ship in which he was to have sailed he relinquished his purpose, and in 1772 paid a visit in company with Dr. Solander to Iceland, where he obtained a large number of botanical specimens, and also purchased a collection of Icelandic manuscripts and printed books, including the library of Halfdan Einarsson, the literary historian of the island, which he gave to the British Museum on his return to England. Ten years later he presented a second collection to that institution. In 1778 Banks succeeded Sir John Pringle as President of the Royal Society, a post he held for upwards of forty-one years. He had been a Fellow since the year 1766. In 1779 he married Dorothea, daughter of William Weston Hugesson of Provender, in the parish of Norton, Kent, and in 1781 he was created a baronet. In 1795 he received the Order of the Bath, and in 1797 he was sworn of the Privy Council. The National Institute of France elected him a member in 1802. He died at his house at Spring Grove, Isleworth, on the 19th of June 1820, leaving a widow but no issue.

Sir Joseph Banks, even when a schoolboy, took great interest in all branches of natural history, and during his residence at Oxford he procured the appointment of a lecturer on natural science in the University. He was always exceedingly generous in his relations with men of science, and the splendid collections in his house in Soho Square were always open to them for study and investigation.

Sir Joseph Banks bequeathed his library, with the exception of some manuscripts which he left to the Royal Society and the Mint, his herbarium, drawings, engravings, and other collections to the Trustees of the British Museum, subject to a life interest and a life use in them by his friend and librarian, Mr. Robert Brown, the eminent botanist. This bequest was accompanied by a proviso that Mr. Brown should be at liberty to transfer the collections to the British Museum during his lifetime, if the Trustees were desirous to receive them, and he were willing to comply with their wishes. An arrangement to this effect was eventually carried out, and in the year 1827 the transfer was effected; Mr. Brown at the same time receiving the appointment of Keeper of the Department of Botany in the Museum, a post he held until his death in 1858.

The number of printed books acquired by the Museum amounted to about sixteen thousand, consisting principally of works on natural history and the journals and transactions of learned societies. The manuscripts numbered but forty-nine, but among them were the log-books of *The Endeavour*, *The Resolution*, and *The Racehorse*, and the journals of Tasman, Carver, Verwey and other navigators.

A catalogue of the library was compiled by Mr. Jonas Dryander, who succeeded Dr. Solander as Sir Joseph's librarian, in five volumes, and published in London in the years 1798-1800.

Sir Joseph Banks was the author of two treatises:—one, *On the Cause of Blight in Corn*, published in 1805; and the other on *Some Circumstances relative to Merino Sheep*, published in 1809; together with some articles contributed to the journals of learned societies. He evidently intended at one time to publish a work embodying the results of his researches, as the plates were engraved, and the text partly prepared for press, but the death of his librarian Dr. Solander in 1782 appears to have caused him to relinquish his purpose. Kaempfer's *Icones Plantarum* was published by him in 1791, and he also superintended the issue of Roxburgh's *Coromandel Plants* in 1795-1819. A statue of Sir Joseph by Sir Francis Chantrey is placed in the Natural History Museum in South Kensington, and a portrait of him by Sir Thomas Lawrence is hung in the board-room of the British Museum. Another portrait of him by Thomas Phillips, R.A., is in the National Portrait Gallery.

Sarah Sophia Banks, the only sister of Sir Joseph Banks, possessed similar tastes to her brother, and amassed a considerable number of books, coins, objects of natural history, etc. She died at her brother's house in Soho Square on the 27th of September 1818; and after her death a portion of her collections, consisting of sixty-six volumes of manuscripts, chiefly relating to heraldic matters, ceremonials, archery, etc., together with several printed books principally treating of chivalry, knighthood, etc., some of them enriched with her MS. notes, were presented to the library of the British Museum by Lady Banks, the wife of Sir Joseph. Several of the volumes were in very fine bindings.

REV. JOHN BRAND, 1744-1806

The Rev. John Brand, the author of *Observations on Popular Antiquities*, was born on the 19th of August 1744 at Washington, in the county of Durham, where his father Alexander Brand was parish clerk. When fourteen years of age he was apprenticed to his uncle Anthony Wheatley, a shoemaker of Newcastle-upon-Tyne, and during his residence in that town he attended the grammar school there. He displayed so much ability and industry that the master of the school, the Rev. Hugh Moises, with the assistance of some friends, sent him to Lincoln College, Oxford, where he graduated B.A. in 1775. He had been ordained some time previously, and, after filling several curacies, in 1784 he was presented by the Duke of Northumberland to the rectory of the united parishes of St. Mary-at-Hill and St. Mary Hubbard in the city of London. In the same year he was elected resident secretary of the Society of Antiquaries, an office he held until his death on the 11th of September 1806. He was buried in the chancel of his church. Brand had a very extensive knowledge of antiquities, and he accumulated a large library, which was very rich in old English literature.

Among the rarer books were the *Knight of the Tower*, printed by Caxton in 1484; the *Dyalogue of Dives and Pauper*, and Arnold's *Chronicle of the Customs of London*, printed by Pynson in 1493 and 1521; *A Plaister for a Galled Horse*, London, 1548; John Byshop's *Beautiful Blossomes*, London, 1577; Thomas Bentley's *Monument of Matrones*, London, 1582; *A Booke of Fishing with hooke and line*, London, 1600; Mrs. Fage's *Poems*, London, 1637; and *A Juniper Lecture*, London, 1639. The collection also contained some curious works on witches.

After Brand's death, the library was sold in two parts by Stewart of 194 Piccadilly. The first sale took place on May 6th, 1807, and thirty-six following days, 'Sundays, the King's Birthday, and May 21-26 excepted.' It consisted of eight thousand six hundred and eleven lots of printed books, and two hundred and forty-three of manuscripts, which realised four thousand three hundred pounds. The second part, containing duplicates and pamphlets, was sold on February the 8th, 1808, and fourteen following days, 'Sundays and the Fastday excepted.' There were four thousand and sixty-four lots in this portion, and the sum obtained for them was eighteen hundred and fifty-one pounds. *The Knight of the Tower* was purchased by Mr. Payne the bookseller for Earl Spencer for one hundred and eleven pounds, six shillings; Arnold's *Chronicle* fetched eighteen guineas; the *Dyalogue of Dives and Pauper*, four pounds, three shillings; Bentley's *Monument of Matrones*, eight pounds, eighteen shillings and sixpence; and Mrs. Fage's *Poems*, five pounds, fifteen shillings and sixpence. A copy of Brand's own work on *Popular Antiquities*, with additions for a new edition, sold, with the copyright, for six hundred and thirty pounds.

In addition to his *Observations on Popular Antiquities*, which appeared in 1777, Brand published a work on the *History and Antiquities of the town and county of Newcastle-upon-Tyne* in 1789; and in 1775 a poem *On Illicit Love, written among the ruins of Godstow Nunnery, near Oxford*—the place where the celebrated Rosamond, the mistress of Henry II., was buried. He also contributed many papers to the *Archæologia* of the Society of Antiquaries.

Nichols, in his *Literary Anecdotes*,[90] says of Brand that 'his manners, somewhat repulsive to a stranger, became easy on closer acquaintance, and he loved to communicate to men of literary and antiquarian taste the result of his researches on any subject in which they might require information.'

JOHN DENT, 1750?-1826

Mr. John Dent was born about the middle of the eighteenth century. His father is said to have been the master of a school in a small town in Cumberland. At an early age he entered the banking-house of Messrs. Child and Co. of London as a clerk, and in 1795 rose to be a partner in the firm. In 1790 he was elected Member of Parliament for the borough of Leicester, and held the seat during five successive Parliaments until the dissolution in 1812. Six years later he was chosen Member for Poole, which he represented till 1826. He died at his residence in Hertford Street, Mayfair, on the 14th of December 1826.

Mr. Dent, who was a Fellow of the Royal Society and of the Society of Antiquaries, accumulated a very fine library, which was very rich in the Greek and Latin Classics and early English literature. It also contained some very beautiful manuscripts. After his death it was sold in two parts by Mr. Evans of Pall Mall. The first sale, which took place on March the 29th, 1827, and eight following days, consisted of fifteen hundred and two lots, and realised six thousand two hundred and seventy-eight pounds, twelve shillings. The second portion of the books was sold on the 25th of the succeeding month and eight following days. There were one thousand four hundred and seventy-four lots in this sale, which brought eight thousand seven hundred and sixty-two pounds, seven shillings. The following are a few of the many very rare books which this noble collection contained, and the prices which were obtained for them:—

Fust and Schoeffer's Latin Bible of 1462, one hundred and seventy-three pounds, five shillings; a vellum copy of the first edition of Livy, printed by Sweynheym and Pannartz at Rome in 1469, two hundred and sixty-two pounds, ten shillings; the first edition of the *Anthologia Græca* on vellum, printed at Florence in 1494, seventy pounds; a perfect copy of Higden's *Polychronicon*, printed by Caxton in 1482, one hundred and three pounds, nineteen shillings; three other imperfect Caxtons, fifty-eight pounds, seventeen shillings and sixpence; Barclay's *Shyp of Folys*, printed by Pynson in 1509, thirty pounds, nine shillings; Bradshawe's *Lyfe of Saynt Radegunde*, printed by Pynson, without date, thirty-two pounds; *The Cronycle of Englonde*, printed by Wynkyn de Worde in 1502, thirty-eight pounds, seventeen shillings; a copy on vellum of the *Orcharde of Syon*, printed by Wynkyn de Worde in 1519, sixty-five pounds, two shillings; *Vitruvius de Architectura*, printed on vellum by P. de Giunta in 1513, one hundred and seven pounds, two shillings; the Coverdale Bible, 1535, eighty-nine pounds, five shillings; and Archbishop Parker's *De Antiquitate Britannicæ Ecclesiæ*, 1573, forty pounds. Mr. Dent possessed the first three Shakespeare folios, and a large number of the separate quarto plays. The folios realised respectively one hundred and ten pounds, five shillings, fifteen pounds, and sixty-five pounds, two shillings. The copy of the third folio had many contemporary manuscript corrections. Of the quarto plays, twenty-six pounds was obtained for the first edition of *Love's Labors Lost*, twenty-two pounds for the first edition of *Othello*, sixteen pounds for the first edition of *The Merchant of Venice*, and four pounds, ten shillings for the first edition of *Midsummer Night's Dream*.

Several of the manuscripts were of exceptional beauty and interest. A Roman Breviary, with illuminations in the finest Flemish style, presented to Queen Isabel of Castile by Francisco de Rojas, sold for three hundred and seventy-eight pounds; a copy of the Gospels in Greek, said to have been written about the end of the eleventh century, for two hundred and sixty-seven pounds, fifteen shillings; an *Office de la Vierge*, written by Nicolas Jarry, the celebrated calligraphist, in 1656 for Anne of Austria, and which afterwards passed into the possession of Madame de Maintenon and the Prince de Conti, for one hundred and ten pounds, five shillings; and a copy of the *Westminster Liber Regalis*, written in the fifteenth century, for fifty-five pounds, thirteen shillings. All these manuscripts were on vellum. The copies of the Roman Breviary and the Greek Gospels are described by Dibdin in his *Bibliographical Decameron* (vol. i. pp. clxiii and xcii).

FOOTNOTES:

[90] Vol. ix. p. 653.

RIGHT HON. THOMAS GRENVILLE, 1755-1846

THOMAS GRENVILLE. After a Portrait by Hoppner.

The Right Hon. Thomas Grenville, who was born on the 31st of December 1755, was the second son of the Right Hon. George Grenville, the statesman, who succeeded Lord Bute as Premier in 1763, and Elizabeth, daughter of Sir William Wyndham. In 1771 he entered Christ Church, Oxford, as a gentleman-commoner, and in 1778 he was appointed ensign in the Coldstream Guards, which he left the following year to become a lieutenant in the 80th foot. In 1780 he was elected Member for Buckinghamshire, and became a follower of Lord Rockingham and Mr. Fox, the latter of whom thought so highly of his talents that he intended, if his India Bill had passed, to have made him Governor-General. Towards the close of the war with the United States, Mr. Grenville was sent to Paris to negotiate terms of peace, but only remained there a short time, being recalled by the death of the Marquis of Rockingham and a change of ministry. On his return to this country he continued for some time to support Mr. Fox, but the course pursued by that statesman with regard to the French Revolution caused him to transfer his allegiance to Mr. Pitt, and in 1794 Mr. Grenville accepted the post of Minister Extraordinary to the Court of Vienna. In 1798 he became a privy councillor, and in 1799 he was sent as Ambassador to Berlin to endeavour to prevent the King of Prussia deserting the coalition against France; but the first vessel in which he sailed was stopped by ice, and the second was wrecked, and the delay which ensued rendered the mission an abortive one. In 1800 he was made Chief Justice in Eyre to the South of the Trent, a sinecure office of two thousand a year, of which he was the last holder. On the fall of Mr. Pitt's ministry in March 1801, Mr. Grenville ceased to support the Tory party, and renewed his political connection with Mr. Fox, and in 1806, shortly after his brother, Lord Grenville, became Prime Minister, he was appointed President of the Board of Control. On the death of Mr. Fox on the 13th of September 1806, he succeeded Lord Howick as First Lord of the Admiralty, a post he held until the formation of the Duke of Portland's administration in April 1807, when he finally retired from office, and devoted the remaining forty years of his life to literature, and to the collection of the splendid library, which is now one of the great glories of the British Museum. From an early age Mr. Grenville was animated by an ardent love for books, and took a great interest in the development of the National Library, of which he was for many years a Trustee. He died at Hamilton Place, Piccadilly, on the 17th of December 1846, at the age of ninety-one. Mr. Grenville had originally bequeathed his library to his great-nephew the Duke of Buckingham, but the circumstance that it was principally purchased from the profits of the sinecure office which he had held for so many years, led him to the conclusion that it was 'a debt and a duty' that the collection so acquired should be devoted to the use of the public. In the autumn of

1845, in the course of a conversation with his friend Mr. Panizzi, afterwards Sir Anthony Panizzi, then Keeper of Printed Books in the British Museum, he informed him of his intention; and after his death it was found that he had revoked the bequest to the Duke of Buckingham, and left his noble collection to the nation. A full and interesting description of the printed books in the library by Sir Anthony Panizzi is to be found in the Report on the accessions to the Museum for the year 1847, and we cannot do better than give the account of them in the words of the famous librarian, who had himself much to do with the acquisition of this magnificent gift: —

'With exception of the Collection of His Majesty George the Third, the Library of the British Museum has never received an accession so important in every respect as the Collection of the Right Honourable Thomas Grenville.... Formed and preserved with the exquisite taste of an accomplished bibliographer, with the learning of a profound and elegant scholar, and the splendid liberality of a gentleman in affluent circumstances, who employed in adding to his library whatever his generous heart allowed him to spare from silently relieving those whose wants he alone knew, this addition to the National Library places it in some respects above all libraries known, in others it leaves it inferior only to the Royal Library at Paris. An idea may be formed of the literary value of Mr. Grenville's Library by referring to its pecuniary value; it consists of 20,240 volumes, forming about 16,000 works, which cost upwards of £54,000, and would sell for more now. During his lifetime, Mr. Grenville's library was most liberally rendered accessible to any person, however humble his condition in life, who could show the least cause for asking the loan of any of his precious volumes. By bequeathing the whole to his country, Mr. Grenville has secured to literary men, even after his death, that assistance, as far as it relates to the use of his books, which he so generously bestowed on them in every way during his long and dignified career: — the career of a man of high birth, distinguished for uniting to a powerful and cultivated intellect a warm and benevolent heart.'

Sir Anthony Panizzi, in describing the contents of the collection, adds: 'It would naturally be expected that one of the editors of the

"Adelphi Homer" would lose no opportunity of collecting the best and rarest editions of the Prince of Poets. Æsop, a favourite author of Mr. Grenville, occurs in his Library in its rarest forms; there is no doubt that the series of editions of this author in that library is unrivalled. The great admiration which Mr. Grenville felt for Cardinal Ximenes, even more on account of the splendid edition of the Polyglot Bible which that prelate caused to be printed at Alcala, than of his public character, made him look upon the acquisition of the Moschus, a book of extreme rarity, as a piece of good fortune. Among the extremely rare editions of the Latin Classics, in which the Grenville Library abounds, the unique complete copy of Azzoguidi's first edition of Ovid is a gem well deserving particular notice, and was considered, on the whole, by Mr. Grenville himself, the boast of his collection. The Aldine Virgil of 1505, the rarest of the Aldine editions of this poet, is the more welcome to the Museum, as it serves to supply a lacuna; the copy mentioned in the Catalogue of the Royal Collection not having been transferred to the National Library.

'The rarest editions of English Poets claimed and obtained the special attention of Mr. Grenville. Hence we find him possessing not only the first and second edition of Chaucer's Canterbury Tales by Caxton, but the only copy known of a hitherto undiscovered edition of the same work printed in 1498 by Wynkyn de Worde. Of Shakespeare's collected Dramatic Works, the Grenville Library contains a copy of the first edition, which, if not the finest known, is at all events surpassed by none. His strong religious feelings, and his sincere attachment to the Established Church, as well as his mastery and knowledge of the English Language, concurred in making him eager to possess the earliest, as well as the rarest, editions of the translations of the Scriptures in the vernacular tongue. He succeeded to a great extent; but what deserves particular mention is the only known fragment of the New Testament in English, translated by Tyndale and Roy, which was in the press of Quentell, at Cologne, in 1525, when the printers were obliged to interrupt the printing, and fly to escape persecution.

'The History of the British Empire, and whatever could illustrate any of its different portions, were the subject of Mr. Grenville's unremitting research, and he allowed nothing to escape him deserving to be preserved, however rare and expensive. Hence his collection of works on the Divorce of Henry VIII.; that of Voyages and Travels, either by Englishmen, or to countries at some time more or less connected with England, or possessed by her; that of contemporary works on the gathering, advance, and defeat of the "Invincible Armada"; and that of writings on Ireland,—are more numerous, more valuable, and more interesting than in any other collection ever made by any person on the same subjects. Among the Voyages and Travels, the collections of De Bry and Hulsius are the finest in the world; no other library can boast of four such fine books as the copies of Hariot's Virginia, in Latin, German, French, and English of the De Bry series. And it was fitting that in Mr. Grenville's library should be found one of the only two copies known of the first edition of this work, printed in London in 1588, wherein an account is given of a colony which had been founded by his family namesake, Sir Richard Grenville.

'Conversant with the language and literature of Spain, as well as with that of Italy, the works of imagination by writers of those two countries are better represented in his library than in any other out of Spain and Italy; in some branches better even than in any single library in the countries themselves. No Italian collection can boast of such a splendid series of early editions of Ariosto's Orlando, one of Mr. Grenville's favourite authors, nor, indeed, of such choice Romance Poems. The copy of the first edition of Ariosto is not to be matched for beauty; of that of Rome, 1533, even the existence was hitherto unknown. A perfect copy of the first complete edition of the *Morgante Maggiore* of 1482, was also not known to exist before Mr. Grenville succeeded in procuring his. Among the Spanish Romances, the copy of that of "Tirant lo Blanch," printed at Valencia in 1490, is as fine, as clean, and as white as when it first issued from the press; and no second copy of this edition of a work professedly translated from English into Portuguese, and thence into Valencian, is known to exist except in the library of the Sapienza at Rome.

'But where there is nothing common, it is almost depreciating a collection to enumerate a few articles as rare. It is a marked feature of this library, that Mr. Grenville did not collect mere bibliographical rarities. He never aimed at having a complete set of the editions from the press of Caxton or Aldus; but Chaucer and Gower by Caxton were readily purchased, as well as other works which were desirable on other accounts, besides that of having issued from the press of that printer; and, when possible, select copies were procured. Some of the rarest, and these the finest, Aldine editions were purchased by him for the same reasons. The Horæ in Greek, printed by Aldus in 16mo in 1497, is a volume which, from its language, size, and rarity, is of the greatest importance for the literary and religious history of the time when it was printed. It is, therefore, in Mr. Grenville's library. The Virgil of 1501 is not only an elegant book, but it is the first book printed with that peculiar *Italic*, known as Aldine, and the first volume which Aldus printed, "forma enchiridii," as he called it, being expressly adapted to give poor scholars the means of purchasing for a small sum the works of the classical writers. This also is, therefore, among Mr. Grenville's books; and of one of the two editions of Virgil, both dated the same year, 1514, he purchased a large paper copy, because it was the more correct of the two.

'It was the merit of the work, the elegance of the volume, the "genuine" condition of the copy, etc., which together determined Mr. Grenville to purchase books printed on vellum, of which he collected nearly a hundred. He paid a very large sum for a copy of the Furioso of 1532, not because it was "on ugly vellum," as he very properly designated it, but because, knowing the importance of such an edition of such a work, and never having succeeded in procuring it on paper, he would rather have it on expensive terms and "ugly vellum," than not at all.

'By the bequest of Mr. Grenville's library, the collection of books printed on vellum now at the Museum, and comprising those formerly presented by George II., George III., and Mr. Cracherode, is believed to surpass that of any other National Library, except the King's Library at Paris, of which Van Pract justly speaks with pride, and all foreign competent and intelligent judges with envy and admiration. Injustice to the Grenville Library, the list of all its vellum books ought here to be inserted. As this cannot be done, some only of the most remarkable shall be mentioned. These are—the Greek Anthology of 1494; the Book of Hawking, of Juliana Berners, of 1496; the first edition of the Bible, known as the "Mazarine Bible," printed at Mentz about 1454; the Aldine Dante of 1502; the first Rationale of Durandus of 1459; the first edition of Fisher On the Psalms, of 1508; the Aldine Horace, Juvenal, Martial, and Petrarca, of 1501; the Livy of 1469; the Primer of Salisbury, printed in Paris in 1531; the Psalter of 1457, which supplies the place of the one now at Windsor, which belonged to the Royal Collection before it was transferred to the British Museum; the Sforziada, by Simoneta, of 1490, a most splendid volume even in so splendid a library; the Theuerdank of 1517; the Aulus Gellius and the Vitruvius of Giunta, printed in 1513, etc., etc. Of this identical copy of Vitruvius, formerly Mr. Dent's, the author of the Bibliographical Decameron wrote, "Let the enthusiastic admirers of a genuine vellum Junta—of the amplest size and in spotless condition—resort to the choice cabinet of Mr. Dent for such a copy of this edition of Vitruvius and Frontinus." The Aulus Gellius is in its original state, exactly as it was when presented to Lorenzo de' Medici, afterwards Duke of Urbino, to whom the edition was dedicated.'

In addition to the printed books, the Grenville Library contains sixty-four manuscripts, many of them being of great interest and value. The finest of them is a volume of exquisite miniature drawings by Giulio Clovio, executed by command of Philip II. of Spain, and representing the victories of the Emperor Charles V. This volume was formerly in the Escurial. Other notable manuscripts are the original drawings for Hariot's Virginia in the De Bry collection, made by John White; Norden's Description of Essex; the Third Voyage of Vespucius in Latin; and two very interesting documents relating to the Spanish Armada—one being an original letter from the Lords of the Council to the Lord High Admiral, regarding the preparation of the fleet, dated July 21, 1588; and the other, a Resolution of a Council of War, held by the admirals and captains of the fleet which dispersed the Armada, dated August 1, 1588. The former of these papers is signed by Chr. Hatton (Cancs.), W. Burghley, F. Knollys, T. Heneage, Poulet, and J. Wolley; the latter by

C. Howard, George Cumberland, T. Howarde, Edmonde Sheffeylde, Fr. Drake, Edw. Hoby, John Hawkyns, and Thomas Fenner.

There is a catalogue of Mr. Grenville's library in three parts (London, 1842-72). Parts 1 and 2 were compiled by Messrs. Payne and Foss, the booksellers of Pall Mall, who bought largely for him; and part 3 by Mr. W.B. Rye, the late Keeper of the Department of Printed Books, British Museum.

A portrait of Mr. Grenville by Hoppner has been engraved for Fisher's *National Portrait Gallery*. There is also a painting of him by Phillips at Althorp, and a miniature by C. Manzini in the National Portrait Gallery.

A bust of him, presented by Sir David Dundas, is placed in the room in the British Museum occupied by his library.

FRANCIS DOUCE, 1757-1834

Francis Douce, who was born in 1757, was a son of Thomas Douce, one of the Six Clerks of the Court of Chancery. He was first sent to a school at Richmond, conducted by a Mr. Lawton, author of a work on Egypt, and afterwards to 'a French academy, kept by a pompous and ignorant Life-Guardsman, with a view to his learning merchants' accounts, which were his aversion.' On leaving school he studied for the bar, and for some time held an appointment, under his father, in the Six Clerks' Office, but the post was not very congenial to him, as from an early age he devoted himself to books and antiquities, and he also had a great passion for music. His father, who died in 1799, bequeathed the greater part of his property, which was very considerable, to his elder son, leaving but a comparatively small amount to be divided between Francis and his sisters, but in 1823 Nollekens, the sculptor, left Douce so large a portion of his fortune that at the decease of the latter his property was valued at nearly eighty thousand pounds. In 1807 he succeeded the Rev. Robert Nares as Keeper of the Manuscripts in the British Museum, but resigned the post in 1812 in consequence of some trifling disagreement with one of the trustees. While holding this office he took part in the preparation of the catalogues of the Harleian and Lansdowne manuscripts. Douce published in 1807 *Illustrations of Shakspeare and Ancient Manners*, and in 1833 *The Dance of Death*, 'exhibited in elegant Engravings on wood, with a Dissertation on the several Representations on that Subject.' The substance of this Dissertation had appeared about forty years before in illustration of Hollar's etchings, published by Edwards of Pall Mall, London. In addition to these works he edited Arnold's *Chronicle* in 1811, two books for the Roxburghe Club in 1822 and 1824, and assisted in the production of Scott's *Sir Tristram*, Smith's *Vagabondiniana*, and the 1824 edition of Warton's *History of English Poetry*. Many papers also by him are to be found in the *Archæologia*, the *Vetusta Monumenta*, and the *Gentleman's Magazine*. Douce was a prominent Fellow of the Society of Antiquaries, and numbered among his friends Isaac D'Israeli, the Rev. C.M. Cracherode, Sir George Staunton, Mr. John Towneley, and Dr. Dibdin, to the last of whom he left five hundred pounds. He is introduced under the name of *Prospero* in Dibdin's *Bibliomania*. Douce died at his residence in Gower Street, London, on the 30th of March 1834, and he left in his will two hundred pounds to Sir Anthony Carlisle 'requesting him either to sever my head or extract the heart from my body, so as to prevent the possibility of the return of vitality.' His valuable collection of printed books, which consisted of sixteen thousand four hundred and eighty volumes, with a quantity of fragments of early English works, including two printed by Caxton, which are unique; three hundred and ninety-three manuscripts, many of them beautifully illuminated; ninety-eight charters; a large number of valuable drawings and prints; together with a collection of coins and medals, were left by him to the Bodleian Library. It is said that this bequest was the result of the courteous reception he received from Dr. Bandinel, the librarian, when Douce visited Oxford with Isaac D'Israeli in 1830. The carvings in ivory or other materials, and the miscellaneous curiosities, were bequeathed to Dr., afterwards Sir Samuel Rush Meyrick, of Goodrich Castle, Wales, who published an account of them, entitled *The Doucean Museum*. To the British Museum Douce left a volume of the works of Albert Dürer which had formerly belonged to Nollekens, his impressions from monumental brasses, and his 'commented copies of the blockhead Whitaker's History of Manchester, and his Cornwall Cathedral.' His will also directs his executor 'to collect together all my letters and correspondence, all my private manuscripts, and unfinished or even finished essays or intended work or works, memorandum books, especially such as are marked in the inside of their covers with a red cross, with the exception only of such articles as he may think proper to destroy, as my diaries, or other articles of a merely private nature, and to put them into a strong box, to be sealed up without lock or key, and with a brass plate inscribed "Mr. Douce's papers, to be opened on the 1st of January 1900," and then to deposit this box in the British Museum, or, if the Trustees should decline receiving it, I then wish it to remain with the other things bequeathed to the Bodleian Library.' The Trustees accepted the charge of the box, and it was opened at the time appointed, but nothing of literary value was found in it.

A catalogue of the printed books, manuscripts, charters and fragments presented by Douce to the Bodleian was published in 1840, and there is also a manuscript catalogue of the prints and drawings.

JAMES EDWARDS, 1757-1816

James Edwards, who was so ardent a collector that he directed that his coffin should be made out of the shelves of his library, was born in 1757. He was the eldest son of William Edwards, an eminent bookseller of Halifax, Yorkshire, who was noted both for his success in collecting rare books, and his skill and taste in binding them. In 1784 James Edwards and, along with him, his younger brother John, were set up by their father as booksellers in Pall Mall, London, under the title of Edwards and Sons. John died soon afterwards, but the business was conducted with great ability and success by the elder brother, who, Dibdin says, 'travelled diligently and fearlessly abroad; now exploring the book-gloom of dusty monasteries, and at other times marching in the rear or front of Bonaparte's armies in Italy.'

Edwards was a bookbinder as well as a bookseller, and in 1785 he took out a patent for 'embellishing books bound in vellum by making drawings on the vellum which are not liable to be defaced but by destroying the vellum itself.' This was accomplished by rendering the vellum transparent, and then painting or impressing the design on the under surface. The British Museum possesses a Prayer Book bound by Edwards in this manner for Queen Charlotte, wife of King George III., which is a very skilful and artistic piece of work. Both he and his father were also celebrated for the pretty paintings with which they decorated the edges of the leaves of the books they bound. In 1788 Edwards, accompanied by his friend and fellow bookseller James Robson, went to Venice for the purpose of purchasing the Pinelli Library, which they brought to England, and sold by auction in the following year. Many other collections of note were sold by him during the twenty years he remained in business. Having amassed a considerable fortune, he determined to retire from trade, and in 1805 purchased the fine old manor-house at Harrow, which for some time was one of the residences of the Archbishops of Canterbury. A part of Dibdin's *Bibliographical Decameron* was written on the garden terrace of this mansion, Edwards being the 'Rinaldo' of that work. In consequence of ill-health he determined in 1815 to part with the remainder of his library (a portion of the books had been disposed of by Christie on his retirement in 1804), and it was sold by his successor in the Pall Mall business, Robert Harding Evans, who became so well known as a book auctioneer. The sale consisted of but eight hundred and thirty lots, but it realised the large sum of eight thousand four hundred and twenty-one pounds, seventeen shillings. Edwards died at Harrow on the 2nd of January 1816, and a monument was erected to his memory in the parish church.

Edwards's collection was not a large one, but it contained some exceedingly rare and choice manuscripts and printed books. Among the most precious of the former was the famous Bedford Book of Hours, which he acquired at the Duchess of Portland's sale in 1786 for two hundred and thirteen pounds, and which was purchased at his own sale by the Marquis of Blandford, afterwards Duke of Marlborough, for six hundred and eighty-seven pounds, fifteen shillings. It is now in the British Museum. Other fine manuscripts were a copy of the Gospels in Greek, written in the tenth century; *Opera Horatii*, executed for Ferdinand I. King of Naples, which realised respectively two hundred and ten and one hundred and twenty-five pounds; and *Regole e Precetti della Pittura*, written by Leonardo da Vinci, and illustrated with original drawings by Nicholas Poussin, which fetched one hundred and two pounds, eighteen shillings.

Among the printed books were the Latin Bible, on vellum, printed at Mentz, by Fust and Schoeffer, in 1462, which realised one hundred and seventy-five pounds; and the first edition of Livy, also on vellum, printed by Sweynheym and Pannartz at Rome about 1469. This copy, the only one known on vellum, belonged to Pope Alexander VI., and was bought by Sir M.M. Sykes for nine hundred and three pounds. It was afterwards acquired by the Right Hon. Thomas Grenville, and bequeathed by him to the British Museum. Luther's own copy of the first edition of his translation of the Bible after his final revision, printed at Wittemberg in 1541, with MS. notes by himself, Bugenhagen and Melanchthon, which is also now in the British Museum, sold for eighty-nine pounds, five shillings; and a splendid set of the *Opere di Piranesi* for three hundred and fifteen pounds. A fine and perfect block-book, the *Biblia Pauperum*, was also among the treasures of the library, and was purchased by the Duke of Devonshire for two hundred and ten pounds.

GEORGE HIBBERT, 1757-1837

George Hibbert was born at Manchester in the year 1757. His father was Robert Hibbert, a West India merchant. Destined from his boyhood to a commercial life, he was educated at a private school, and on leaving Lancashire he joined a London firm engaged in the West India trade, in which, first as a junior partner, and afterwards as the head of the firm, he remained nearly half a century. In 1798 Mr. Hibbert was elected an alderman, but resigned his gown in 1803, and in 1806 he entered Parliament as one of the members for Seaford, Sussex, and sat for that borough until 1812. He was also chairman of the West India merchants, and agent for Jamaica. The construction of the West India Docks was largely owing to his exertions, and as one of the original members of the committee of the London Institution, he took a prominent part in its foundation and management, and for many years he filled the office of president. Mr. Hibbert was elected a Fellow of the Royal Society in 1811, and a Fellow of the Society of Antiquaries in the following year. He was also a Fellow of the Linnæan Society, and formed at his residence at Clapham a large collection of exotic plants, many of which were first introduced into this country by the agents he employed in almost every part of the globe. He married Elizabeth Margaret, daughter of Mr. Philip Fonnereau, by whom he had a large family. Mr. Hibbert died on the 8th of October 1837, at Munden House, near Watford, Hertfordshire, and was buried in the churchyard of Aldenham, in the same county.

Mr. Hibbert, who was the 'Honorio' of Dibdin's *Bibliographical Decameron*, was a patron of art, and an enthusiastic collector of books, pictures, and prints and drawings. He formed a splendid library at his houses at Clapham, and in Portland Place, London, which is believed to have cost him at least thirty-five thousand pounds. It contained a large number of early printed Bibles, and was particularly rich in rare editions of the French Romances, and of English and Italian Poetry. No fewer than eighty of the books were printed on vellum. The collection also comprised twenty-five manuscripts.

When, in 1829, Mr. Hibbert retired to his estate of Munden, which had been bequeathed to him by Mr. Roger Parker, an uncle of his wife, he found that the size of his new residence rendered it necessary that he should dispose of the greater part of his collections, and his library was sold by auction by Mr. Evans at 93 Pall Mall in three divisions. The sales occupied altogether forty-two days. The first commenced on the 16th of March, and the last on the 25th of May 1829. There were eight thousand seven hundred and ninety-four lots, representing about twenty thousand volumes; and the total amount realised was twenty-one thousand seven hundred and fifty-three pounds, nine shillings. The books sold for comparatively small sums. A copy of the sale catalogue, with the prices obtained for the books and the names of the purchasers, is preserved in the library of the British Museum.

The following are a few of the principal books in this magnificent collection, together with the prices they fetched at the sale: —

The Gutenberg Bible, two hundred and fifteen pounds.

The Mentz Psalter of 1459, ninety pounds, six shillings.

The Latin Bible printed by Fust and Schoeffer at Mentz in 1462, one hundred and twenty-eight pounds, two shillings.

The Latin Bible, printed at Paris in 1476, thirty-two pounds, eleven shillings.

The Latin Bible, printed by Jenson at Venice in 1479. A very fine copy, which formerly belonged to Pope Sixtus IV., ninety-eight pounds, fourteen shillings.

The Complutensian Polyglot Bible, said to have been Cardinal Ximenes's own copy, for which Mr. Hibbert gave sixteen thousand one hundred francs at the sale, five hundred and twenty-five pounds.

Luther's own copy of the first edition of his translation of the Bible after his final revision. This volume, which is now in the British Museum, contains his autograph, and also the autographs of Bugenhagen, Melanchthon, and G. Major, two hundred and sixty-seven pounds.

The first and second editions of Cicero's *Officia*, printed by Fust and Schoeffer at Mentz in 1465 and 1466, eighty-two pounds, ten shillings; and fifty-nine pounds.

Cicero's *Epistolæ ad Familiares*, printed by Joannes de Spira at Venice in 1469, eighty pounds.

Petrarch's *Sonetti, Canzoni e Trionfi*, printed by Jenson at Venice in 1473; the only copy known on vellum, eighty pounds, seventeen shillings.

A presentation copy to Cardinal Sforza of the *Sforziada*, printed at Milan in 1490; in the original velvet binding, with silver knops, one hundred and sixty-eight pounds. The last two volumes are now preserved in the Grenville Library in the British Museum.

Poliphili Hypnerotomachia, printed by Aldus at Venice in 1499, eighty-two pounds, nineteen shillings.

Missale Vallisumbrose, printed by Lucantonio di Giunta at Venice in 1503, sixty-four pounds, one shilling.

All the above books are printed on vellum. The library also contained several fine block-books: the first edition of the *Speculum Humanæ Salvationis*, the *Apocalypsis*, and the first edition of *Ars Memorandi*, which sold respectively for eighty pounds; thirty-one pounds, ten shillings; and twenty-six pounds, ten shillings. The *Catholicon* of Joannes Balbus de Janua, printed at Mentz in 1460, and five Caxtons: the first edition of the *Dictes or Sayings of the Philosophers*, *Fayts of Arms*, the second edition of the *Mirrour of the World*, the *Recuyell of the Histories of Troye*, and the *Royal Book*, were to be found in the collection. Thirty-six pounds, four shillings and sixpence was obtained for the *Catholicon*, and three hundred and thirty-nine pounds, thirteen shillings and sixpence for the Caxtons. Of these the *Recuyell* fetched the highest price—one hundred and fifty-seven pounds, ten shillings. Some other notable books in this marvellous library were the Dante, printed at Florence in 1481, which realised forty pounds, nineteen shillings; the first edition of the *Teseide* of Boccaccio, which was disposed of for one hundred and sixty pounds; a very fine copy of Smith's *Historie of Virginia*, which sold for thirteen guineas; and the first four folio Shakespeares. The prices obtained for these were eighty-five pounds, one shilling; thirteen pounds; twenty-four pounds; and three pounds, nine shillings.

The more important manuscripts were *Præparatio ad Missam*, written and illuminated for Pope Leo X., which fetched ninety-nine pounds, fifteen shillings; *Droits d'Armes et de Noblesse*, ninety-four pounds, ten shillings; *Roman de la Rose*, eighty-four pounds; *Missale Romanum*, sixty-one pounds, nineteen shillings; and *Romant des Trois Pelerinages*, thirty-one pounds, ten shillings. These were all written on vellum.

In 1819 Mr. Hibbert printed for the Roxburghe Club, from a manuscript preserved in the Pepysian Library at Magdalen College, Cambridge, *Six Bookes of Metamorphoseos by Ovyde*, translated from the French by Caxton, together with some prefatory remarks by himself.

REV. CHARLES BURNEY, D.D., 1757-1817

Charles Burney, the second son of Charles Burney, the author of *The History of Music*, was born at Lynn, Norfolk, in the early part of December (the exact date is uncertain) 1757. He was educated at the Charterhouse, and Caius College, Cambridge, but left the University without taking a degree. He afterwards became a student of King's College, Aberdeen, where he graduated M.A. in 1781. After leaving the College he devoted himself to educational work, and for a short time was an assistant master at Highgate School, which he left to join Dr. William Rose, the translator of Sallust, in his school at Chiswick. In 1786, having married Rose's second daughter in 1783, he opened a school of his own at Hammersmith, which he carried on until 1793, when he removed to Greenwich, and there established a very flourishing academy, which in 1813 he made over to his son, the Rev. Charles Parr Burney. Late in life (1807) Burney took orders, and was appointed to the Rectory of St. Paul's, Deptford, Kent, and in a short time after to the Rectory of Cliffe in the same county. In 1811 he was made Chaplain to the King, and in 1817, a few months before his death, he was collated to a prebendal stall in Lincoln Cathedral. He received the degree of LL.D. from the Universities of Aberdeen and Glasgow in 1792, the degree of M.A. was conferred on him by Cambridge University in 1808, and that of D.D. by the Archbishop of Canterbury in 1812. Burney, who was the friend and companion of Dr. Parr and Professor Porson, wrote several works on the Greek and Latin Classics, as well as one or two of a theological nature. He died of apoplexy at Deptford on the 28th of December 1817, and a monument to his memory was erected in Westminster Abbey by a number of his old scholars.

Dr. Burney realised a considerable fortune by his scholastic work, and the money which he thus acquired enabled him to form a library of nearly thirteen thousand five hundred volumes of printed books, and five hundred and twenty manuscripts. Among the latter was the Towneley Homer, believed to be of the thirteenth century, and valued at six hundred guineas. The library was particularly rich in the Greek Classics, especially the dramatists; comprising as many as one hundred and sixty-six editions of Euripides, one hundred and two of Sophocles, and forty-seven of Æschylus, the margins of a large proportion of the classical books being covered with notes in Burney's hand, in addition to those by the Stephens, Bentley, Markland, and others. Another very interesting feature of the library was the large number of English newspapers it contained. These papers, which reached from the reign of James I. until nearly the end of that of George III., were bound in about seven hundred volumes, and now form the basis of the splendid collection in the British Museum. Dr. Burney also amassed from three to four hundred volumes containing materials for a history of the British Stage, and several thousand portraits of literary and theatrical personages. On the death of the Doctor his library was purchased for the British Museum for the sum of thirteen thousand five hundred pounds.

GEORGE JOHN, SECOND EARL SPENCER, 1758-1834

George John, second Earl Spencer, was born on the 1st of September 1758. He was the only son of John Spencer, who was created Viscount Spencer of Althorp in 1761, and Earl Spencer in 1765, and grandson of John, the youngest son of Charles Spencer, third Earl of Sunderland. At seven years of age he was placed under the tutorship of William Jones, the famous Orientalist, who was afterwards knighted, with whom he made two Continental tours. Jones resigned his charge in 1770, when Lord Althorp was sent to Harrow, and, on leaving school, to Trinity College, Cambridge. In 1780 he entered Parliament as member for Northampton, and on the formation of the second Rockingham Ministry in March 1782 he became a Commissioner of the new Treasury Board. On the death of his father in 1783, Lord Althorp (who had married in 1781 Lavinia, eldest daughter of Charles, first Lord Lucan) succeeded to the title, and in 1784 was sent with Mr. Thomas Grenville on a special mission to the Court of Vienna. During his absence from England, on the 19th of July in that year, he was made Lord Privy Seal in Mr. Pitt's Ministry, which office he resigned in the following December for that of First Lord of the Admiralty, a post which he held with great credit for upwards of six years. After his retirement from the Admiralty in February 1801, Lord Spencer remained out of office until February 1806, when he accepted the Secretaryship of State for the Home Department in the Grenville-Fox Ministry. On the dissolution of that ministry in March 1807, he finally retired from office, but continued to take part in the debates in the House of Lords. He died on the 10th of November 1834, and was succeeded by his eldest son John Charles.

Lord Spencer was a most energetic and enlightened collector of books, and the magnificent library which, until the year 1892, was one of the glories of Althorp, testifies to the skill and liberality with which he collected them. A taste for literature and a love of books were developed in Lord Spencer at an early age, and he was but thirty-two when he acquired the choice collection of Count Reviczky, a Hungarian nobleman, which at once placed his library among the more important private collections of the time. He also bought largely at the Mason, Herbert, Roxburghe, Alchorne, and other sales, and after the dispersion of the famous library at White Knights in 1819 he was able to acquire, at a cost of seven hundred and fifty pounds, the copy of the Valdarfer Boccaccio for which he had vainly bid two thousand two hundred and fifty pounds seven years before at the Roxburghe sale. In the years 1819 and 1820 he made a bibliographical tour on the Continent, during which, among other purchases, he acquired the library of the Duke of Cassano-Serra, which contained some very rare fifteenth century books.

Lord Spencer was considerably assisted in the formation of his famous collection by his librarian, the well-known Dr. Thomas Frognall Dibdin, the author of *Bibliomania*, *The Bibliographical Decameron*, and other pleasant and gossiping, but somewhat verbose and not particularly accurate, works on books, their printers and owners. Dibdin's services were liberally rewarded; and Edwards, in his work *Libraries and Founders of Libraries*, states that in addition to his stipend as librarian, 'Lord Spencer insured his librarian's life for the advantage of his family. Lord Spencer also gave him the vicarage of Exning, in Suffolk, in 1823, and obtained for him, on Episcopal recommendation, the rectory of St. Mary, Bryanstone Square, at the end of the same year.' Dibdin was the first to suggest the establishment of the Roxburghe Club, of which he became vice-president. He died in 1847.

The collection at Althorp, which Renouard described as 'the most beautiful and richest private library in Europe,' amounted in 1892 to about forty-one thousand five hundred volumes. Other private libraries have possessed more books, but none could boast of choicer ones. It contained the earliest dated example of wood-engraving — the figure of St. Christopher, with the date 1423; and no less than fourteen block-books, comprising three editions of the *Ars Moriendi*, three of the *Speculum Humanæ Salvationis*, two of the *Apocalypsis S. Johannis*, together with copies of the *Biblia Pauperum*, *Ars Memorandi*, *Historia Virginis ex Cantico Canticorum*, *Wie die fünfzehen zaichen kimen vor dem hingsten tag*, the *Enndchrist*, and *Mirabilia Romæ*. It was particularly rich in Bibles, among which were the Gutenberg and

Bamberg Bibles, the Coverdale Bible of 1535, and a magnificent copy of the Antwerp Polyglot, once the property of De Thou. It also contained the first and second Mentz Psalters. The Classics, too, were splendidly represented. The editions of works by Cicero numbered upwards of seventy, about fifty of which were printed before 1473; while fifteen of those of Virgil were prior to the year 1476. Among these were the second edition by Sweynheym and Pannartz, most probably printed in 1471, which is not less rare than the first, and the famous 'Adam' edition, which issued from the press in that year. These two volumes were obtained from the library of the King of Wirtemberg, Dibdin making a special journey to Stuttgart to purchase them. The library also possessed a large number of the early editions of Dante, Petrarch, Boccaccio, and other Italian Classics; and no less than fifty-two Caxtons, three of them unique, were to be found on its shelves. A splendid descriptive catalogue of the library, entitled 'Bibliotheca Spenceriana,' was compiled by Dibdin in the years 1814-23.

Lord Spencer maintained his interest in his books to the end of his life, and in the year before that of his death he wrote to Dibdin, 'I am trying my hand at a Classed Catalogue.'

In August 1892 this noble collection was purchased by Mrs. Rylands, widow of the late Mr. John Rylands, of Longford Hall, near Manchester, for a sum which was said to be little less than a quarter of a million sterling; and on the 6th of October 1899 she presented it, together with a handsome building for its reception, to the city of Manchester, in memory of her husband. An excellent catalogue, both of the printed books and the manuscripts, in three handsome quarto volumes, compiled by Mr. Gordon Duff, the librarian, accompanied this munificent gift.

SIR RICHARD COLT HOARE, Bart., 1758-1838

Sir Richard Colt Hoare, Bart., the historian of Wiltshire, was born on the 9th of December 1758. He was the son of Richard Hoare, Esq., of Barn Elms, Surrey (who was created a baronet in 1786), by Anne, second daughter of Henry Hoare, Esq., of Stourhead, Wiltshire, and of Susanna, daughter and heiress of Stephen Colt, Esq. He was privately educated, and at an early age entered the family bank (Messrs. Hoare's Bank, Fleet Street, London). In his work, *Pedigrees and Memoirs of the Families of Hore*, etc., he writes:—'Blessed by my parents with the advantages of a good education, I thereby acquired a love of literature and of drawing; of which, in my more advanced years, I feel the inestimable advantage. Destined, as I imagined, for an active and commercial life, I was unexpectedly and agreeably surprised to hear, shortly after my marriage, that my generous grandfather had intentions to remove me from the banking business, and to settle me on his estate in Wiltshire; which he put into execution during his lifetime, by making over to me all his landed property, with their appendages, at Stourhead and in the adjoining counties.' In 1783 Hoare married Hester, only daughter of Lord Westcote, afterwards created Lord Lyttelton, who died in 1785, leaving a son Henry Richard. In 1787, on the death of his father, he succeeded to the baronetcy. After the decease of his wife he made an extensive tour on the Continent, visiting France, Italy, Switzerland and Spain. In 1787 he returned home, but in the following year he paid a second visit to the Continent, and did not return to England until August 1791. During these tours he made a large number of drawings of interesting objects, and 'for the gratification of his family and friends' printed an account of his travels in four volumes. When he was no longer able to travel on the Continent in consequence of the French revolutionary war, Sir R.C. Hoare made a tour through Wales, taking Giraldus Cambrensis as a guide, and in 1806 he published a translation of the *Itinerarium Cambriæ* of Giraldus in two handsome volumes. He also contributed sixty-three drawings to Archdeacon Coxe's *Historical Tour in Monmouthshire*, which appeared in 1801. In 1807 he paid a visit to Ireland, and printed a short account of his excursion. In 1812 Hoare published in London the first part of his great work, the *Ancient History of Wiltshire*, which he completed in two volumes in 1821. This was followed by the *Modern History of Wiltshire* in fourteen parts, London, 1822-24, which was left unfinished at the time of his death. Hoare was the author of many works in addition to those already mentioned, some of which were intended only for private circulation. A list of them will be found in the Catalogue of the Hoare Library at Stourhead, compiled by John Bowyer Nichols in 1840. Hoare, who was a Fellow of the Royal Society and of the Society of Antiquaries, died at Stourhead on the 19th of May 1838. His only son predeceased him, and the baronetcy and estates devolved on his eldest half-brother, Henry Hugh Hoare of Wavendon, Buckinghamshire.

Sir R.C. Hoare possessed a noble library at Stourhead. The foundation of it no doubt was laid by his grandfather, Henry Hoare, whose bookplate occurs on many of the volumes, but it was Sir R.C. Hoare who brought together the magnificent collection of books on British topography, which was probably the finest private one ever formed. The water-colour drawings, the books of prints, and the engravings in the library were remarkable for their beauty, and had been selected with great judgment and taste. During his travels on the Continent between the years 1785 and 1791 Hoare acquired a large number of books relative to the history and topography of Italy. Of these he printed in 1812 a separate catalogue, the impression of which was limited to twelve copies. In 1825 he presented this collection to the British Museum, together with a copy of the catalogue, upon the fly-leaf of which he has written:—'Anxious to follow the liberal example of our gracious monarch George the Fourth, of Sir George Beaumont, Bart., of Rich^d. Payne Knight, Esq. (tho' in a very humble degree) I do give unto the British Museum, this my Collection of Topography, made during a residence of five years abroad—and hoping that the more modern publications may be added to it hereafter. Rich. Colt Hoare, A.D. 1825.' The Stourhead library was sold by auction on Monday, the 30th of July 1883 and seven following days, by Sotheby, Wilkinson and Hodge. The books, engravings and drawings, of which there were one thousand nine hundred and seventy-one lots, realised ten thousand and twenty-eight pounds, six shillings and sixpence. On the 9th of December 1887, and three following days, some more books belonging to the library were sold for one thousand three hundred and ninety-two pounds, eleven shillings and sixpence. The prices obtained for many of the books were exceptionally high.

WILLIAM BECKFORD, 1759-1844

William Beckford, the author of *Vathek*, was born at Fonthill, Wiltshire on the 29th of September 1759. He was the only legitimate child of Alderman William Beckford, who was twice Lord Mayor of London, and who died in 1770, leaving his son property worth upwards of one hundred thousand pounds a year. Beckford amassed at his residence at Fonthill a magnificent collection of books, pictures, furniture and curiosities of all kinds, but his extravagance and the depreciation of his West India property compelled him in 1823 to sell Fonthill and the greater part of its contents. He, however, retained a portion of his library and the best of his pictures, and removed them to Lansdown Tower, Bath, which he built on leaving Fonthill, and where he continued to add to his collections. Beckford married in 1783 Margaret, daughter of Charles, fourth Earl of Aboyne, by whom he had two daughters—Margaret and Susan Euphemia—the elder of whom married Colonel Orde, and the younger the Marquis of Douglas, who afterwards became Duke of Hamilton. The elder daughter having offended her father by her marriage with Colonel Orde, he left all his property to the Duchess of Hamilton. After Beckford's death on May the 2nd, 1844, the Duke of Hamilton wished to sell the library to Mr. Henry Bohn, who was willing to give thirty thousand pounds for it, but the Duchess objected to part with her father's books, and they were removed to Hamilton Palace, but kept separate from the noble library which already existed there. In the years 1882, 1883 and 1884 both these splendid collections were sold. The sale, or rather sales, of the Beckford books, for the collection was divided into four portions, took place at the auction rooms of Sotheby, Wilkinson and Hodge, and lasted altogether forty days; the first sale commencing on the 30th of June 1882 and lasting twelve days, and the last on the 27th of November 1883, and continuing for four days. The total number of lots in the four sales was nine thousand eight hundred and thirty-seven, and the amount realised seventy-three thousand five hundred and fifty-one pounds, eighteen shillings.

WILLIAM BECKFORD. From a Medallion by Singleton.

Beckford's library was rich in fine early printed books, rare voyages and travels, and choice French, Spanish and Italian works, but it was chiefly remarkable for its superb collection of beautiful and historical bindings. It contained a large number of volumes from the libraries of Grolier, Maioli, Lauwrin, Canevari, De Thou, Peiresc, and other distinguished collectors, and also examples of bindings bearing the arms and devices of Francis I. of France, Henry II. and Diana of Poitiers, Charles IX., Henry III., Henry IV., Louis XIII., Anne of Austria, etc.; many of the volumes being bound by Nicolas and Clovis Eve, Le Gascon, Padeloup, Derome, Monnier and other famous French binders. Very high prices were obtained for many of these splendid books—*Lactantii Opera*, printed in the Monastery of Subiaco by Sweynheym and Pannartz in 1465, sold for two hundred and eighty-five pounds; *Biblia Latina*, printed on vellum by N. Jenson at Venice in 1476, three hundred and thirty pounds; *Livre de Bien Vivre*, on vellum, finely illuminated, Paris, A. Verard, 1492, three hundred and thirty pounds; *Philostrati Vita Apollonii Tyanei*, printed by Aldus at Venice in 1502, Grolier's copy, bound in red morocco, three hundred pounds; *Lucanus*, printed by Aldus in 1515, Grolier's copy, bound in marbled calf, two hundred and ninety pounds;

Tirante il Bianco, Vinegia, 1538, red morocco, from the library of Demetrio Canevari, one hundred and eleven pounds; *Entree de Henry II. en Paris 6 Juing* 1549, etc., with the arms and cypher of de Thou on the binding, four hundred and seventy pounds; *Psalmorum Paraphrasis Poetica,* by G. Buchanan, beautifully bound in olive morocco, with the arms and cypher of De Thou, three hundred and ten pounds; *Livre de la Conqueste de la Toison d'Or par le Prince Jason,* par J. Gohory, Paris, 1563, in a beautiful binding by Nicolas Eve, with the arms of the Duke of Guise painted on the covers, four hundred and five pounds; *Poliphile Hypnerotomachie,* Paris, 1561, bound in blue morocco by Nicolas Eve for Louise de Lorraine, two hundred and twenty pounds; *Portraits des Rois, Hommes et Dames Illustres,* etc., a series of the engraved works of Sir Anthony Vandyck, including his own etchings, in three large folio volumes, two thousand eight hundred and fifty pounds; *Decor Puellarum,* printed by N. Jenson at Venice in 1471, in a splendid binding by Monnier—blue morocco, with flowers in various leathers, and with silk linings, five hundred and thirty pounds; and *Longi Pastoralia,* printed on vellum by P. Didot at Paris for Junot, Duke of Abrantes, with drawings by Prud'hon and F. Gérard, nine hundred pounds.

Beckford wrote other works besides *Vathek,* several of which he left in manuscript, and a large number of his books contained notes in his handwriting.

FREDERICK NORTH, FIFTH EARL OF GUILFORD, 1766-1827

Frederick North, fifth Earl of Guilford, was born on the 7th of February 1766. He was the third and youngest son of Frederick, second Earl, Prime Minister from January 1770 to March 1782. When his health, which was very delicate, permitted, he went to Eton, and afterwards became a student of Christ Church, Oxford. He was created D.C.L. in 1793, and received the same degree by diploma in 1819. In 1779, through his father's interest, he obtained the sinecure of one of the Chamberlains of the Tally Court of the Exchequer, and in 1794 he was appointed to the Comptrollership of the Customs of the Port of London, when he resigned the representation of the family borough of Banbury, to which he had succeeded when his eldest brother, George Augustus, came to the Earldom in 1792. North was Secretary of State to the Viceroy of the Ionian Islands during 1795 and 1796, and in 1798 he was made Governor of Ceylon, a post he held until July 1805. On the death of his brother Francis, the fourth Earl, in 1817, he succeeded to the Earldom of Guilford, and in 1819 he was created a Knight Grand Cross of the Order of St. Michael and St. George. He was a Fellow of the Royal Society and a Member of the Eumelean Club. Lord Guilford, who had been received into the Eastern Church at Corfu in 1791, died unmarried in London on the 14th of October 1827, and was succeeded by his cousin, the Rev. Francis North, Prebendary of Winchester and Master of the Hospital of St. Cross. Lord Guilford was a distinguished scholar, and a most accomplished linguist. He took the greatest interest in everything relating to Greek literature and art, and it was principally through his exertions, and with his money, that a University was founded in 1824 at Corfu, of which he was the first chancellor, and in which he resided until 1827, when he was obliged to return to England on account of his health. He left his collections of printed books, manuscripts, etc., at Corfu to the University, but in consequence of its failure to comply with certain conditions which accompanied the bequest, it was not carried out. Lord Guilford's fine library was sold by Evans, in seven parts, in the years 1828, 1829, 1830, andPg 323] 1835. The first sale took place on December 15th, 1828, and eight following days; and the others on

January 12th, 1829, and five following days; February 28th, 1829, and two following days; December 8th, 1830, and four following days; December 20th, 1830, and four following days; January 5th, 1831, and three following days; and November 9th, 1835, and seven following days. The last three sales were of the manuscripts and books removed from Corfu. There were eight thousand five hundred and eleven lots in the seven sales, which realised twelve thousand one hundred and seventy-eight pounds, ten shillings and sixpence.

Lord Guilford's collection was an excellent one, and, as might be expected, the Greek manuscripts in it were particularly numerous and choice. The printed books were good, but they were not equal to the manuscripts either in interest or value. Among the latter was the original manuscript of Tasso's *Gerusalemme Liberata*, with some alterations of verses in the margin, likewise in the handwriting of Tasso. This sold for two hundred and four pounds, fifteen shillings. Four Greek manuscripts of the eleventh century: a copy of the Four Gospels; the Greek Offices, with Intonations or Musical Directions for Chanting; an Evangelistarium and Menologium of the Greek Church; and Josephus's *Historia de Bello Judaico*, deserve special notice on account of their beauty and rarity. These fetched at the sale respectively one hundred and two pounds, eighteen shillings; one hundred and seventy-three pounds, five shillings; seventy-three pounds, ten shillings; and two hundred and seventy-three pounds. Another interesting manuscript was a copy of the New Testament in Glagolitic characters, which realised one hundred and sixty-eight pounds. Among the printed books may be mentioned a large paper copy of the first edition of the Sixtine Bible, printed at Rome in 1590, and suppressed by order of Gregory XIV., on account of the numerous inaccuracies in it, which realised sixty-three pounds; and the Duke of Northumberland's *Concio ad Populum Londinensem*, printed at Rome in 1570, of which the only other known copy is in the library of the Vatican, for which forty-two pounds was obtained.

GEORGE SPENCER CHURCHILL, FIFTH DUKE OF
MARLBOROUGH, 1766-1840

George Spencer Churchill, fifth Duke of Marlborough, the collector of the famous library at White Knights, near Reading, Berkshire, was the elder son of George, fourth Duke of Marlborough, by Caroline, only daughter of John, fourth Duke of Bedford. He was born on the 6th of March 1766, and was educated at Eton, and subsequently at Christ Church, Oxford, graduating M.A. in 1786 and D.C.L. in 1792. At the general election in 1790 he was returned to Parliament as one of the members for Oxfordshire, and in August 1804 he was appointed a Lord of the Treasury, which office he held until February 1806. On the 12th of March in the same year he was called to the House of Lords as Baron Spencer of Wormleighton, and on the death of his father on the 29th of January 1817 he succeeded to the dukedom. In the May following he was authorised to take and use the name of Churchill after that of Spencer, and to bear the arms of Churchill quarterly with those of Spencer, in order to perpetuate in his family the surname of his celebrated ancestor, John, first Duke of Marlborough. He married, on the 15th of September 1791, Susan, second daughter of John, seventh Earl of Galloway, by whom he had issue four sons and two daughters. He died on the 5th of March 1840, and was succeeded by his eldest son, George.

The splendid library which the Duke of Marlborough, while Marquis of Blandford, collected at White Knights was one of the finest in the kingdom. Its two great treasures were the Bedford Book of Hours, now in the British Museum, purchased by the Duke in 1815 at the sale of the library of James Edwards, for the sum of six hundred and ninety-eight pounds, five shillings; and the edition of Boccaccio's *Decameron*, printed by Valdarfer at Venice in 1471, which he acquired at the Duke of Roxburghe's sale in 1812, after a spirited contest with his relative, Earl Spencer, at the enormous price of two thousand two hundred and sixty pounds. This copy, Edward Edwards tells us (*Libraries and Founders of Libraries*), had been offered to Lord Sunderland for a hundred guineas just a century before one of his great-grandsons offered more than two thousand guineas for it, and was outbidden by another. Among many other choice manuscripts and rare books the library contained a beautiful Missal, said to have been executed for Diana of Poitiers; no fewer than eighteen Caxtons; the *Bokys of Hawkyng and Huntyng*, printed at St. Albans in 1486; a large number of very rare books from the presses of Machlinia, Pynson, Wynkyn de Worde, and other early English printers; a copy on vellum of the first edition of Luther's translation of the Bible after his final revision; a collection of Churchyard's Works in two volumes; many of the early editions of Shakespeare's plays, together with the first edition of his *Sonnets*; and Ireland's account of the Shakesperian Forgery, in his own handwriting. The collection was especially rich in missals, books of emblems, and Italian, Spanish, and French romances of chivalry, poetry, and facetiæ.

The extravagance of the Duke compelled him to dispose of his magnificent collection during his lifetime, and it was sold in two parts by Mr. Evans at 26 Pall Mall. The sale, which consisted of four thousand seven hundred and one lots, commenced on the 7th of June 1819 and lasted till the 3rd of July following. It realised but fourteen thousand four hundred and eighty-two pounds, ten shillings and sixpence, a much less sum than that paid for the books by the Duke. The Valdarfer Boccaccio sold for nine hundred and eighteen pounds, fifteen shillings, and the Caxtons fetched one thousand three hundred and sixteen pounds, twelve shillings and sixpence; the highest prices being obtained for Gower's *Confessio Amantis*, and Chaucer's *Troylus and Creside*, which realised two hundred and five pounds, sixteen shillings, and one hundred and sixty-two pounds, fifteen shillings. The Book of St. Albans, which was imperfect, fetched eighty-four pounds; Luther's translation of the Bible, two hundred and twenty pounds, ten shillings; Churchyard's Works, eighty-five pounds, one shilling; and Shakespeare's *Sonnets*, thirty-seven pounds. The Missal said to have been written for Diana of Poitiers sold for one hundred and ten pounds, five shillings.

ALEXANDER, TENTH DUKE OF HAMILTON, 1767-1852

A good library had no doubt existed in Hamilton Palace for a considerable period of time, but Alexander, tenth Duke of Hamilton, who was born on the 5th of October 1767, and died on the 18th of August 1852, was the first of his line who was a book-collector on an extensive scale. He formed a large and very choice collection of printed books, but that of his manuscripts was of still greater interest and value. It was wonderfully rich in Bibles and portions of the Scriptures, Missals, Breviaries and Books of Hours, many of them having been written and illuminated for Francis I., King of France, the Emperor Maximilian, Pope Leo X., the Duke of Guise, and other distinguished personages. The finest of these was a copy of the Gospels in Latin, known as 'The Golden Gospels,' written about the end of the eighth century in gold letters upon purple vellum, which was at one time the property of King Henry VIII. Another famous manuscript in the library, valued at five thousand pounds, was the *Divina Commedia* of Dante, illustrated with upwards of eighty original designs attributed to Sandro Botticelli, now in the Royal Library at Berlin.

In addition to his own books, the Duke acquired the whole of William Beckford's splendid collection by his marriage with Beckford's daughter Susan Euphemia. William, the eleventh Duke, who was born on February the 19th, 1811, and died on July the 15th, 1863, added considerably to the library, but his successor was reluctantly obliged to part with it, and it was advertised to be sold by auction on June 30th, 1882. Before, however, the time appointed for the sale, the Royal Museum at Berlin, by a private arrangement, acquired the whole of the manuscripts for a sum which is believed to have amounted to about seventy-five thousand pounds, and they were divided between that Institution and the Royal Library at Berlin. A portion of them, which related to Scottish history, was purchased of the Prussian authorities by the British Museum; and ninety-one other manuscripts which were not required by the Berlin Museum, including the 'Golden Gospels,' were sent to Sotheby, Wilkinson and Hodge, by whom they were sold on the 23rd of May

1889 for fifteen thousand one hundred and eighty-nine pounds, ten shillings and sixpence. The 'Golden Gospels' was bought by Mr. Quaritch for one thousand five hundred pounds. The printed books were sold by the same auctioneers on May 1st, 1884, and seven following days. The sale consisted of two thousand one hundred and thirty-six lots, and realised twelve thousand eight hundred and ninety-two pounds, twelve shillings and sixpence. The following are a few of the rarest and most interesting books, and the prices they fetched—*Boecius de Consolatione Philosophie*, printed by Caxton in 1477-78, one hundred and sixty pounds; Dante's *Commedia*, printed at Florence in 1481, with twenty engravings by Baccio Baldini, three hundred and eighty pounds; the Poems of Pindar in Greek, printed by Aldus in 1513, with the arms of France and the monogram and devices of Henry II. and Diana of Poitiers on the binding, one hundred and forty-one pounds; the Prince of Condé's copy of *L'Hystoire du Roy Perceforest*, Paris, 1528, with his arms on the covers, one hundred and eighteen pounds; a dedication copy, printed upon vellum, and bound for James V., King of Scotland, of Hector Boece's *History and Croniklis*, translated by Bellenden, and printed at Edinburgh in 1536, the binding having on the upper cover IACOBVS QVINTVS, and on the lower REX SCOTORVM, eight hundred pounds; a Collection of Architectural Designs, executed with pen and ink by J. Androuet du Cerceau, in a beautiful binding attributed to Clovis Eve, two hundred and forty pounds; De Bry's *Collectiones Peregrinationum*, in eleven volumes, bound in blue morocco by Derome, five hundred and sixty pounds; Book of Common Prayer, 1637, folio—King Charles I.'s copy, with numerous alterations in his own handwriting which were used in printing the Scottish Prayer-book of the same year, usually termed Laud's Book. Prefixed to the Order for Morning Prayer the King has written: 'Charles R.—I gave the Archbᴾ. of Canterbury comand to make the alteracons expressed in this Book and to fit a Liturgy for the Church of Scotland, and wheresoever they shall differ from another Booke signed by us at Hampᵗ. Court Septembʳ. 28, 1634, our pleasure is to have these followed rather than the former; unless the Archbᴾ. of St. Andrews and his Brethren who are upon the place shall see apparent reason to the contrary. At Whitehall, April 19, 1636'—one hundred and thirty-seven pounds.

The paintings and objects of art belonging to the Duke of Hamilton were sold in July 1882, and realised three hundred and ninety-seven thousand pounds.

SIR MARK MASTERMAN SYKES, BART., 1771-1823

Sir Mark Masterman Sykes, Bart., was the eldest son of Sir Christopher Sykes, second baronet, of Sledmere, Yorkshire. He was born on the 20th of August 1771, and in his seventeenth year was sent to Brasenose College, Oxford. In 1795 he served the office of High Sheriff of Yorkshire, and on the death of his father in 1801 he succeeded to the title and estates. He was elected Member of Parliament for the city of York in 1807; was again returned in 1812 and 1813, and retired on account of ill health in 1820. Sir M. Masterman Sykes was twice married. His first wife was Henrietta, daughter and heiress of Henry Masterman of Settrington, Yorkshire, and on his union with her in 1795 he assumed the additional name of Masterman. She died in 1813, and in the following year he married Mary Elizabeth, daughter of William Tatton Egerton, and sister of Wilbraham Tatton Egerton, of Tatton Park, who survived him. Sir Mark died at Weymouth, on his way to London, on the 16th of February 1823. He had no children, and was succeeded by his brother, Sir Tatton Sykes.

Sir M. Masterman Sykes early developed a love for books, and the magnificent library which he formed, one of the finest private collections in England, was the result of upwards of thirty years' unremitting and careful work. Some of the rare volumes it contained, we are informed in the preface to the sale catalogue of his library written by the Rev. H.J. Todd, 'were procured during the collector's travels abroad, but many of them were acquired at the dispersion of the libraries of Major Pearson, Dr. Farmer, Steevens, Reed, the Rev. Mr. Brand, the Duke of Roxburghe and others, but especially of that of the late Mr. Edwards, from whom the celebrated Livy of 1469 was obtained—the only known copy of the first edition of Livy on vellum.'

Among the principal treasures of the collection were the Gutenberg Bible; the Psalter of 1459, on vellum; the *Rationale Divinorum Officiorum* of Durandus, on vellum, 1459; the *Catholicon* of Joannes

Balbus de Janua, 1460; the Latin Bible of 1462, on vellum; and the Epistles of St. Jerome, on vellum, 1470: all printed at Mentz.

The library was especially rich in early editions of the Greek and Latin Classics, and on its shelves were to be found the only copy known to exist on vellum of the first edition of Livy, printed at Rome by Sweynheym and Pannartz about 1469, to which we have already referred; the first edition of Pliny, printed by Joannes de Spira at Venice in 1469; that printed at Rome by Sweynheym and Pannartz in 1470; a copy on vellum of the beautiful 1472 edition from the press of Nicolas Jenson of Venice; and the earliest editions of Homer, Cicero, Horace, Virgil, Tacitus, Terence, and Valerius Maximus.

The library also contained the Dante printed at Foligno in 1472, and that printed at Florence in 1481; the first issue of the Latin translation of the Letter of Columbus, printed at Rome in 1493; a fine copy of the *Poliphili Hypnerotomachia*, printed by Aldus at Venice in 1499; the Aldine Petrarch of 1501; several rare Missals and Books of Hours, the most notable of them being a vellum copy of the Vallombrosa Missal, printed at Florence in 1503; and a copy of the *Tewrdannck*, also on vellum, printed at Nuremberg in 1517.

There were several Caxtons, among them being *The Myrrour of the World* and Higden's *Polychronicon*.

The literature of the reigns of Elizabeth and James I. was well represented, and the library contained a copy of that rare work, Archbishop Parker's *De Antiquitate Ecclesiæ Britannicæ*.

The collection also comprised several fine and interesting manuscripts. Deserving especial notice were a beautiful illuminated Office, on vellum, of the Virgin Mary, executed for Francis I., King of France; the original Report of Convocation to Henry VIII. on the Legality of his proposed Divorce from Anne of Cleves, subscribed with the autograph signatures of the Archbishop and all the Bishops and Clergy assembled in Convocation, dated July 9th, 1540; and an autograph manuscript of Dugdale's Visitation of the County of York in 1665-66.

Sir M. Masterman Sykes possessed an immense collection of prints. It included a complete set of Bartolozzi's engravings which is said to have cost Sir Mark nearly five thousand pounds; his collection of portraits was considered to be one of the best in the kingdom; and Dibdin declared that his 'Faithornes and Hollars almost defied competition.' He also accumulated a considerable number of pictures, bronzes, coins and medals.

All the collections were dispersed by sale in 1824. The books were sold by Mr. Evans of Pall Mall in three parts, commencing on the 11th of May and continuing until the 28th of June. The total amount realised was eighteen thousand seven hundred and twenty-nine pounds, sixteen shillings. The prices obtained were by no means high. The Gutenberg Bible, which was a very fine one, fetched less than two hundred pounds, and the copy of the Mentz Psalter, for which Mr. Quaritch subsequently gave four thousand nine hundred and fifty pounds at Sir J. H. Thorold's sale in 1884, sold for one hundred and thirty-six pounds, ten shillings. The Latin Bible of 1462 was disposed of for the same sum; and the unique vellum Livy, which cost Sir Mark nine hundred and three pounds at the sale of Mr. Edwards's books in 1815, realised but four hundred and seventy-two pounds, ten shillings. This volume was bought by Messrs. Payne and Foss, who sold it to Mr. John Dent, and at the sale of his collection in 1827 it was acquired for two hundred and sixty-two pounds, ten shillings by the Right Hon. Thomas Grenville, who bequeathed it to the British Museum in 1846. The three manuscripts mentioned—The Office of the Virgin Mary, the Report of Convocation on Henry VIII.'s divorce from Anne of Cleves, and Dugdale's Visitation of the County of York—fetched respectively one hundred and sixty-three pounds, sixteen shillings; two hundred and fifteen pounds, five shillings; and one hundred and fifty-seven pounds, ten shillings.

Sir M. Masterman Sykes was one of the original members of the Roxburghe Club, and in 1818 printed for presentation to the members a portion of Lydgate's Poems. He was the 'Lorenzo' of Dibdin, who describes him as 'not less known than respected for the suavity of his manners, the kindness of his disposition, and the liberality of his conduct in all matters connected with books and prints.'

RICHARD HEBER, 1773-1833

Richard Heber, styled by Sir Walter Scott 'Heber the Magnificent, whose library and cellar are so superior to all others in the world,' was the eldest son of Reginald Heber, lord of the manors of Marton in Yorkshire, and Hodnet in Shropshire, and was half-brother to Reginald Heber, Bishop of Calcutta. He was born in Westminster on the 5th of January 1773, and was first educated under the private tuition of the Rev. George Henry Glasse; afterwards proceeding to Brasenose College, Oxford, where he graduated B.A. in 1796, and M.A. in the following year. In 1822 the University conferred on him the degree of D.C.L. On the death of his father in 1804, Heber succeeded to the estates in Yorkshire and Shropshire, which he considerably augmented and improved. He was one of the founders of the Athenæum Club, and in 1821 he was elected a representative in Parliament for the University of Oxford, but resigned his seat in 1826. From his earliest years he was an ardent collector, and Dibdin says that he had seen a catalogue of Heber's books, compiled by him at the age of eight; and when ten years old he requested his father to buy some volumes at a certain sale, where 'there would be the best editions of the classics.' Of many of his books he possessed several copies, and on being asked by a friend why he purchased them, he seriously replied: 'Why, you see, Sir, no man can comfortably do without *three* copies of a book. One he must have for his show copy, and he will probably keep it at his country house. Another he will require for his own use and reference; and unless he is inclined to part with this, which is very inconvenient, or risk the injury of his best copy, he must needs have a third at the service of his friends.' Soon after the peace of 1815 Heber paid a visit to the Continent to collect books for his library, and in 1825 he again left England for a considerable period for the purpose of still further adding to his literary stores. On his return in 1831 he spent his time in seclusion between his country residence at Hodnet, near Shrewsbury, and his house at Pimlico, devoting himself to the last days of his life to the increase of his immense collection. He died at Pimlico of an attack on the lungs, accompanied with jaundice, on the 4th of October 1833, and was buried at Hodnet on the 16th of the following month. The

Rev. Mr. Dyce in a letter to Sir Egerton Brydges, gives a melancholy account of his end. 'Poor man,' he writes, 'he expired at Pimlico, in the midst of his rare property, *without a friend to close his eyes*, and from all I have heard I am led to believe he died broken-hearted: he had been ailing for some time, but took no care of himself, and seemed indeed to court death. Yet his ruling passion was strong to the last. The morning he died he wrote out some memoranda for Thorpe about books which he wished to be purchased for him. He was the most liberal of book-collectors: I never asked him for the loan of a volume, *which he could lay his hand on*, he did not immediately send me.[91] Heber, who was a man of deep learning, numbered among his friends Porson, Cracherode, Canning, Southey, Dr. Burney, Sir Walter Scott, and many other distinguished persons. Sir Walter dedicated the sixth canto of *Marmion* to him, and alludes to his library in the following lines: —

> 'Thy volumes, open as thy heart,
> Delight, amusement, science, art,
> To every ear and eye impart;
> Yet who, of all who thus employ them,
> Can like the owner's self enjoy them? —
> But, hark! I hear the distant drum!
> The day of Flodden Field is come. —
> Adieu, dear Heber! Life and health,
> And store of literary wealth.'

The number of volumes accumulated by Heber was enormous. He collected manuscripts as well as printed books. At the time of his death he possessed eight houses overflowing with books. At Hodnet he had built a new library which he is said to have filled with volumes selected on account of their fine condition; and so careful was he of these, that occasionally he used to engage the whole of the inside places of the coach for their conveyance from London. The walls of all the rooms and passages of his house at Pimlico were lined with books; and another house in York Street, Westminster, which he used as a depository for newly purchased books, was literally crammed with them from the floors to the ceilings. He had a library in the High Street, Oxford; an immense collection at Paris, which was sold in the years 1834 to 1836; another at Ghent, sold in 1835; and others at Brussels and Antwerp, together with smaller gatherings in several places on the Continent. Dibdin estimated the total number of volumes in Heber's collections in England at one hundred and twenty-seven thousand five hundred, but other calculations have placed it at a somewhat lower figure. The whole of the libraries which he possessed in England and on the Continent probably contained from one hundred and forty-five thousand to one hundred and fifty thousand volumes, as well as a very large number of pamphlets; and they are believed to have cost him about a hundred thousand pounds. As Heber was an accomplished scholar as well as a collector, his books were chosen with ability and judgment. He was a purchaser at every great sale, and so keen was he in the prosecution of his favourite pursuit, that on hearing of a rare book he has been known to undertake a coach journey of several hundred miles to obtain it. His library was particularly rich in the works of the early English poets, and his collection of Greek and Latin Classics, Spanish, Italian, Portuguese and French books was very extensive and choice, but he had a great objection to large paper copies, because they occupied so much room on his shelves. He possessed also a number of books printed in Mexico; and among his manuscripts were to be found the letters and papers of Sir Julius Cæsar, the autograph manuscript of *The Monastery*, by Sir Walter Scott, and a large collection of the letters of distinguished men. For a considerable period his will could not be found, although diligent search was made for it, both at home and abroad, and his sister, Mrs. Cholmondeley, was on the point of taking out letters of administration, when it was accidentally discovered by Dr. Dibdin among some books on an upper shelf at Pimlico. As it did not contain any directions as to the disposal of his books, those in England, together with some brought from Holland, were sold by Sotheby and Son, Evans, and Wheatley at a series of sales extending over four years, and realised fifty-seven thousand five hundred and fifty-four pounds, twelve shillings. The catalogue is in thirteen parts, bearing the dates 1834-37. His books on the Continent, with the drawings and coins, fetched about ten thousand pounds more.

Heber edited the works of Persius Flaccus, Silius Italicus, and Claudianus. He also reprinted the *Caltha Poetarum, or the Bumble Bee,* of T. Cutwode, from the edition of 1599, for the Roxburghe Club, and assisted in the preparation of the third edition of Ellis's *Specimens of the Early English Poets.*

FOOTNOTES:

[91] *The Book Fancier.* By Percy Fitzgerald (London, 1887), p. 230.

RICHARD GRENVILLE, FIRST DUKE OF BUCKINGHAM, 1776-1839

Richard Temple Nugent Brydges Chandos Grenville, first Duke of Buckingham, was born in London on the 20th of March 1776. He was the eldest son of George Grenville, Earl Temple, who was made Marquis of Buckingham in 1784. He began collecting books at a very early age, and in 1798 had already commenced the formation of a library at Stowe; and the acquisition of the manuscripts and papers of Thomas Astle, Keeper of the Records in the Tower; the Irish manuscripts from Belanagare, the seat of The O'Conor Don; the State Papers of Arthur Capel, Earl of Essex, Lord-Lieutenant of Ireland in the reign of Charles II., together with some other purchases, placed his library among the finest private collections in the kingdom.[92] On the death of his father in 1813 he succeeded to the title, and nine years later he was created Duke of Buckingham and Chandos. In 1827, in consequence of his great expenditure on his various collections, and the munificence with which he had entertained the royal family of France, he found himself in embarrassed circumstances, and left England, remaining abroad about two years. In 1834 he was compelled to sell his furniture, pictures, and articles of virtù, but did not part with his books, which, on his death on the 17th of January 1839, passed into the possession of his only son, Richard Plantagenet Temple Nugent Brydges Chandos Grenville, who was born on February the 11th, 1797. The habits of the son were not less extravagant than those of his father, and in 1847 the effects at Stowe and his other residences were seized by bailiffs, and in August and September 1848 the pictures, furniture, china, plate, etc., were sold by auction, realising over seventy-five thousand five hundred pounds. The printed books in the library were sold by Sotheby and Wilkinson, on January 8th, 1849, and eleven following days, and January 29, and eleven following days. There were six thousand two hundred and twelve lots in the two sales, which brought ten thousand three hundred and fifty-five pounds, seven shillings and sixpence. The extensive and valuable series of engraved portraits contained in the Duke's illustrated copy of the *Biographical History of England*, by the Rev. James Granger, was sold by the same auctioneers on March 5th and eight following days, and a continuation of it by the Rev. Mark Noble, together with some other engravings, on the 21st of March and five following days. There were two thousand two hundred and one lots in these two sales, for which the sum of three thousand seven hundred and ninety-nine pounds, eighteen shillings and sixpence was obtained. The manuscripts were bought by the Earl of Ashburnham for eight thousand pounds. The collection of printed books in the Stowe library was inferior in interest to that of the manuscripts, but it contained some rare and choice volumes. Amongst them was a block-book, *The Apocalypse*, which sold for ninety-four pounds; *Missale ad usum Ecclesiæ Andegavensis*, on vellum, printed in 1489, sixty-three pounds; Le Fevre's *Recuyles of the Hystoryes of Troye*, printed by Wynkyn de Worde in 1503, fifty-five pounds; a complete set of the twenty-five parts in eight volumes of De Bry's *Collectiones Peregrinationum*, printed at Frankfurt in 1590-1634, eighty-one pounds; De Bry's *Relation of Virginia*, translated by Hariot, printed at Frankfurt in 1590, sixty-three pounds; the first Shakespeare folio (mended, and the title-page slightly imperfect), seventy-six pounds; fine, large, and perfect copies of the second and third folios, eleven pounds, five shillings and thirty-five pounds; Shakespeare's *Poems*, 1640, seven pounds, ten shillings; Prynne's *Records*, three volumes, 1665-70, one hundred and forty pounds; the fourth volume, printed in 1665 or 1666, believed to be unique, three hundred and thirty-five pounds; Houbraken's *Heads of Illustrious Persons*, two volumes, 1756, folio, large paper, with first states and duplicate proofs of the plates, etc., ninety-one pounds; Bartolozzi's Engravings, a collection of six hundred and sixty plates in various proof states, bound in eight folio volumes, sixty-two pounds; Boydell's Prints, five hundred and forty fine impressions, bound in nine folio volumes, seventy-eight pounds, fifteen shillings; Lysons's *Topographical Account of Buckinghamshire*, inlaid in eight volumes, atlas folio, and super-illustrated with four hundred and eighty drawings, etc., five hundred and forty pounds; and Lysons's *Environs of London*, large paper, eighteen volumes quarto, super illustrated with eight hundred drawings and a large number of plates, one hundred and thirty-three pounds. The Duke, who died at the Great Western Hotel, London, on July the 29th, 1861, was the author of *Memoirs of the Court and Cabinets of George III.*, 1853-

55, two volumes; *Memoirs of the Court of England during the Regency,* 1856, two volumes; *Memoirs of the Court of George IV.,* 1859, two volumes; *Memoirs of the Courts and Cabinets of William IV. and Victoria,* 1861, two volumes; and *Private Diary of Richard, Duke of Buckingham and Chandos,* 1862, four volumes; together with a few political works.

FOOTNOTES:

[92] A descriptive catalogue of the manuscripts in the Stowe library by the Rev. Charles O'Conor, D.D., the Duke's librarian, was printed in 1818-19.

HENRY PERKINS, 1778-1855

Henry Perkins, who was born in 1778, was a partner in the well-known firm of Barclay, Perkins and Co., brewers, but he does not appear to have taken an active part in the business, and he spent the later part of his life in retirement among his books at Hanworth Park, Middlesex. He died at Dover on the 15th of April 1855.

Mr. Perkins, who was a Fellow of the Linnean, Geological and Horticultural Societies, possessed a small but exceedingly valuable library, which, among many other extremely rare books, contained two copies of the Gutenberg Bible, one on vellum and the other on paper; a copy on vellum of Fust and Schoeffer's Latin Bible of 1462; a copy of the Coverdale Bible; several works from the press of Caxton, and the first four editions of Shakespeare's Plays. It also comprised many fine manuscripts, some of them superbly illuminated. Mr. Henry Perkins bequeathed his books to his son, Mr. Algernon Perkins, and after his death in 1870 they were sold by auction at Hanworth by Gadsden, Ellis and Co. on the 3rd, 4th, 5th and 6th of June 1873. There were but eight hundred and sixty-five lots in the sale, but they realised an average of thirty pounds, or a total of twenty-five thousand nine hundred and fifty-four pounds, four shillings, the largest sum ever obtained for a library of the same extent. The vellum copy of the Gutenberg Bible was purchased for the Earl of Ashburnham for three thousand four hundred pounds; and the paper copy, now in the Huth library, fetched two thousand six hundred and ninety. Fust and Schoeffer's Latin Bible of 1462, which Mr. Perkins acquired at the sale of Mr. Dent's books for one hundred and seventy-three pounds, five shillings, sold for seven hundred and eighty pounds; while the copy of Coverdale's Bible, which wanted the title and two following leaves and the map, realised four hundred pounds; and the 1623 edition of Shakespeare's Plays brought five hundred and eighty-five pounds. The manuscripts also went for large sums. John Lydgate's *Sege of Troye*, a magnificently illuminated manuscript on vellum of the fifteenth century; *Les Œuvres Diverses* of Jehan de Meun; and *Les Cent Histoires de Troye* of Christine de Pisan, of about the same period, sold respectively for thirteen hundred and twenty, six hundred and ninety, and six hundred and fifty pounds. The prices obtained for the books were generally greatly in excess of those given by Mr. Perkins for them.

FREDERICK PERKINS, 1780-1860

Frederick Perkins of Chepstead, Kent, born in 1780, was a brother of Henry Perkins, and a partner in the same firm. He also formed a good library, which contained the first four Shakespeare folios, and a considerable number of the separate plays in quarto. Among them were the first editions of *Love's Labour Lost*, *Much Ado about Nothing*, the Second Part of *Henry the Fourth*, *Troilus and Cressida*, *Pericles*, *Othello*, and the second or first complete edition of *Romeo and Juliet*, as well as the first edition of *Lucrece*. Three Caxtons were to be found in the collection: the *Mirrour of the World*, the *Chastising of Goddes Children*, and Higden's *Polycronicon*, but they were not good copies. The library also comprised some fine illuminated Horæ and other manuscripts, including a copy on vellum of Chaucer's *Canterbury Tales* of the fifteenth century. Mr. Perkins died on the 10th of October 1860, and his library was sold by Sotheby, Wilkinson and Hodge on July 10th, 1889, and six following days. There were two thousand and eighty-six lots in the sale, which realised eight thousand two hundred and twenty-two pounds, seven shillings. The first Shakespeare folio fetched four hundred and fifteen pounds, the second forty-seven pounds, the third one hundred pounds, and the fourth fourteen pounds. Of the quarto plays, the Second Part of *Henry the Fourth* sold for two hundred and twenty-five pounds, *Othello* for one hundred and thirty pounds, and *Romeo and Juliet* for one hundred and sixty-four pounds. The copies of *Love's Labour Lost*, *Much Ado about Nothing*, *Troilus and Cressida*, and *Pericles* were poor ones, and realised but comparatively small sums. The *Lucrece* fetched two hundred pounds.

JOHN BELLINGHAM INGLIS, 1780-1870

John Bellingham Inglis was born in London on the 14th of February 1780. His father, a partner in the firm of Inglis, Ellice and Co., merchants, Mark Lane, London, was a Director of the East India Company, and was at one time its Chairman. In consequence of the failure of his father young Inglis set up in business on his own account in the wine trade, but this not proving successful, he retired after a short time on the money rescued from the wreck of the fortune of his father, who died soon after his failure. He resided for many years in St. John's Wood, but afterwards removed to Hampstead Heath. He died at 13 Albion Road, N.W., on the 9th of December 1870.

Mr. Inglis, who was a good classical scholar, an excellent linguist, and a man of considerable literary ability, commenced collecting books at a very early age, and soon formed a very valuable and important library, which was especially rich in works from the presses of the early English printers. Unlike some possessors of libraries, he read the books which he had collected; and the Duke of Sussex, at one of his literary dinners at Kensington Palace, is reported to have said: 'Gentlemen, you are all very learned about titles, editions, and printers, but none of you seem to have read anything of the books except Mr. Inglis here.' In 1832 he translated into English, for the first time, the *Philobiblon* of Richard de Bury, and presented it to Thomas Rodd, the bookseller, who published it. He also made translations of several other mediæval printed books and manuscripts, which have never been published. A biographical notice of him appears in *The Bookworm* of December 1870, by J.P. Berjeau, the editor of that periodical. A portion of Inglis's books was sold anonymously by Sotheby on June 9th, 1826, and seven following days. The title-page of the catalogue reads: 'Catalogue of a singularly curious and valuable selection from the Library of a Gentleman, including three extraordinary specimens of Block Printing; Books printed in the Fifteenth Century; Books printed on vellum; Fine copies of Works from the Presses of Caxton, Machlinia, Wynkyn de Worde, Pynson, Julyan Notary, Verard, etc.; an extensive

Collection of Old English Poetry; Romances; Historical and Theological Tracts; early Voyages and Travels; curious Treatises on Witches and Witchcraft; some of the earliest Dictionaries and Vocabularies in the English Language, etc. Likewise several Manuscripts on vellum, most beautifully illuminated, etc.' The number of lots in this sale was sixteen hundred and sixty-five, and the sum realised three thousand three hundred and thirty-three pounds, nine shillings and sixpence. The prices obtained for the books were extremely low. The three block-books:—the first edition of the *Speculum Humanæ Salvationis, Historia Sancti Johannis Evangelistæ ejusque Visiones Apocalypticæ*, and the *Biblia Pauperum* fetched but ninety-five pounds, eleven shillings; forty-seven pounds, five shillings, and thirty-six pounds, fifteen shillings respectively; while no more than four hundred and thirty-one pounds, fifteen shillings and sixpence could be obtained for the thirteen Caxtons in the sale—about thirty-three pounds each. The following are a few of the other notable books in this fine collection, and the prices they fetched: *Les Faits de Maistre Alain Chartier, imprimez a Paris par Pierre le Caron pour Anthoine Verard*, printed on vellum, with capital letters painted in gold and colours, fifty-six pounds, fourteen shillings; *Le Recueil des Histoires Troiennes, imprime a Paris par Anthoine Verard*, presentation copy to Charles VIII., printed on vellum, ornamented with eighty-three miniatures, twenty-seven pounds; Vincent, *Les cinq volumes du Miroir Hystorial, imprime a Paris par Anthoine Verard*, 1495-96, forty-six pounds, four shillings; *Speculum Christiani*, printed by Machlinia, sixteen pounds, sixteen shillings; *Promptorius Puerorum*, printed by Pynson in 1499, thirty-eight pounds, seventeen shillings; *The Floure of the Commandments of God*, Wynkyn de Worde, 1521, thirteen pounds, thirteen shillings; *The Catechisme, set furth by ... Johne, Archbischop of Sanct Androus, etc. Prentit at Sanct Androus, 1552*, sixteen pounds, five shillings and sixpence; *Mary of Nemmegen*, printed at Antwerp by Jan Van Doesborgh in 1518 or 1519, the only copy known, twenty-four pounds; Painter, *The Palace of Pleasure*, London, Thomas Marshe, 1575, a very fine copy, twenty-three pounds; and Shakespeare's *Sonnets*, London, 1609, forty pounds, nineteen shillings. Perhaps the finest of the manuscripts were a beautifully illuminated copy on vellum of the *Liber de Proprietatibus Rerum, Anglice*, by Bartholomæus de Glanvilla, written towards the end of the fourteenth century, which fetched fifty-one pounds, nine shillings; and Boccaccio's *Tragedies of the Falle of Unfortunate Princes*, translated into English verse, written on vellum in England in the early part of the fifteenth century, and richly illuminated. Thirty pounds, nine shillings was all that was obtained for this fine manuscript. After Inglis's death, his son, Dr. C. Inglis, sold such books as he could not find room for. They were disposed of by Sotheby, Wilkinson and Hodge on the 31st of July 1871, and five following days, and realised two thousand seven hundred and sixty-six pounds, thirteen shillings and sixpence. Among the fifteen hundred and eighty-eight lots in the sale were a few rare books and some fine papyri. A third sale of the books in this splendid library, by order of Dr. C. Inglis, took place on June 11th, 1900, and three following days, by the same auctioneers. In this sale there were eight hundred and forty-nine lots, for which the sum of seven thousand five hundred and nineteen pounds, twelve shillings and sixpence was obtained. Although no Caxtons were to be found among the books, there were many rare and interesting examples from the presses of Machlinia, Pynson, Wynkyn de Worde, Julian Notary and other early English printers. The foreign printers were also well represented, and the collection contained several beautiful Books of Hours, both printed and in manuscript. Some very high prices were obtained for the more important books, as the following list of a few of the most notable will show:—*Speculum Humanæ Salvationis*, printed by G. Zainer at Augsburg in 1471, eighty-four pounds; Turrecremata, *Meditationes*, Romæ, 1473, one hundred pounds; the first edition of the *Philobiblon* of Richard de Bury, Coloniæ, 1473, eighty pounds; *Rolle de Hampole super Job*, attributed to the Oxford press of Rood and Hunt, about 1481-86, three hundred pounds; *Chronicle of England*, printed by Machlinia about 1484, one hundred and seventy-five pounds; *Heures de lusaige de Romme*, with cuts printed in various colours, Paris, Jehan du Pré, 1490, two hundred and seventy-two pounds; First Letter of Columbus (Latin) 1493, Vespuccius, *Mundus Novus*, 1502, and other rare tracts in one volume, two hundred and thirty pounds; *Verardus in Laudem Fernandi Hispaniarum Regis*, etc., containing the letter of Columbus to King Ferdinand on his discovery of America, 1494, ninety pounds; *Vitas Patrum*, printed by Wynkyn de Worde in 1495, fifty pounds;

Hoefken van Devotien, Antwerpen, 1496, one hundred and one pounds; *Postilla Epistolarum et Evangeliorum Dominicalium*, printed by Julian Notary in 1509, fifty pounds; *Mirrour of Oure Ladye*, R. Fawkes, 1530, forty-nine pounds; *Heures de Rome*, with illustrations by Geoffroy Tory, Paris, 1525, one hundred and forty-four pounds; and Spenser's *Faerie Queene, Foure Hymnes, Prothalamion*, etc., all first editions, 1590-96, one hundred and seventy pounds.

WILLIAM HENRY MILLER, 1789-1848

Mr. William Henry Miller, who was born in 1789, was the only child of Mr. William Miller of Craigentinny, Midlothian. In 1830 he entered Parliament as one of the Members for Newcastle-under-Lyme, which seat he held until the year 1841. He died unmarried at his residence, Craigentinny House, near Edinburgh, on the 31st of October 1848, and was buried, according to his desire, in a mausoleum on his estate. Mr. Miller formed a fine collection of very choice books at Britwell Court, Buckinghamshire, many of which he acquired at the Heber and other important sales of the first half of the nineteenth century. He was very particular about the condition and size of the volumes he purchased, and from his habit of carrying a foot-rule about him for the purpose of ascertaining their dimensions he became known as 'Measure Miller.' The library was bequeathed to his cousin Miss Marsh, from whom it passed to Mr. Samuel Christie-Miller, who was Member for Newcastle-under-Lyme from 1847 to 1859, and on his death on the 5th of April 1889 to Mr. Wakefield Christie-Miller, who died at Dublin on the 22nd of February 1898. Many rare books have been added to the Britwell Library by its later possessors. The additions made by the last owner were especially important, notably that of the larger portion of the Elizabethan rarities discovered in 1867 at Lamport Hall, the seat of Sir Charles Isham; and the collection may now be considered unrivalled among private libraries for the number of choice examples of English and Scottish literature which it contains, particularly in the division of English poetry. The finest copy known of the *Dictes or Sayings of the Philosophers*, one of the three extant copies of the *Morale Prouerbes of Cristyne*, and nine other works printed by Caxton, are to be found on the shelves of the library, as well as a large number of books from the presses of Wynkyn de Worde, Pynson, Julyan Notary, and other early English printers. Among them are many editions of the grammatical treatises of Robert Whitinton and John Stanbridge, printed by Wynkyn de Worde, and unique copies of Fitzherbert's *Boke of Husbandrie*, the romance of *Oliver of Castile*, and *Fysshynge with an Angle*, all by the same printer. The library contains also a fine series of the early editions of the English Chronicles, and of the works of Chaucer. Among the treasures of the Elizabethan and Jacobean periods are the first Shakespeare folio (the second, third, and fourth folios are also in the library); an unique copy of an edition of *Venus and Adonis*, printed for William Leake at London in 1599, from the Isham collection; all the early editions of Sidney's *Arcadia*; fine examples of the early editions of the works of Edmund Spenser; the only perfect copy known of the first edition of the *Paradyse of Daintie Devises*; and remarkably complete sets of the works of Churchyard, Breton, Greene, Dekker, Wither and Brathwaite. Other notable books in this splendid library are a copy on vellum, with coloured maps, of Ptolemy's *Cosmographia*, printed at Ulm in 1482, and bound by Derome; the Aldine edition of *Poliphili Hypnerotomachia*, in the original binding, and an unique copy of the English translation printed in London by Samuel Waterson in 1592; a fine and perfect set in nine parts of the *Mirrour of Princely Deedes and Knighthood* (a translation of the Spanish *Espejo de Principes y Cavalleros*); editions of Hakluyt's *Voyages*; a beautiful and tall copy of *Purchas his Pilgrimes*; the finest and most complete set which has been formed of De Bry's *Voyages*; the first issue of Milton's *Paradise Lost*; the first edition of Walton's *Compleat Angler* in the original sheepskin binding; the Kilmarnock edition of Burns's *Poems*; and several of the original editions of Shelley's works, including the excessively rare *[OE]dipus Tyrannus*. There is a fine collection of early English music in the Britwell Library, and it possesses the greater portion of the Heber ballads and broadsides, and a large number of books which once belonged to De Thou. Many of the volumes are masterpieces of the work of Bedford, Riviere, Lortic, and other English and foreign binders.

GEORGE DANIEL, 1789-1864

George Daniel was born in London on the 16th of September 1789. After receiving an education at Mr. Thomas Hogg's boarding-school at Paddington Green, he became a clerk to a stockbroker in Tokenhouse Yard,[93] and afterwards followed the profession of an accountant; but he employed all his leisure time in literary pursuits, and in the collection of books, works of art and curiosities. He commenced writing at a very early age, and was the author of a novel *The Adventures of Dick Distich*, and a considerable number of poetical and dramatic pieces. He also contributed many articles to *Ackerman's Poetical Magazine*, *Bentley's Miscellany*, and other magazines, and was the editor of Cumberland's *British Theatre*, and Cumberland's *Minor Theatre*. His first printed production, *Stanzas on Lord Nelsons Victory and Death*, written in conjunction with a young friend, appeared in 1805, but he tells us that he wrote some verses when he was but eight years of age on the death of his father. In 1811 he published a poem called *The Times, or the Prophecy*, and in 1812 a poetical squib founded on the reputed horse-whipping of the Prince of Wales by Lord Yarmouth, entitled *R-y-l Stripes; or, a Kick from Yar—th to Wa—s*, for the suppression of which a large sum was paid by the Prince Regent. In the same year appeared *The Adventures of Dick Distich* in three volumes, which was written by the author before he was eighteen, and a volume of *Miscellaneous Poems*; and in 1814 *The Modern Dunciad*, in which he sings the praises of 'old books, old wines, old customs, and old friends.' He continued to write during the whole of his life, and his last work, *Love's Last Labour not Lost*, was published in 1863. Daniel was fond of convivial society, and numbered Charles Lamb and Robert Bloomfield among his acquaintances, and he was also intimate with many of the principal actors of the day. He died at his son's house, The Grove, Stoke Newington, on the 30th of March 1864. The cause of his death was apoplexy.

Daniel formed a very choice and valuable library in his residence, 18 Canonbury Square, Islington, which was chiefly remarkable for rare editions of old English writers, and very fine collections of

Elizabethan black-letter ballads and Shakespeariana. The Elizabethan ballads would alone be sufficient to render any library famous. They were one hundred and forty-nine in number, and he is said to have purchased them for fifty pounds from Mr. William Stevenson Fitch, Postmaster at Ipswich, who is believed to have obtained them from the housekeeper at Helmingham Hall, Suffolk, the residence of the Tollemache family. Of these ballads seventy-nine were sold to Mr. Heber by Mr. Daniel for seventy pounds, and the remaining seventy were bought at the sale of his library for seven hundred and fifty pounds by Mr. Huth, who had them printed for presentation to the members of the Philobiblon Society. The Shakespearian collection comprised splendid copies of the first four folios and eighteen of the quarto plays, together with the 1594 and 1655 editions of *Lucrece*, the 1594 and 1596 editions of *Venus and Adonis*, and the first editions of the *Sonnets* and *Poems*. The library also contained a large number of early Jest-Books, Drolleries, Garlands and Penny-Histories; and among the rare editions of English writers were works by John Skelton, Edmund Spenser, Anthony Chute, Robert Chester, Anthony Munday, Ben Jonson, Patrick Hannay, George Herbert, Robert Herrick, John Milton, and many others. Several very beautiful manuscripts were also to be found in it.

Daniel's library was sold by auction by Sotheby, Wilkinson and Hodge on the 20th of July 1864, and the nine following days. There were eighteen hundred and seventeen lots, which realised thirteen thousand nine hundred and eighty-four pounds, eleven shillings; the water-colour drawings, engravings, portraits, coins, etc., of which there were four hundred and sixty-one lots, were sold at the same time, and produced one thousand eight hundred and eighty pounds, eleven shillings more.

The sale excited great interest, and many of the books went for large sums; but the prices obtained for others were small compared with those the volumes would fetch at the present time: a fine copy of the first edition of Walton's *Compleat Angler* realised no more than twenty-seven pounds, ten shillings. All the Shakespeares sold well. The first folio, probably the finest example extant, was bought by the Baroness Burdett-Coutts for six hundred and eighty-two guineas, till recently the highest price ever obtained for a copy;[94] and the second, third and fourth folios fetched respectively one hundred and forty-eight pounds, forty-six pounds, and twenty-one pounds, ten shillings. The third folio was a good copy, but had the title in facsimile, which accounts for the small sum it realised. Of the quarto plays, the first edition of *King Richard the Third*—a very fine copy—sold for three hundred and fifty-one pounds, fifteen shillings; the first editions of the *Merry Wives of Windsor* and *Love's Labour Lost* for three hundred and forty-six pounds, ten shillings each, and the first edition of *King Richard the Second* for three hundred and forty-one pounds, five shillings. The 1594 and 1596 editions of *Venus and Adonis* realised two hundred and forty pounds and three hundred and fifteen pounds; a copy of the *Sonnets* two hundred and twenty-five pounds, fifteen shillings; and the first edition of *Lucrece* one hundred and fifty-seven pounds, ten shillings. The copy of *Love's Labour Lost*, and the 1596 edition of *Venus and Adonis*, of which the Bodleian Library possesses the only other copy, were secured for the British Museum.

The following are a few of the other more notable books in the library, together with the prices they fetched at the sale:—Unique copy of *The Boke of Hawkynge and Huntynge and Fysshynge*, printed by Wynkyn de Worde, without date, one hundred and eight pounds; *Rychard Cuer de Lyon*, also printed by Wynkyn de Worde, 1528, ninety-two pounds; *Complaynt of a Dolorous Lover*, printed by Robert Wyer about 1550, unique, sixty-seven pounds, four shillings; *The Tragicall Historie of Romeus and Juliet* (London, 1562), seventy-seven pounds, fourteen shillings; *Merry Jeste of a shrewde and curste Wyfe* (London, about 1575), unique, sixty-four pounds; Munday's *Banquet of Daintie Conceits* (London, 1588), unique, two hundred and twenty-five pounds; Chute's *Beawtie Dishonoured*, written under the title of *Shores Wife* (London, 1593), unique, ninety-six pounds; *Maroccus Extaticus, or Bankes Bay Horse* (London, 1595), eighty-one pounds; Chester's *Loves Martyr, or Rosalins Complaynt* (London, 1601)—this work contains a poem (Threnos) by Shakespeare at p. 172—one hundred and thirty-eight pounds; *Meeting of Gallants at an Ordinarie, or the Walkes in Powles* (London, 1604), unique, eighty-one pounds; *Sejanus, his Fall*, by Ben Jonson, first edition (London, 1605), printed on large paper, a presentation copy from the author with the following autograph inscription—

> 'To my perfect friend Mr. Francis Crane
> I erect this Altar of Friendship,
> and leave it as an eternall witnesse of my Love.
> BEN JONSON'—

unique, one hundred and six pounds; Hannay's *Philomela, the Nightingale*, etc. (London, 1622), ninety-six pounds.

A carved casket made out of the mulberry tree in Shakespeare's Garden, and presented to Garrick with the freedom of the borough of Stratford-on-Avon, was purchased at Charles Mathews's sale in 1835 by Daniel for forty-seven guineas, and presented by him to the British Museum.

FOOTNOTES:

[93] *Dictionary of National Biography.*

[94] At a sale at Sotheby's on July 11th, 1899, Mr. M'George of Glasgow gave seventeen hundred pounds for a copy; and two years later Mr. Quaritch purchased another copy at Christie's for seventeen hundred and twenty pounds.

WILLIAM, SIXTH DUKE OF DEVONSHIRE, 1790-1858

All the Dukes of Devonshire were men of letters and collectors of books. William, the first Duke, acquired many volumes which had belonged to De Thou, and William, the third Duke, bought largely at the sales of the libraries of Colbert, Baluze, Count von Hoym and other collectors of his time; but William, the sixth Duke, who was born on May the 21st, 1790, may justly be regarded as the founder of the Chatsworth Library in its present form. 'He imbibed a taste for literature and books,' says Sir J.P. Lacaita in his preface to the catalogue of the Library, 'from his mother, Lady Georgiana Spencer, the "beautiful Duchess of Devonshire," and from his uncle George John, second Earl Spencer, who formed what is perhaps the finest private library in existence.' In 1811 he succeeded to the Dukedom, and shortly afterwards endeavoured to add to his library Count M'Carthy's collection, for which he offered twenty thousand pounds, but the offer was declined. He purchased the choicer portion of the books of Thomas Dampier, Bishop of Ely, and he bought largely at the sales of the Edwards, Roxburghe, Towneley and other libraries. In 1815 the Duke removed the books from his other residences to Chatsworth with a view to the formation of a great library there,[95] and in 1821 he purchased John Philip Kemble's splendid collection of plays for two thousand pounds, adding to it four years later the first edition of *Hamlet*, which he purchased of Messrs. Payne and Foss, the booksellers of Pall Mall, for one hundred pounds. But one other copy of this precious little volume is known to exist, that in the British Museum, which wants the title-page, while that acquired by the Duke is without the last leaf. After the death of the Duke on January the 18th, 1858, the collection at Chatsworth was further enlarged by his successor, who transferred to it some choice books from the library at Chiswick, and also added to it a select portion of the books of his brother, Lord Richard Cavendish, who died in 1873.[96] In 1879 a catalogue of the books at Chatsworth was compiled by Sir J.P. Lacaita, the librarian, in four volumes, and printed at the Chiswick Press. The library is rich in choice and early editions of the Greek and Latin Classics, and the productions of the Aldine Press are particularly numerous and fine.

Of the Bibles, the Latin Bible of 1462, and a vellum copy of that printed by Jenson in 1476, are perhaps the most important. As many as twenty-five works from the press of Caxton, and twenty-four from that of Wynkyn de Worde are to be found in the catalogue. Among the Caxtons is a copy of the *Recuyell of the Histories of Troye*, which once belonged to Elizabeth Grey, wife of Edward IV. This volume was bought at the Roxburghe sale for one thousand and sixty pounds, ten shillings. A magnificent copy of De Bry's *Collectiones Peregrinationum*, which formerly belonged to François César Le Tellier, Marquis de Courtanvaux, is also deserving of special notice. A large proportion of the books are in handsome and historical bindings, and no fewer than twenty-four volumes from the library of Grolier are to be found on the shelves of the collection, which also contains a nearly complete set of County Histories. Among the manuscripts is one of great interest. It is a Missal given by King Henry VII. to his daughter Margaret, Queen Consort of James IV., King of Scotland, and mother of the Lady Margaret Douglas, who later presented the volume to the Archbishop of St. Andrews. The book contains two notes in the handwriting of Henry. On the recto of the fourteenth leaf he has written, 'Remember yor kynde and louyng fader an yor good prayers, Henry Ky'; and on the reverse of leaf 32, 'Pray for your louyng fader that gave you this booke, and I geve you att all tymes godds blessỹg and myne, Henry Ky.' On the reverse of leaf 156 Lady Margaret Douglas has written, 'My good lorde of Saynt Andrews i pray you pray for me that gaufe yow thys buuk—yowrs too my pour, Margaret.'

The Devonshire library also contains a magnificent series of drawings by the old masters, and prints by the early engravers, which were acquired by William, the second Duke. The gem of the collection of drawings is the *Liber Veritatis*, a set of original designs by Claude Lorrain, which Louis XIV. endeavoured in vain to purchase.

DUKE OF DEVONSHIRE.

FOOTNOTES:

[95] Preface to the catalogue of the library at Chatsworth, by Sir J.P. Lacaita.

[96] *Ibid.*

SIR THOMAS PHILLIPPS, BART., 1792-1872

Sir Thomas Phillipps, Bart., who was the son of Thomas Phillipps, of Broadway, Worcestershire, was born at Manchester on the 2nd of July 1792. He was educated at Rugby, and in 1811 proceeded to University College, Oxford, graduating B.A. in 1815 and M.A. in 1820. In 1818, on the death of his father, he succeeded to the family estates, and in 1821 he was created a baronet. Phillipps died at Thirlestaine House, Cheltenham, on the 6th of February 1872, and was buried at Broadway. He was twice married, and by his first wife had three daughters. Phillipps, who was a Trustee of the British Museum and a Fellow of the Royal Society and of the Society of Antiquaries, and also a member of the principal learned societies, both English and foreign, began at a very early age to collect books. While at Rugby he formed a small library, the catalogue of which is still in existence, and the inheritance of his father's property in 1818 enabled him to commence the formation of his magnificent collection of manuscripts. With a view to their acquisition, in 1820 he paid a visit to the Continent, and remained abroad until 1825, during which time he made large purchases of manuscripts, especially at the sale of the famous Meerman collection at the Hague in 1824, and he also privately bought the manuscripts belonging to the extensive and important collection of Professor Van Ess of Darmstadt, together with a number of his early printed books. Phillipps was indefatigable in the acquirement of his treasures, and at the time of his death his library contained some sixty thousand manuscripts, and a goodly collection of printed books. He writes: 'In amassing my collection of manuscripts, I commenced with purchasing everything that lay within my reach, to which I was instigated by reading various accounts of the destruction of valuable manuscripts.... My principal search has been for historical, and particularly unpublished manuscripts, whether good or bad, and particularly those on vellum. My chief desire for preserving vellum manuscripts arose from witnessing the unceasing destruction of them by goldbeaters; my search for charters or deeds by their destruction in the shops of glue-makers and tailors. As I advanced the ardour of the pursuit increased, until at last I became a perfect vello-maniac (if I may coin a word), and I gave any price that was asked. Nor do I regret it, for my object was not only to secure good manuscripts for myself, but also to raise the public estimation of them, so that their value might be more generally known, and consequently more manuscripts preserved. For nothing tends to the preservation of anything so much as making it bear a high price. The examples I always kept in view were Sir Robert Cotton and Sir Robert Harley.'

Sir Thomas Phillipps's collection was not confined to European manuscripts. It contained several hundred Oriental ones, and he also acquired those relating to Mexico belonging to Lord Kingsborough. The illuminated manuscripts were particularly fine, and some of them had been executed for regal and other distinguished persons, and were beautifully bound. Many of the manuscripts which related to Ireland and Wales were of special interest and great value. For many years Phillipps kept his library, together with his fine collections of pictures, drawings, and coins at his residence at Middle Hill, Worcestershire; but in 1862, in consequence of their ever-increasing size, he removed them to Thirlestaine House, Cheltenham, which he purchased from Lord Northwick. On Sir Thomas's death his entailed Middle Hill estates went to his eldest daughter, Henrietta Elizabeth Molyneux, the wife of James Orchard Halliwell, the Shakespearian commentator, but in a will made shortly before his death he left Thirlestaine House, together with his books, manuscripts, pictures, and other collections, to his third daughter, Katherine Somerset Wyttenbach, wife of the Rev. J.E.A. Fenwick, at one time vicar of Needwood, Staffordshire. This bequest was, however, encumbered with the singular condition, that neither his eldest daughter, nor her husband, nor any Roman Catholic should ever enter the house.[97] His second daughter, Maria Sophia, who married the Rev. John Walcott of Bitterley Court, Shropshire, predeceased her father. Since the manuscripts came into the possession of Mrs. Fenwick, portions have been sold by private arrangement to several of the foreign governments; amongst these, however, were no English ones. A large number of the remainder have been disposed of by auction at a series of sales by Sotheby, Wilkinson and Hodge, but the immense collection is by no means exhausted. The first sale took place on August 3rd, 1886, and seven following days; and the others on January 22nd, 1889, and two following days; July 15th, 1891, and following day; December 7th, 1891, and following day; July 4th, 1892, and two following days; June 19th, 1893, and three following days; March 21st, 1895, and four following days; June 10th, 1896, and six following days; May 17th, 1897, and three following days; June 6th, 1898, and five following days; and June 5th, 1899, and five following days. The total amount realised at all these auction sales is upwards of thirty-six thousand six hundred pounds. The printed books in Phillipps's library, which 'included a complete set of the publications privately printed by him at Middle Hill; important heraldic and genealogical works, county histories and topography, Welsh books, valuable dictionaries and grammars, and a large collection of rare articles relating to America; history, voyages and travels,' were sold in three parts by Sotheby, Wilkinson and Hodge on August 3rd, 1886, and seven following days; January 22nd, 1889, and two following days; and December 7th, 1891, and following day. There were five thousand four hundred and sixty-two lots in the three sales, which realised three thousand two hundred and fourteen pounds, thirteen shillings and threepence.

About 1822 Sir Thomas Phillipps set up a private printing-press in Broadway Tower, situated on his Middle Hill estate, where he printed a large number of his manuscripts. Among the more important of these were:—*Institutiones Clericorum in Comitatu Wiltoniæ*, 1297-1810, two volumes, 1821-25, folio; *Monumental Inscriptions in the County of Wilton*, two volumes, 1822, folio (only six copies of this work were printed, one of which realised fourteen pounds, ten shillings at the sale of the books); *A Book of Glamorganshire Antiquities, by Rice Merrick, Esq., 1578, now first published by Sir T. Phillipps, Bart., 1825*, folio; and *Collectanea de Familiis Diversis quibus nomen est Phillipps*, etc., two volumes, 1816-40, folio (a copy of which fetched sixteen pounds at the sale). Phillipps also printed catalogues of his manuscripts and printed books. A fair but not complete list of the works will be found in Lowndes's *Bibliographer's Manual of English Literature*. In 1862 the printing-press was removed with the library and other collections to Thirlestaine House.

FOOTNOTES:

[97] *Athenæum*, February 17, 1872.

REV. THOMAS CORSER, 1793-1876

The Rev. Thomas Corser was the third son of George Corser, banker, of Whitchurch, Shropshire. He was born at Whitchurch in 1793, and received his early education first at the school of his native place, and afterwards at the Manchester Grammar School, from whence he was admitted a commoner of Balliol College, Oxford. He took the degree of B.A. in 1815 and that of M.A. in 1818. In 1816 Corser was ordained to the curacy of Condover, near Shrewsbury, and after filling several other curacies he was appointed in 1826 to the rectory of All Saints' Church, Stand, Manchester, which living he held, together with the vicarage of Norton-by-Daventry in Northamptonshire, for nearly half a century. He died, after a long illness, at Stand Rectory on the 24th of August 1876.

The Rev. T. Corser was elected a Fellow of the Society of Antiquaries in 1850, and he was one of the founders of the Chetham Society, for which he edited four works: *Chester's Triumph*, James's *Iter Lancastrense*, Robinson's *Golden Mirrour*, and *Collectanea Anglo-Poetica*. The last-named work, of which a portion was written by Corser and the remainder by James Crossley, is an elaborate account of Corser's splendid collection of early English poetry.

Corser was one of the most learned and enthusiastic book-collectors of his day, and his noble library contained, besides a wonderful collection of unique and rare editions of the works of the early English poets and dramatists, a fine block-book, 'Apocalypsis Sancti Johannis,' seven Caxtons, and a large number of books printed by Machlinia, Wynkyn de Worde, Pynson, Notary, Redman, and other early English printers. The library also comprised a large number of books of emblems, drolleries, jest-books, garlands, and many other scarce and curious works in all classes of literature. Mr. Corser also possessed a few choice manuscripts.

In 1868 Mr. Corser, in consequence of ill health and failure of his eyesight, which precluded him from the further enjoyment of his books, determined to part with his library, and it was sold in eight parts by Sotheby, Wilkinson and Hodge. The first portion was sold on the 28th of July 1868, and two following days; and the last portion on June the 25th, 1873, and three following days. There were six thousand two hundred and forty-four lots in the eight sales, and the total amount realised was nineteen thousand seven hundred and eighty-one pounds. Catalogues, with the prices, of all the sales are preserved in the British Museum. The sums obtained for the books were not large. The block-book sold for four hundred and forty-five pounds, and the seven Caxtons—the first edition of the *Dictes or Sayings, Tully of Old Age, Knight of the Tower, Golden Legend, Life of Our Lady, Speculum Vitæ Christi,* and *Fayts of Arms*—realised but thirteen hundred and forty-three pounds; the *Knight of the Tower* and *Fayts of Arms* fetching the highest prices—five hundred and sixty pounds, and two hundred and fifty pounds. Several of the Caxtons were, however, imperfect. *The Dyalogue of Dives and Pauper,* 1493, until recently believed to be the first dated book printed by Pynson, brought one hundred and four pounds, and *The Recuyles of the historyes of Troye,* 1503; *Bartholomæus de proprietatibus rerum,* about 1495; and *The Example of Vertue,* 1530, all printed by Wynkyn de Worde, one hundred and fourteen pounds, sixty pounds, and fifty-eight pounds. Mr. Corser's four Shakespeare folios sold for one hundred and sixty pounds, forty-nine pounds, seventy-seven pounds, and twelve pounds, while the first edition of the *Sonnets* realised forty-five pounds, and the 1636 edition of *Venus and Adonis* fifty-five pounds. Some other rare books, and the prices obtained for them, were the *Sarum Missal,* printed at Paris in 1514, eighty-seven pounds; *Biblia Pauperum* (A. Verard, Paris, about 1503), ninety-nine pounds; *Guy de Waruich* (Paris, 1525), two hundred and eighty-two pounds; unique copy of an edition of *Huon of Bordeaux,* thought to have been printed by Pynson, eighty-one pounds; *Nurcerie of Names,* by Guillam de Warrino (William Warren) (London, 1581), one hundred pounds; Daye's *Daphnis and Chloe* (London, 1587), unique, sixty pounds; *The Three Ladies of London,* by W.R. (London, 1592), seventy-six pounds; *The Phœnix Nest* (London, 1593), sixty-four pounds, ten shillings; Chute's *Beawtie Dishonoured* (London, 1593), one hundred and five pounds; *Maroccus Extaticus, or Bankes Bay Horse* (London, 1595), one hundred and ten pounds; the first five editions of Walton's *Compleat Angler,* one hundred and forty pounds;

and twenty early ballads in black letter, bound in a volume, eighty-nine pounds.

The more important manuscripts in the collection were *Le Romant des Trois Pelerinages*, by Guillaume de Guilleville, written on vellum in the fourteenth century, and ornamented with many illuminations and drawings, two hundred and ten pounds; *Bartholomæus De Proprietatibus Rerum*, vellum, richly illuminated, fourteenth century, ninety-one pounds; a *Poem on the Lord's Prayer*, by John Kylyngwyke, vellum, fourteenth century, seventy pounds; *Lyf of Oure Lady*, by John Lydgate, fifteenth century, written and illuminated on vellum, forty-six pounds; and *Officium Beatæ Mariæ Virginis*, fifteenth century, illuminated, sixty-four pounds.

Some additional manuscripts and books which had belonged to Mr. Corser were sold after his death, at Manchester, by Capes, Dunn and Pilcher on December the 13th, 1876, and two following days. These realised one thousand four hundred and eight pounds, sixteen shillings and sixpence. Among them was the original manuscript of Cavendish's *Life of Wolsey*, which fetched sixty guineas.

DAVID LAING, 1793-1878

David Laing, the eminent Scottish antiquary, was the second son of William Laing, a bookseller in Edinburgh, and was born in that city on the 20th of April 1793. He was educated at the Canongate Grammar School, and afterwards attended the Greek classes of Professor Dalzel at the Edinburgh University.[98] At an early age he was apprenticed to his father, and in the year 1821 he entered into partnership with him. His father died in 1832, and David Laing continued to carry on the business until 1837, when, having been elected librarian to the Society of Writers to H.M. Signet, he gave it up, and disposed of his stock by public sale. Laing was Honorary Secretary of the Bannatyne Club from its foundation by Sir Walter Scott in 1823 to its dissolution thirty-eight years later, and himself edited a large number of its publications. He also edited papers for the Spalding, Abbotsford, and Hunterian Clubs, and the Shakespeare and Wodrow Societies; while his contributions to the *Proceedings* of the Society of Antiquaries of Scotland, of which he was elected a Fellow in 1826, consisted of upwards of one hundred separate papers. In 1864 the University of Edinburgh conferred on him the degree of LL.D. He died unmarried on the 18th of October 1878.

Laing's life was one of great literary activity, and although he did not produce any large original work, he edited many of the writings of the old Scottish authors. His acquaintance with the early literary and ecclesiastical history, as well as the art and antiquities, of Scotland was very extensive; and Lockhart, in *Peter's Letters to his Kinsfolk*, states that he possessed a 'truly wonderful degree of skill and knowledge in all departments of bibliography.' A list of the various publications issued under his editorial superintendence from 1815 to 1878 inclusive, together with his lectures on Scottish art, appear in a collection of privately printed notices of him edited by T.G. Stevenson, Edinburgh, 1878.

Laing availed himself of his exceptional opportunities to form a very large and fine library, which was particularly rich in books illustrative of the history and literature of Scotland, many of which were of excessive rarity, and several unique. Nearly every publication relating to Mary Queen of Scots was to be found in it. After Laing's death his library, with the exception of his manuscripts, which he bequeathed to the University of Edinburgh, was sold in four portions by Sotheby, Wilkinson and Hodge.

First Sale—

December 1st, 1879, and ten following days. Three thousand seven hundred and ninety-nine lots = thirteen thousand two hundred and eighty-eight pounds, eight shillings and sixpence.

Second Sale—

April 5th, 1880, and ten following days. Four thousand and eighty-two lots = one thousand seven hundred and thirty-eight pounds, three shillings.

Third Sale—

July 20th, 1880, and four following days. Two thousand four hundred and forty-three lots = seven hundred and seventy-one pounds, nine shillings and sixpence.

Fourth Sale—

February 21st, 1881, and three following days. One thousand four hundred and nineteen lots = seven hundred and thirty-eight pounds, eighteen shillings.

Large prices were obtained for many of the books, especially for the early ones printed in Scotland.

The following are a few of the rarest of the volumes, together with the amounts for which they were sold:—

A Roman Breviary on vellum, printed by N. Jenson at Venice in 1482, and ornamented with borders to the pages, drawn by a pen, ninety-three pounds; *Lo Doctrinal de Sapiensa*, in the Catalan dialect, by Guy de Roye, printed about 1495, one hundred pounds; *Missale pro usu totius Regni Norvegiæ* (Haffniæ, 1519), with the arms and cypher of the King of Denmark on the back of the binding, one hundred and thirty-two pounds; *The Falle of Princis*, etc., by Boccaccio, translated by John Lydgate, and printed by Pynson in 1527, seventy-eight pounds; *The Catechisme* of Archbishop Hamilton, printed at 'Sanct Androus' in 1552, one hundred and forty-eight pounds; *Tractate concerning ye Office and Dewtie of Kyngis*, etc., written by William Lauder, and printed by John Scott at Edinburgh in 1556, seventy-seven pounds; *Confessione della Fede Christiana*, by Theodore Beza, printed in 1560, containing the autograph of Sir James Melville, and having MARIA R. SCOTOR[V] stamped in gold on each cover, one hundred and forty-nine pounds; *The Forme and Maner of Examination before the Admission to ye Tabill of ye Lord, usit by ye Ministerie of Edinburge* (Edinburgh, 1581), seventy pounds; the first edition of the author's corrected text of *Don Quixote* (Madrid, 1608), together with the first edition of the second part (Madrid, 1615), one hundred and ninety-two pounds; dedication copy to King Charles II. of the *Institutions of the Law of Scotland*, by Sir James Dalrymple of Stair, afterwards Viscount Stair, two volumes (Edinburgh, 1681), in a remarkably fine contemporary Scotch binding, with the royal arms in gold on the covers, two hundred and ninety-five pounds; a first edition of *Robinson Crusoe*, three volumes (London, 1719-20), thirty-one pounds; one of the twelve copies, printed at a cost of upwards of ten thousand pounds, of the *Botanical Tables* of the Earl of Bute, nine volumes, with the arms of the Earl impressed in gold on the bindings, seventy-seven pounds; the first edition of Burns's *Poems* (Kilmarnock, 1786), with lines in the autograph of Burns, and a letter from J.G. Lockhart, ninety pounds; and a fine collection of Scots Ballads and Broadsides, one hundred and thirty in number, issued between 1669 and 1730, many of great rarity, one hundred and thirty-three pounds. Laing left a collection of drawings to the Royal Scottish Academy of Painting, of which he had been elected Honorary Professor of Ancient History and Antiquities in 1856. His prints were sold by Sotheby, Wilkinson and Hodge on the 21st of

February 1880, in two hundred and thirteen lots, and realised two hundred and seventy pounds, thirteen shillings.

FOOTNOTES:

[98] *Dictionary of National Biography.*

BERTRAM, FOURTH EARL OF ASHBURNHAM, 1797-1878

Bertram, fourth Earl of Ashburnham, who was born on the 23rd of November 1797, and died on the 22nd of June 1878, was one of the greatest and most ardent of English book-collectors. He developed a taste for book-buying at a very early age. It is said that his first purchase was made in 1814, when, a boy at Westminster School, he bought a copy of the *Secretes* of Albertus Magnus for eighteenpence at Ginger's well-known shop in Great College Street, and at the time of his death he had amassed a library which ranked among the first in the kingdom. Magnificent as was his collection of printed books, the library was even still more notable for the manuscripts it contained, which amounted to nearly four thousand, and were remarkable for their value and importance. In addition to those which he bought separately, Lord Ashburnham acquired in 1847 the manuscripts of Count Guglielmo Libri for eight thousand pounds, and in 1849 he purchased the Stowe manuscripts for the same sum, and those of Jean Barrois for six thousand pounds. Five years after the death of Lord Ashburnham, his successor, the present Earl, offered the manuscripts, for one hundred and sixty thousand pounds, to the Trustees of the British Museum, who were anxious to purchase them for that sum. The Chancellor of the Exchequer, however, declined to find the money for the entire collection, but the Stowe manuscripts were acquired by the Government for forty-five thousand pounds, and divided between the British Museum and the library of the Royal Irish Academy in Dublin. To the latter institution were given the Irish manuscripts and certain volumes specially relating to Ireland. It had long been suspected that many of the manuscripts in the Libri and Barrois collections had been abstracted from French and Italian public libraries, and when this was proved to have been the case, principally through the researches of M. Delisle, the Director of the Bibliothèque Nationale, it was arranged between the Trustees of the British Museum and the French authorities that should the former become possessors of the manuscripts, they would return the stolen volumes for the sum of twenty-four thousand pounds. As the Treasury refused to sanction the purchase of the whole of the Ashburnham manuscripts, this arrangement could not be carried out, and in 1887 the manuscripts, one hundred and sixty-six in number, stolen from the French and Italian libraries, were bought by Mr. Karl Trübner, acting as agent for the Grand Duke of Baden and the German Imperial authorities, for the same sum as the French had been willing to pay for them. The primary object of this transaction, says Mr. F.S. Ellis in his excellent account of the library in Quaritch's *Dictionary of English Book-Collectors*, 'was to recover the famous Manesse Liederbuch, a thirteenth century MS. carried away by the French from Heidelberg in 1656, the loss of which had ever since been regarded as a national calamity in Germany. For £6000 in cash and this precious volume, he handed over the 166 Libri and Barrois MSS. to the Bibliothèque Nationale. By a simple arithmetical process, we can conclude that £18,000 was the net cost to the German Exchequer of a single volume of old German ballads—the highest price ever paid for a book.' The stolen manuscripts which were not required to replace those taken from the French libraries, were purchased by the Italian Government.

Mr. Yates Thompson is understood to have purchased that portion of the other manuscripts in the library known as 'The Appendix,' for about forty thousand pounds, and after selecting those he required for his own collection, to have sent the remainder to the auction rooms of Sotheby, Wilkinson and Hodge, where they were sold on May the 1st, 1899. There were one hundred and seventy-seven lots in the sale, which realised eight thousand five hundred and ninety-five pounds, five shillings. The choicest manuscript in the catalogue was an important text of the later version (1400-40) of 'Wycliffe's English Bible,' known as the 'Bramhall Manuscript,' which was knocked down to Mr. Quaritch for seventeen hundred and fifty pounds. Other fine manuscripts were a copy of the *Historia Ecclesiastica* of the Venerable Bede, written in the eighth century; an *Evangeliarium* of the twelfth century, with beautiful illuminations; *Officia Liturgica*, fifteenth century; and *Horæ Beatæ Mariæ Virginis*, written in the sixteenth century, richly illuminated. These realised respectively two hundred and thirty pounds, three hundred pounds, four hundred and sixty-seven pounds, and three hundred pounds. On the 10th of June 1901 and the four following days the manuscripts in the Barrois

Collection, not previously disposed of, were sold by the same auctioneers. There were six hundred and twenty-eight lots in this sale, and the very large sum of thirty-three thousand two hundred and seventeen pounds, six shillings and sixpence was obtained for them, the choicest manuscripts fetching exceptionally high prices. The manuscripts were of great importance and much interest. Among them were to be found early copies of the Gospels and Epistles, and beautifully illuminated manuscripts of the Latin and Italian Classics, Books of Devotion, and early French Romances and Chronicles. The collection also contained a number of papers relating to Mary, Queen of Scots, and a valuable series of Anglo-Norman Charters, etc. The following are a few of the more interesting and valuable manuscripts, together with the prices they realised: — *Roman du Saint Graal et Lancelot du Lac*, on vellum, in three folio volumes, with beautifully painted miniatures and initials, fourteenth century — eighteen hundred pounds; *Psalterium Latinum*, on vellum, fourteenth century, with paintings attributed to Giotto — fifteen hundred and thirty pounds; *Vie du vaillant Bertrand du Guesclin*, written on vellum in the fourteenth century, with miniatures in *camaïeu gris* — fifteen hundred pounds; *La Légende Dorée*, translated by Jehan de Vignay, fifteenth century, on vellum, with a large number of very fine illuminated miniatures and ornamental initials — fifteen hundred pounds; *Chronique Generale dite de la Bourcachardiere*, by Jehan de Courcy, in two large folio volumes, on vellum, with large illuminations, fifteenth century — fourteen hundred and twenty pounds; *Horæ Beatæ Mariæ Virginis*, with very fine illuminations, fifteenth century — eleven hundred and sixty pounds; *Histoire Universelle*, on vellum, in two volumes, with miniatures in *camaïeu gris*, fifteenth century — nine hundred and ten pounds; *Dante*, vellum, richly illuminated, fourteenth century — six hundred and thirty pounds. The collection of Anglo-Norman Charters fetched three hundred and five pounds, and the Letters and Papers relating to Mary, Queen of Scots, one hundred and ninety-six pounds.

For upwards of fifty years Lord Ashburnham availed himself of every opportunity of acquiring the finest and most perfect copies obtainable of the rarest and choicest books, and he brought together a collection of printed volumes which was well worthy of being associated with that of his manuscripts. It was especially rich in Bibles, and in Missals, Horæ and other Service Books, and in the early editions of Dante, Boccaccio and Chaucer. Among the Bibles and portions of the Scriptures were a block-book, a copy of the *Biblia Pauperum*, regarded by Heinecken as the second edition of that work; vellum and paper copies of the Gutenberg Bible; a vellum copy of the 1462 Latin Bible; a perfect copy of Tyndale's translation of the Pentateuch, printed at 'Marlborow' by Hans Loft in 1534; and the Coverdale Bible of 1535. Of foreign incunabula there was a large number; of Caxtons a very goodly list,[99] but comparatively few of them perfect; and the rarest productions of the press of St. Albans, and of those of Machlinia, Lettou, Pynson, Wynkyn de Worde, Copland, and other early English printers were to be found in the library. The collection of the editions of the *Book of Hawking, Hunting*, etc., attributed to Dame Juliana Berners, may be considered to have been unique, for it included the *Book of St. Albans*, printed in 1486, the extremely rare edition printed by Wynkyn de Worde in 1496, the three editions printed by William Copland, those of William Powell and John Waley, and the only known copy of the first separate edition of *Fysshynge with an Angle*, printed by Wynkyn de Worde in 1532. Other rare English books were the first edition of the first *Reformed Primer*, printed in 1535; an *Abridgement of the Chronicles of Englande*, printed by Grafton in 1570, which belonged to Thomas Howard, Duke of Norfolk, who was beheaded in 1572, with an interesting letter written by him on the blank space of the reverse of the last leaf, shortly before his death; *The Principal Navigations, etc., of the English Nation*, by Richard Hakluyt, printed in 1598-1600, with the very rare map having the Voyage of Sir Francis Drake, 1577, and that of Standish, 1587, and the original suppressed pages of the Voyage to Cadiz; the four Shakespeare folios, and the first five editions of Walton's *Compleat Angler*, in the original bindings (three sheep and two calf) as issued by the publisher. Books also worthy of special notice were the beautifully illuminated copies of Boccaccio's *Ruine des Nobles Hommes*, printed by Colard Mansion at Bruges in 1476; the *Opera Varia Latine* of Aristotle, printed on vellum by Andrea de Asula at Venice in 1483; and *Heures de la Vierge Marie*, also printed on vellum, by Geoffroy Tory in 1525. A catalogue of the more rare and curious printed books in the library was privately printed in 1864.

Although bookbindings did not form a special feature of the library, Lord Ashburnham possessed some remarkably fine and interesting examples of them. That on a tenth century manuscript of the Gospels, which for many centuries belonged to the Abbey of Noble Canonesses at Lindau, on the Lake of Constance, is one of the finest specimens of gold and jewelled bindings to be found in any collection. This beautiful work of art, the lower cover of which is of the eighth century and the upper of the ninth, is of gold or silver gilt, and is profusely decorated with jewels. It is described in the *Vetusta Monumenta* of the Society of Antiquaries, and was shown at the Exhibition of Bookbindings at the Burlington Fine Arts Club in 1891.[100] The collection also contained a particularly fine mosaic binding, with doublures, by Monnier, and many volumes from the libraries of Grolier, Maioli, the Emperor Charles V., De Thou, etc.

Lord Ashburnham's printed books were sold in three portions in 1897 and 1898 by Sotheby, Wilkinson and Hodge. The first sale took place on June 25th, 1897, and seven following days; the second on December 6th, 1897, and five following days, and the third on May 9th, 1898, and five following days. There were four thousand and seventy-five lots in the three sales, and the total amount realised was sixty-two thousand seven hundred and twelve pounds, seven shillings and sixpence.

Very high prices were obtained for the books. The *Biblia Pauperum* block-book sold for a thousand and fifty pounds; the vellum copy of the Gutenberg Bible for four thousand pounds, the largest sum paid for a copy of this Bible, and the highest but one ever given for a printed book (Lord Ashburnham's copy on paper was sold privately to Mr. Quaritch for three thousand pounds); the Latin Bible of 1462 for fifteen hundred pounds; and the Coverdale Bible and Tyndale's Pentateuch for eight hundred and twenty pounds, and two hundred pounds. The illuminated copies of Boccaccio's *Ruine des Nobles Hommes*, printed by Colard Mansion; Aristotle's *Opera Varia Latine*, printed by Andrea de Asula; and the *Heures de la Vierge Marie*, printed by Geoffroy Tory, realised six hundred and ninety-five pounds, eight hundred pounds, and eight hundred and sixty pounds.

Of the Caxtons the *Life of Jason* and the *Dictes* fetched the highest prices—two thousand one hundred pounds, and thirteen hundred and twenty pounds; the former being the largest sum ever paid for any Caxton book. Three hundred and eighty-five pounds were obtained for the 'Book of St. Albans'; one thousand pounds for Chaucer's *Canterbury Tales*, printed by Wynkyn de Worde in 1498, believed to be the only copy extant; and three hundred and sixty pounds for the *Treatyse of Fysshing with an Angle*, by the same printer. This little book, which consists of sixteen leaves, and without the covers weighs about two ounces, sold for nearly forty-five times its weight in gold. The first edition of the *Reformed Primer* sold for two hundred and twenty-five pounds; Grafton's *Chronicle*, with the letter of the Duke of Norfolk, for seventy pounds; and a vellum copy of the *Tewrdannck* for three hundred and ten pounds.

The first folio Shakespeare, which was slightly imperfect, was bought by Mr. Sotheran for five hundred and eighty-five pounds, for presentation to the Memorial Library, Stratford-on-Avon. The second folio fetched ninety pounds, and the third one hundred and ninety pounds. Hakluyt's *Navigations* sold for two hundred and seventy-five pounds, and the set of the first five editions of the *Compleat Angler* for eight hundred pounds. At the Corser sale they realised but one hundred and forty pounds. The copy of *Merlin* with the Monnier binding brought seven hundred and sixty pounds, and a collection of early impressions of sixty-two prints by Albert Dürer three hundred and fifty pounds.

FOOTNOTES:

[99] Eighteen are mentioned in Blades's *Life and Typography of Caxton*. London, 1861-63.

[100] This volume was recently sold for the Earl of Ashburnham by Sotheby, Wilkinson and Hodge to a private purchaser for ten thousand pounds.

SIR WILLIAM TITE, C.B., 1798-1873

Sir William Tite, C.B., was the son of Mr. Arthur Tite, a London merchant. He was born in London in 1798, and after receiving his education at private schools, became a pupil of David Laing, the architect of the Custom House. Sir William Tite designed many buildings in London and the provinces, and a considerable number of the more important railway stations; but the work with which his name is especially associated was the rebuilding of the Royal Exchange, which cost £150,000, and was opened by the Queen on the 28th of October 1844. In 1838 he was elected President of the Architectural Society, and of the Royal Institute of British Architects from 1861-63, and from 1867-70. He entered Parliament in 1855 as Member for Bath, and continued to represent that constituency until his death. In 1869 he was knighted, and in the following year he received the Companionship of the Bath. Sir William was a Fellow of the Royal Society, and also of the Society of Antiquaries. He died at Torquay on April 20th, 1873, and was buried in Norwood Cemetery.

Sir William Tite was an ardent collector of manuscripts, books, and works of art, and he formed a very large and choice library, which contained many valuable manuscripts, and a great number of rare early English books. It was sold by Sotheby, Wilkinson and Hodge, in May and June 1874. The sale occupied sixteen days, and realised nineteen thousand nine hundred and forty-three pounds, six shillings. There were three thousand nine hundred and thirty-seven lots.

Among the more notable manuscripts in the library were a richly illuminated *Lectionarium*, written on vellum about A.D. 1150 at the monastery of Ottenbeuren in Suabia, which sold for five hundred and fifty pounds; a Wycliffe New Testament on vellum of the first half of the fifteenth century, which brought two hundred and forty-one pounds; a copy of the Four Gospels of about the same period, which fetched one hundred and eight pounds; a number of Horæ and other service books, and three devotional works written by Jarry, the famous French calligraphist. There were also the original manuscripts of three of the novels of Sir Walter Scott—*Peveril of the Peak*, the first volume of the *Tales of my Landlord (The Black Dwarf)*, and *Woodstock*, which together realised three hundred and ninety-eight pounds. The collection also contained a block-book, *The Apocalypse*, which brought two hundred and eighty-five pounds; four Caxtons, the most important of which—a perfect copy of the second edition of the *Mirrour of the World*—sold for four hundred and fifty-five pounds; and many books from the presses of Machlinia, Pynson, Wynkyn de Worde, Notary, and other early English printers. Shakespeare was well represented. The first three folios were to be found in the library, as well as the first editions of *Lucrece* and the *Sonnets*, and a large number of the quarto plays. The first folio and *Lucrece* realised respectively four hundred and forty pounds and one hundred and ten pounds. There was also a choice collection of the works of other writers of the time of Elizabeth and James I. A copy of the first edition of *Don Quixote*; and a set of the first five editions of Walton's *Compleat Angler*, which sold for sixty-eight pounds, also deserve especial notice. A series of autographs in thirteen folio volumes realised three hundred and twenty-five pounds; and the sale catalogue contained as many as two hundred and fourteen lots of autograph letters of Mary Queen of Scots, Lord Bacon, Cromwell, and other celebrities.

Sir William Tite was the author of a 'Report of a Visit to the Estates of the Honourable Irish Society in Londonderry and Coleraine in the year 1834,' and of a 'Descriptive Catalogue of the Antiquities found in the Excavations at the New Royal Exchange,' which he published in 1848. Several of his papers and addresses, which principally treated of bibliographical or antiquarian subjects, were privately printed. He was a liberal promoter of all schemes for the advancement of education, and he founded the Tite Scholarship in the City of London School.

JAMES THOMSON GIBSON-CRAIG, 1799-1886

Mr. James Thomson Gibson-Craig, who was born in March 1799, was the second son of Mr. James Gibson, the political reformer, who, on succeeding under entail to the Riccarton estates in 1823, assumed the name of Craig, and in 1831 was created a baronet. He was educated at the High School and the University of Edinburgh, and after spending some time in foreign travel, he became a Writer to the Signet, and joined the firm afterwards known as Gibson-Craig, Dalziel and Brodies, of Edinburgh, of which he continued a member until about the year 1875. Mr. Gibson-Craig was well known for his literary and antiquarian tastes, and it was principally owing to his exertions that the Historical Manuscripts of Scotland were reproduced and issued during the time his brother, Sir William Gibson-Craig, held the office of Lord Clerk Register. He was a friend of Sir Walter Scott, of Lord Jeffrey, and Lord Cockburn, and at a later period of Lord Macaulay; and he was also intimate with most of the principal Scottish artists and antiquaries of his time. He died at Edinburgh on the 18th of July 1886. Mr. Gibson-Craig, who began to collect during his student days, formed an extensive and valuable library of choice books, many of which were bound by celebrated binders, and were once to be found in such famous libraries as those of Grolier, Canevari, Diana of Poitiers, Mary Queen of Scots, Robert Dudley, Earl of Leicester, De Thou, Count von Hoym, Longepierre, and Madame de Pompadour. After his death his collection was sold by Sotheby, Wilkinson and Hodge in three portions. The first portion was sold on June the 27th, 1887, and nine following days; the second on March the 23rd, 1888, and five following days, and on April 6th and eight following days; and the third on November the 15th, 1888, and two following days. There were altogether nine thousand four hundred and four lots, and the amount realised was fifteen thousand five hundred and nine pounds, four shillings and sixpence.

The following are some of the more notable books and manuscripts in the collection, and the prices obtained for them: —

Bartholomæi Camerarii de Prædestinatione dialogi tres. Parisiis, 1556. Bound in white morocco, the sides blind-tooled with the various emblems of Diana of Poitiers, and the initial of Henry II., King of France, surmounted by a crown. In the centre of the upper cover are the words CONSEQVITVR QVOD CVNQVE PETIT, and on the lower cover NIHIL AMPLIVS OPTAT. One hundred and forty-six pounds.

Cronique de Savoye, par Maistre Guillaume Paradin. Lyon, 1552. This volume formerly belonged to Mary Queen of Scots. It is in the original calf binding, and has in the centre of each cover a shield bearing the arms of Scotland, surmounted by a crown, with a crowned M above, below, and on each side of them, as well as at the corners of the book, and also on the panels of the back. Two hundred and sixty-five pounds.

Larismetique et Geometrie de Estienne de la Roche. Lyon, 1538. The binding bears the arms of James Hepburn, Earl of Bothwell, third husband of Mary Queen of Scots. Eighty-one pounds.

The XIII. Bukes of Eneados, translated out of Latyne verses into Scottish metir bi Mayster Gawin Douglas, Bishop of Dunkel, and unkil to the Erie of Angus. [W. Copland], London, 1553. Seventy-five pounds, ten shillings.

Poliphili Hypnerotomachia. Aldus, Venetiis, 1499. Ninety pounds.

Tewrdannck. Augsburg, 1519. Thirty-nine pounds.

Walton's *Compleat Angler.* First edition. London, 1653.

Cotton's *Complete Angler.* First edition. London, 1676. Together, one hundred and ninety-five pounds.

Burns's *Poems.* Kilmarnock, 1786. One hundred and eleven pounds.

The more important of the manuscripts were:—

Horæ B. Mariæ Virginis, written in the thirteenth century on vellum by an Anglo-Saxon or Scottish scribe. Three hundred and twenty-five pounds.

The First and Second Series of Sir Walter Scott's *Chronicles of the Canongate*. An autograph manuscript presented by the author to R. Cadell. One hundred and forty-one pounds.

A collection of valuable and interesting correspondence and memoranda relating to the Rebellion of 1715, comprising many of the original letters and despatches from the Earl of Mar, etc. Ninety-nine pounds.

In 1882 Mr. Gibson-Craig issued, in an edition of twenty-five copies, *Fac-similes of Old Book Binding* in his collection; and in the following year a facsimile reprint of the *Shorte Summe of the whole Catechisme*, by his ancestor John Craig, accompanied by a memoir of the author by Thomas Graves Law, of the Signet Library. He also printed for the Bannatyne Club 'Papers relative to the marriage of King James the Sixth of Scotland with the Princess Anna of Denmark A.D. MDLXXXIX, and the Form and Manner of Her Majesty's Coronation at Holyroodhouse A.D. MDXC.'

ALEXANDER WILLIAM, TWENTY-FIFTH EARL OF CRAWFORD, 1812-1880

It is about three hundred years since the founder of the Bibliotheca Lindesiana died. John Lindsay, the Octavian, better known by his title of Lord Menmuir, the ancestor of the Earls of Balcarres, had a distinguished though but brief career. He was not quite forty-seven years old when he died. During his short though eventful life he took a leading part in State affairs, being much trusted by his Sovereign, King James VI. He was a man of varied talents—lawyer, statesman, man of business, scholar, man of letters, and a poet. He seems to have been familiar with Greek, and to have corresponded in the Latin language. Besides these he acquired a knowledge of French, Italian and Spanish. He accumulated many State papers and letters from distinguished persons both at home and abroad.[101] These, now known as 'the Balcarres Papers,' were presented by Colin, Earl of Balcarres, to the Advocates' Library in 1712. A summary account of them is given in the First Report of the Historical Manuscripts Commission. Lord Menmuir's library is now represented at Haigh[102] by two volumes and three fragments, all of which bear his autograph. Lord Menmuir was succeeded by a son, who died whilst yet a youth and unmarried. The second son, David, who after his brother's death inherited the estate of Balcarres, may be termed the second founder of the library. The father's love of books and learning seems to have in a very large measure descended to the son. He added to the library until it became one of the best in the kingdom. A very charming letter from William Drummond of Hawthornden to David Lindsay, sent with a copy of the *Flowers of Zion*, which the poet had privately printed, is clear evidence of the terms on which Lindsay lived with his friends and fellow book-lovers. The original letter is preserved in the Muniment Room at Haigh, but the identical copy of Drummond's work has, alas! been lost sight of.

THE SMALL BOOK-STAMP OF THE FIRST LORD BALCARRES.

The library of Sir David Lindsay, Lord Balcarres, continued at the family seat on the shores of the Firth of Forth until comparatively recent times. Sibbald in 1710 mentions the 'great bibliothek' at Balcarres. In Sibbald's time the owner, Colin, third Earl of Balcarres, had added many books to the library, and spent the evening of his days in the pursuit of letters. When Lady Balcarres, great-grandmother of the present Earl of Crawford, left Fife and removed to Edinburgh, whilst her son was in the West Indies, the greater portion of the library was literally thrown away and dispersed—torn up for grocers as useless trash, by her permission. Of the library collected by generations of Lindsays, all that now remains is a handful of little over fifty volumes. The books of David Lindsay, first Lord Balcarres, who died in 1641, are recognisable from his signature, and on many of them his arms are impressed in gold on the sides.

Of the present library at Haigh, the nucleus of it may be said to be the books inherited by the grandfather of the present Earl, whose wife was the heiress of the first Baron Muncaster. These Muncaster books, although not of the greatest value, formed a basis on which the late Earl of Crawford, who was born in 1812, built up the present library, which will be always associated with his memory. When a boy he was fired with enthusiasm for books, and determined to form a great library in which every branch of human knowledge in every language should have a place. He began collecting about 1826, shortly after going to Eton, and continued most assiduously to gather of all that was best until his death in 1880. His success may be judged in some measure by the remarkable collections dispersed in 1887 and 1889, which together consisted of three thousand two hundred and fifty-four lots, and realised twenty-six thousand three hundred and ninety-seven pounds, fourteen shillings. Family burdens rendered it needful for the present possessor of the library to put his hands on some available assets, and this necessity coming at a period of great commercial depression, a portion of the literary treasures unfortunately suffered. But the work was again renewed, and the present state of the library will not compare ignobly with its past. The number of manuscripts is very considerable, probably about six thousand, not a few of which are of the greatest interest and value, many of them having covers of the precious metals or carved ivory, enriched with gems and crystals. There are also many papyri, a great number of Oriental manuscripts, collections of French autograph letters of the Revolutionary and Napoleonic periods, and of English autograph letters. The printed books amount to about one hundred thousand, and among them are to be found several block-books and a large number of incunabula, including books printed by Caxton, Machlinia, Wynkyn de Worde, Pynson, Rood, and other early English printers. The library is particularly rich in the productions of the early Italian presses, especially those of Rome and Venice; and it also contains a fine collection of rare works on the languages of North and South America, many of them printed in Mexico and Lima, and a series of books printed in Aberdeen from 1622 to 1736. Of other printed matter there are collections of broadside ballads; broadside proclamations illustrative of English, French, Dutch, German and Italian history; a long series of Papal Bulls; early English newspapers from 1631 to the Restoration; Civil War tracts; tracts by, for and against Martin Luther; newspapers and periodicals published during the various French revolutions; and a large number of caricatures issued in France and Germany during the Second Empire and the Commune.

THE LARGE BOOK-STAMP OF THE FIRST LORD BALCARRES.

It is not an easy task to pick out the choicest gems from the abundant treasures of this splendid collection, but the following are a few of the most interesting and valuable of the manuscripts:

A Legal Instrument of Donation from Johannes, the Primicerius, or Captain of a company of soldiers, to the Church of Ravenna; written on papyrus, probably about A.D. 580-600, at Ravenna. Five feet four inches long by eleven and a half inches broad.

The Four Gospels in Syriac, in the original Peshitto version, written on vellum about 550.

St. Cyprian, Bishop of Carthage, *Epistolæ et Opuscula*, written in the seventh or eighth century in rude Merovingian characters, often mixed with uncial letters. One of the oldest manuscripts in existence of this Father of the Church.

The Four Gospels in Latin, written about 850.

A Textus or Book of the Gospels, probably written at the Benedictine monastery of St. Gall, Switzerland, in the ninth or tenth century. In the centre of the upper cover, which is intended to be used as a pax at Mass, is an ivory panel of the Crucifixion, with figures of the Virgin Mary and St. John the Evangelist. The border is of gilt copper engraved with a floriated pattern, and studded with silver bosses and jewels; at the corners are Limoges enamel plaques with the four Evangelists. The ivory carving is of the tenth or eleventh century, the border early thirteenth.

The New Testament in Syriac: the Gospels of the Peshitto version, and the remaining books of the Heraclean version, written about 1000. Remarkable as being the only complete Syriac New Testament of any antiquity in any library in Europe.

The Old Testament in Latin, written by a German scribe in the eleventh century. The upper cover consists of a carved ivory panel of the thirteenth century, with a border of silver gilt, decorated with filigree work and figures in *repoussé*, and enriched with crystals *en cabochon*.

St. Beatus, *Commentarius in Apocalypsim*, written in Spain about 1150; with one hundred and ten very large miniatures and a circular map of the world.

Bible Historiée, executed in the south of France about 1250; a series of full-page paintings on a background of burnished gold, representing scenes from the Book of Genesis.

Psalterium, written in Paris about 1260. This volume belonged at one time to Joan of Navarre, Queen Consort of Henry IV., King of England, whose autograph is on one of the blank leaves.

Roman de la Rose, written for, and presented to, Christina de Lindesay, Dame de Coucy, 1323.

Rime di Petrarca et Cançoni di Dante. One of the most important manuscripts of the two poets, written during the lifetime of Petrarch, or immediately after his death, by Paul the Scribe for Lorenzo, the son of Carlo degli Strozzi, a member of one of the noblest families of Florence.

Lydgate's *Siege of Troy*, probably written for William Carent, of Carent's Court, in the Isle of Purbeck, about 1420. The volume has illuminated borders and seventy miniatures, and bears the arms of Carent at the end.

Missale Romanum, six volumes folio, written on vellum in 1510-17 for Cardinal Pompeo Colonna. The tradition handed down by the family was that the large full-page illuminations with which the manuscript is adorned were executed by Raphael about the year 1517, when the owner was made a cardinal; and there is no doubt that, if not actually by his hand, the work was done by his followers under his supervision. In all probability, we may say that the large miniatures are painted by Timoteo Viti, and the illuminations and arabesques by Litti di Filippo de' Corbizi.[103]

Some of the more notable of the incunabula are two block-books— the first Dutch edition of the *Speculum Humanæ Salvationis*, and a copy of the *Ars Memorativa* printed before 1474-75. Cicero, *Officiorum libri tres*, printed at Mentz by Fust and Schoeffer in 1465. Lactantius, *Opera*, printed in the Monastery of Subiaco, near Rome, by Sweynheym and Pannartz in 1465. Higden's *Polychronicon* and the *Boke of Eneydos*, printed by Caxton in 1482 and 1490. The *Chronicles of England* and the *Speculum Christiani*, printed by Machlinia. Lyndewode, *Constitutiones provinciales ecclesiæ anglicanæ*, printed at Oxford by Rood and Hunte in 1483-85. The *Croniclis of Englōde with the frute of timis*, from the St. Albans press.

Among other books of later dates deserving of special notice may be mentioned—Vespucci, *Paesi novamente retrovati*, Vicenza, 1507. The first and very rare edition of the celebrated Thesis of Luther against the system of indulgences, which he affixed to the gate of the University of Wittemberg, 1517. *Huon of Bordeaux*, printed by Wynkyn de Worde about 1534—believed to be unique. Archbishop Parker's *De Antiquitate Britannicæ Ecclesiæ*, London, 1572. A magnificent set of De Bry's *Grands et Petits Voyages*, in one hundred and eighty-two volumes, 1590-1644. A Booke containing all such Proclamations as were published during the Raigne of Elizabeth (and James I.); collected by Humphrey Dyson, London, 1618. The first and second Shakespeare folios. Three copies of the first edition of Milton's *Paradise Lost*, with the first, third and fourth title-pages.

The immense collection of broadsides forms one of the most remarkable features of this magnificent library. In volume iv. p. 201 of the *Transactions of the Bibliographical Society*, published in 1898, Lord Crawford informs us that 'in the last fourteen or fifteen years he had managed to collect something like nineteen thousand of them, including English, French, German and Venetian Proclamations (3000), Papal Bulls (11,000) and English Ballads (3000).' Among them are several very rare indulgences printed by Wynkyn de Worde and Pynson, and a large number of proclamations and ballads of special interest and value, far too numerous to mention.

The present Earl of Crawford, who is a Trustee of the British Museum, President of the Camden Society, a Fellow of the Royal Society and the Society of Antiquaries, and who was formerly President of the Royal Astronomical Society, has printed catalogues of the English broadsides and ballads, and of the Chinese books and manuscripts in his collection, together with hand-lists to the Oriental manuscripts, the early editions of the Greek and Latin writers, and the proclamations issued by authority of the kings and queens of Great Britain and Ireland. He has also printed collations and notes of some of the rare books in the library.

FOOTNOTES:

[101] Mainly contributed by Mr. J.P. Edmond, Librarian to Lord Crawford.

[102] Lord Crawford's Seat, near Wigan.

[103] Since the above was printed it has been announced that Lord Crawford's MSS. have become by purchase the property of Mrs. Rylands of Manchester.

HENRY HUTH, 1815-1878

Mr. Henry Huth, who was born in London in 1815, was the third son of Mr. Frederick Huth of Hanover, who settled at Corunna, in Spain; but on the occupation of that town by the French in 1809 he came to England, where he became a naturalised British subject, and founded the well-known firm which is still carried on by his descendants. Mr. Henry Huth, we are informed in the preface to the Catalogue of the Huth Library, written by his son, Mr. Alfred Henry Huth, was intended for the Indian Civil Service, and was sent to Mr. Rusden's school at Leith Hill in Surrey, where he 'learned Greek, Latin, and French (Spanish was his mother-tongue), and had also got well on with Hindustani, Persian, and Arabic'; but in 1833, the East India Company having lost their Charter, his father removed him from the school and took him into his business. Office-work proving distasteful to him, he travelled for some years on the Continent and in America, rejoining his father's firm as partner in 1849. From his early years Mr. Henry Huth had been a collector of books, and on his return home he set energetically to work to form that splendid library which ranks among the finest in England, and which has been carefully preserved and augmented by his son, Mr. Alfred Henry Huth. Mr. Henry Huth gave commissions at most of the important book-sales, and we are told that 'he called daily at all the principal booksellers on his way back from the city, a habit which he continued up to the day of his death.' He was a member of the Philobiblon Society, and in 1867 printed for presentation to the members a volume of *Ancient Ballads and Broadsides published in England in the Sixteenth Century*, reprinted from the unique original copies he had bought at the Daniel sale. He was also a member of the Roxburghe Club. Mr. Huth died on the 10th of December 1878, and was buried in the churchyard of Bolney, in Sussex. He married Augusta Louisa Sophia, third daughter of Frederick Westenholz of Waldenstein Castle, in Austria, by whom he had three sons and three daughters.

Among the treasures in Mr. Huth's library are block-books of the *Ars Moriendi, Ars Memorandi,* and the *Apocalypse;* the superb copy of the

Gutenberg Bible which was formerly in the libraries of Sir M. Masterman Sykes and Mr. Henry Perkins; two copies of the Fust and Schoeffer Bible of 1462, one on vellum; and a particularly fine copy of St. Augustine's *De Civitate Dei*, printed at Rome in 1468. The collection also comprises several of the pre-Reformation German Bibles; the first edition of Luther's Bible; the Coverdale Bible of 1535, and the Icelandic Bible printed at Holum in 1584; together with upwards of one hundred other Bibles, a large number of New Testaments, and various portions of the Scriptures in all languages.

In books from the presses of Caxton and other early English printers the library is remarkably rich. It contains no less than twelve Caxtons; about fifty Wynkyn de Wordes, of which several are unique; sixteen Pynsons, and a Machlinia. A vellum copy—the only one known—of the *Fructus Temporum*, printed at St. Albans about 1483; and the *Exposicio Sancti Jeronimi in Symbolum Apostolorum*, printed at Oxford, and bearing the date 1468 (a typographical error for 1478), are also found on its shelves.

Among the books printed by Caxton are the first editions of *The Dictes or Sayings of the Philosophers*, Chaucer's *Canterbury Tales*, *Tully of Old Age*, Gower's *Confessio Amantis*, and Christine de Pisan's *Fayts of Arms*.

The books from the presses of foreign printers are both numerous and fine. Some of the most notable examples are the Dantes of Foligno and Mantua, both printed in the year 1472; the first edition of Homer, printed at Venice in 1488; a magnificent copy on thick paper, with the original binding, of the *Poliphili Hypnerotomachia*, printed by Aldus at Venice in 1499; the Aldine Virgil of 1501, with the book-plate of Bilibald Pirkheimer; and two copies of the *Tewrdannck*, one on vellum, printed at Nuremberg in 1517. There is also a copy of the first edition of *Don Quixote*, with the Privilege only for Madrid.

Few collections are richer than the Huth Library in old English poetry and dramatic literature. It contains the first four folio Shakespeares, and a goodly gathering of quarto plays, many of which were acquired at the Daniel sale in 1864. Among them are the first editions of *Richard II.* and *Richard III.*, printed in 1597; *Henry V.*, *Much Ado about Nothing, Midsummer Night's Dream*, and the *Merchant of Venice*, all printed in 1600; the first sketch of *The Merry Wives of Windsor*, printed in 1602; the second edition of *Hamlet*, printed in 1604; and the first editions of *Pericles*, printed in 1609, and *Othello*, printed in 1622. Other rare Shakespeareana are the first editions of *Lucrece*, the *Sonnets*, and the *Poems*, printed respectively in 1594, 1609, and 1640. It is only possible to mention a few of the rare English books in this grand library; but the *Hundred Merry Tales*, published by Rastell about 1525; the unique copy of Munday's *Banquet of Daintie Conceits*, printed in 1588; a first folio of Ben Jonson's *Works* on large paper, of which only one other copy is known in that state, and a perfect set of the editions of Walton's *Compleat Angler* from 1653 to 1760, cannot be passed over without notice. The unique collection of Elizabethan ballads, to which reference has already been made, would be considered a great treasure in any library. The collection of Voyages and Travels is believed to be the richest private one in Europe. It comprises the early letters of Columbus and Vesputius, and perfect editions of De Bry, Hulsius, Hakluyt, Purchas, etc., together with the voyages of Cortes, Drake, and other famous travellers.

The fine and large collection of manuscripts contains many choice and interesting examples. Several beautifully written Bibles, and a number of Books of Hours are to be found in it. Some of the latter are most charmingly illuminated; two of them, written in the fifteenth century, of Flemish execution, are especially good. One of these contains the coats of arms of Philip the Good, Duke of Burgundy, and Isabella his wife. There are also three handsomely illuminated Petrarchs, and a remarkable manuscript on vellum in four volumes, with very beautiful illustrations of beasts, birds, fish, and insects, painted by George Hoefnagel for the Emperor Rudolph II. A collection of Madrigals for three voices, the words by John Milton, Thomas Tompkins, and others, is of especial interest, for Mr. A.H. Huth informs us that several of the songs by Milton in it have never been published, and that he composed some of the music.

The library also contains a considerable number of interesting letters, and a very fine collection of engravings; the series by Albert Dürer being nearly complete. A somewhat recent addition to the collection is 'a proof set before numbers of the engravings to the Landino Dante of 1481, by Baccio Baldini, after the designs of Botticelli, and separately printed on slips.'[104]

Many of the volumes once formed part of the libraries of Grolier, Maioli, Canevari, Diana of Poitiers, Henry IV. of France, De Thou, Count Mansfeld, Louis XIII., and other celebrated collectors, and bear on their covers the arms or devices of their former owners. There are fine examples of the work of all the great binders, and many books bound in silver, needlework, etc.

The admirable catalogue of the library in five volumes was compiled by Mr. F.S. Ellis and Mr. W.C. Hazlitt, and partly revised by Mr. Henry Huth himself.

FOOTNOTES:

[104] Account of additions to the Huth Library, by Mr. A.H. Huth, in Mr. Quaritch's *Dictionary of English Book-Collectors*.

ROBERT SAMUEL TURNER, 1818-1887

Mr. Robert Samuel Turner was born in 1818. Although engaged in commercial affairs from his youth he was a most enthusiastic book-collector, and at a very early age began to form that noble library, with which only a few collections of his time could vie in value, extent or condition. Mr. Turner principally directed his attention to the acquisition of rare Italian, French and Spanish books. His English books were not numerous, and there were but few German ones in the collection, but some of them were of much interest. He possessed one of the finest copies in existence of the first folio of Shakespeare's Plays, and an exceptionally good example of the *Tewrdannck*. He always endeavoured to obtain the best and choicest copies possible, and many of them, especially the French volumes, were clothed in beautiful bindings, bearing the arms or devices of Grolier, Maioli, Diana of Poitiers, Count Mansfeld, Cosmo de' Medici, Thomas Wotton, Longepierre, Count von Hoym, and other famous collectors. Mr. Turner resided for some years in Park Square West, Regent's Park, London, but in 1878 he removed to the Albany, Piccadilly. In anticipation of his change of residence he determined to part with a portion of his collection of French books, and on the valuation of the late M. Potier, of Paris, he offered it to an eminent French amateur *en bloc* for four thousand pounds. This offer was declined, and he sent the books to Paris to be sold by auction. The sale took place at the Salle Drouot on the 12th of March 1878, and the four following days, when the lots, seven hundred and seventy-four in number, realised three hundred and nineteen thousand one hundred francs — considerably more than three times the sum Mr. Turner was willing to take for them. After his death, which occurred at Brighton on the 7th of June 1887, the remainder of his library was disposed of in two sales by Messrs. Sotheby, Wilkinson and Hodge: the first on June 18th, 1888, and the eleven following days, and the second on November 23rd, 1888, and the thirteen following days. They realised respectively thirteen thousand three hundred and seventy pounds, thirteen shillings, and two thousand eight hundred and seventy-four pounds, seventeen shillings and sixpence. The prices obtained for the books, especially at the French sale, were very high. A dedication copy to Mademoiselle de Montpensier, with the signature of Charles de Lorraine on the title-page, of *Recueil des Portraits et Éloges en vers et en prose (de personnages du temps par Mademoiselle de Montpensier et autres)*, Paris, 1659, with a morocco binding of the seventeenth century, ornamented with *fleurs-de-lis*, fetched fourteen thousand francs; La Fontaine's *Fables Choisies*, five volumes, Paris, 1678, 1679 and 1694, bound by Boyet, eleven thousand nine hundred and fifty francs; *Les Fais de Jason*, par Raoul Le Febvre, printed at Lyons about 1480, seven thousand six hundred francs; *Le Livre appelle Mandeville*, Lyon, 1480, six thousand two hundred and fifty francs; *Les [OE]uvres de Guillaume Coquillant*, Paris, 1532, five thousand four hundred and fifty francs; and *Les [OE]uvres de Molière*, eight volumes, Paris, 1739, with additional plates, five thousand francs. Among the books at the English sales the exceptionally fine and large copies of the *Tewrdannck*, Nuremberg, 1517, and the Aldine *Poliphili Hypnerotomachia*, sold respectively for two hundred and fifty pounds and one hundred and thirty-seven pounds; a copy of *Paesi Novamente Retrovati*, Vicentia, 1507, with the title in facsimile, for one hundred and eighty-six pounds; and Shakespeare's *Poems*, 1640, for one hundred and six pounds. The first folio of Shakespeare Mr. Turner sold privately to an American collector. A Grolier binding realised three thousand francs; another binding with the devices of Diana of Poitiers, four thousand four hundred francs; a book from the library of Longepierre, two thousand five hundred francs; two sets of volumes with *doublures* by Boyet, respectively four thousand francs and three thousand nine hundred francs; and Rogers's *Italy and Poems*, with beautiful bindings by Bedford, sixty-one pounds.

Mr. Turner was an accomplished linguist, and he possessed a wide and accurate knowledge of the literary history and bibliography of France, Italy and Spain. He was also a collector of rare and beautiful bindings before the interest and value of these works of art were generally appreciated.

FREDERICK LOCKER-LAMPSON, 1821-1895

MR. LOCKER LAMPSON.

Mr. Frederick Locker, the author of *London Lyrics* and other volumes of delightful light and social verse, was born in 1821. His father was Mr. E.H. Locker, a Civil Commissioner of Greenwich Hospital, and founder of the Naval Gallery there. For some years Mr. Locker was Précis Writer in the Admiralty. He was twice married: first in 1850 to Lady Charlotte Christian, a daughter of the seventh Earl of Elgin, and secondly in 1874 to Hannah Jane, a daughter of the late Sir Curtis Miranda Lampson, Bart., of Rowfant, Sussex. On the death of his father-in-law in 1885 he added the name of Lampson to his own. He died at Rowfant on May the 30th, 1895.

ONE OF MR. LOCKER-LAMPSON'S BOOK-PLATES.

Mr. Locker-Lampson tells us in his interesting autobiography entitled *My Confidences*, that he first collected pictures and rare sixteenth century engravings, but collectors with long purses outbid him, so he turned to old books: 'little volumes of poetry and the drama from about 1590 to 1610.' These formed the nucleus of his collection, which soon grew wide enough to include Caxtons and the works of the poets of the last century. Rare editions of Sidney, Spenser, Churchyard, Middleton, Herbert, Herrick, Dekker, Chapman, and many other writers of the sixteenth and seventeenth centuries, are to be found in it, and Shakespeare is splendidly represented by a perfect copy of the first folio, the first editions of *Lucrece*, the *Sonnets* and the *Poems*, and a large number—some thirty in all—of the quarto plays, many of which are the original editions. Mr. Locker-Lampson's folio wanted Ben Jonson's verses, and he gives an amusing account in *My Confidences* of an unsuccessful attempt to purchase a copy of them from a Mr. Dene, who possessed an imperfect first folio. He ultimately bought the precious leaf, which had been pasted in a scrap-book, for one hundred pounds, and so completed his copy. The library is also very rich in first editions of Byron, Tennyson, Browning, and other English poets of recent times, many of the volumes containing autograph inscriptions to Mr. Locker-Lampson himself. Mr. Locker-Lampson placed his library, together with his collections of autograph letters, pictures and drawings, in his residence at Rowfant, the beautiful home which he and his wife inherited from the lady's father; and a handsome catalogue of them published in 1886 by Mr. Quaritch, with an introduction by their owner, tells us of the treasures they contain. An etched portrait of Mr. Locker-Lampson and a sketch of his study are inserted in the volume, and Mr. Andrew Lang has prefixed some charming lines descriptive of the library:—

> 'The Rowfant books, how fair they show,
>   The Quarto quaint, the Aldine tall;
> Print, autograph, Portfolio!
>   Back from the outer air they call
> The athletes from the Tennis ball,
>   The Rhymer from his rod and hooks;
> Would I could sing them, one and all,

The Rowfant books!

The Rowfant books! In sun and snow
    They're dear, but most when tempests fall;
The folio towers above the row
    As once, o'er minor prophets—Saul!
What jolly jest books, and what small
    "Dear dumpy Twelves" to fill the nooks.
You do not find in every stall
    The Rowfant books!

The Rowfant books! These long ago
    Were chained within some College hall;
These manuscripts retain the glow
    Of many a coloured capital;
While yet the Satires keep their gall,
    While the *Pastissier* puzzles cooks,
There is a joy that does not pall,
    The Rowfant books!

ENVOY.

The Rowfant books,—ah magical
    As famed Armida's golden looks.
They hold the Rhymer for their thrall—
    The Rowfant books!'

In 1900 was published an Appendix to the Catalogue, the work of Mr. Frederick Locker-Lampson's son, Mr. Godfrey Locker-Lampson, consisting of additions to the library since the printing of the Catalogue in 1886, to which Mr. Andrew Lang again contributed some verses:—

'How often to the worthy Sire
    Succeeds th' unworthy son!
Extinguished is the ancient fire,
Books were the idols of the Squire,

The graceless heir has none.

To Sotheby's go both old and new,
   Bindings, and prose, and rhymes,
With Shakespeare as with Padeloup
The sportive lord has naught to do,
   He reads *The Sporting Times*.

Behold a special act of grace,
   On Rowfant shelves behold,
The well-loved honours keep their place,
And new-won glories half efface
   The splendours of the old.'

The volume also contains verses by Mr. Austin Dobson, the Earl of Crewe, and Mr. Wilfrid Blunt.

WILLIAM MORRIS, 1834-1896

William Morris, the poet, art-designer, and manufacturer, was born at Elm House, Clay Hill, Walthamstow, Essex, on the 24th of March 1834. His father William Morris, a partner in the firm of Sanderson and Co., discount brokers, London, died in 1847, leaving him a considerable fortune. Young Morris was first educated at a preparatory school at Walthamstow, and afterwards at Marlborough, from whence he proceeded to Exeter College, Oxford. On leaving the University he wished to become a painter, but his studies were not sufficiently successful to warrant him carrying out his intention. He also paid some attention to the study of architecture. In 1858 he published a small volume entitled *The Defence of Guenevere and other Poems*, which received but little notice at the time; but *The Life and Death of Jason*, published in 1867, attracted general attention, and his reputation was further greatly increased by *The Earthly Paradise*, a poem in four volumes, which appeared in 1868-70. From that period until the time of his death Mr. Morris published a considerable number of other works, and, in collaboration with Mr. Eirikr Magnusson, some translations from the Icelandic. In 1863, in conjunction with D.G. Rossetti, E. Burne-Jones, and Ford Madox Brown, he established a factory for the production of artistic glass, tiles, wall-paper, etc., which has greatly contributed to the improvement of household decoration in England. A large number of the designs were the work of Mr. Morris himself, his leisure hours being devoted to literature, and it has been said of him 'that his poems were by Morris the wall-paper maker, and his wall-papers by Morris the poet.'

In 1891 Morris established a printing-press near his residence, Kelmscott House, on the Upper Mall, Hammersmith, from which he issued a series of beautiful and sumptuous reprints, principally of old books, with ornamentations by himself, and illustrations chiefly by Sir E. Burne-Jones. Of these reprints, which at the present time fetch large prices, that of *Chaucer's Poems* is considered the finest. In 1898 the trustees of Mr. Morris published 'A Note on his aims in founding the Kelmscott Press. Together with a short description of the Press by C.S. Cockerell, and an annotated list of the books printed thereat.' The list gives fifty-three works in sixty-three volumes and nine leaflets. This was the last book printed at the Kelmscott Press. It was finished at No. 14 Upper Mall, Hammersmith, on the 4th of March 1898. In it the aims of Morris in founding the Press are given in his own words. 'I began printing books,' he writes, 'with the hope of producing some which would have a definite claim to beauty, while at the same time they should be easy to read, and should not dazzle the eye, or trouble the intellect of the reader by eccentricity of form in the letters.' Mr. Morris, who died at Kelmscott House on the 3rd of October 1896, collected a fine and extensive library, which passed into the hands of a Manchester collector for, it is said, the sum of twenty thousand pounds. The purchaser, after selecting the books he required—about half of the MSS. and one-third of the printed books—sent the others to Sotheby, Wilkinson and Hodge, by whom they were sold on December 5th, 1898, and five following days. There were twelve hundred and fifteen lots in the sale, and the sum obtained for them was ten thousand nine hundred and ninety-two pounds, eleven shillings. All the books realised good prices, but the manuscripts were of greater interest and value than the printed volumes. The following are a few of the principal manuscripts, and the prices they fetched:— *Testamentum Novum Latinum*, Sæc. xii., vellum, handsomely illuminated, two hundred and twenty-five pounds; Hegesippus, *De Excidio Judæorum*, Sæc. xii., vellum, in the original Winchester binding, one hundred and eighty pounds; *Biblia Sacra Latina*, written on vellum about 1280, with handsomely painted initials, one hundred and thirty-nine pounds; *Biblia Sacra Latina*, vellum, written about 1300 by an Anglo-Norman scribe, with finely illuminated initials, three hundred and two pounds; *Josephi Antiquitates Judaicæ et de Bello Judaico Libri*, written on vellum by a French scribe in the thirteenth century, and beautifully illuminated, three hundred and five pounds; *Missale Anglicanum*, called the Sherbrooke Missal on account of it having belonged to the Sherbrooke family of Oxton, County Notts, a member of the family having inscribed his name in it about 1600; it was written in the fourteenth century on vellum, and has illuminated capitals and fine marginal decorations, three hundred and fifty pounds; Gratianus, *Decretales*, Sæc. xiv., vellum, with finely painted and illuminated initials, two hundred and fifty-five pounds; Virgilius Maro, *Georgica et Æneis*, written on vellum at the end of the fourteenth or beginning of the fifteenth century by an Italian scribe, with beautiful illuminated decorations, one hundred and sixty-four pounds; and *Legenda Sanctæ Catherinæ de Senis*, Sæc. xv., vellum, handsomely illuminated, one hundred and forty-nine pounds.

Some of the more notable printed books were:—*S. Hieronymi Epistolæ*, printed by Sweynheym and Pannartz at Rome in 1468, fifty-three pounds; *Speculum Humanæ Salvationis Latino-Germanicum*, printed by G. Zainer at Augsburg about 1471, one hundred pounds; *Ptolomæi Cosmographia*, Ulmæ, 1486, ninety-one pounds; *Dives and Pauper*, printed by Pynson in 1493, fifty-five pounds; Higden's *Policronicon*, 1495, *Thordinary of Crysten Men*, 1502, and *The Orcharde of Syon*, 1519, all from the press of Wynkyn de Worde, realised respectively thirty-eight pounds, fifty pounds, and one hundred and fifty-one pounds; *Hystoire du Chevallier Perceval le Galloys*, Paris, 1530, seventy-nine pounds; *Epistole et Evangelii et Letioni Vulgari in lingua Thoscana*, Firenze, 1551, eighty-nine pounds; and the *Historie of the four Sonnes of Aimon*, printed by William Copland in 1554, eighty-one pounds. Among the manuscripts retained were a twelfth-century English Bestiary, for which Mr. Morris gave nine hundred pounds; the 'Windmill' Psalter, written about 1270, which cost him upwards of a thousand pounds; the Huntingdon Psalter, and the Tiptoft Missal.

Lightning Source UK Ltd.
Milton Keynes UK
UKHW012159060721
386714UK00012B/14